Southern SONS, *Northern* SOLDIERS

★ ★ ★

Southern SONS, Northern SOLDIERS

The Civil War Letters of the Remley Brothers,
22nd Iowa Infantry

★ ★ ★

Edited by Julie Holcomb

Introduction by Steven E. Woodworth

NORTHERN ILLINOIS
UNIVERSITY
PRESS

DeKalb

© 2004 by Northern Illinois University Press
Published by the Northern Illinois University Press, DeKalb, Illinois 60115
Manufactured in the United States using acid-free paper
All Rights Reserved
Design by Julia Fauci

Library of Congress Cataloging-in-Publication Data
Remley, George A., b. 1841
Southern sons, northern soldiers : the Civil War letters of the Remley brothers, 22nd Iowa infantry / edited by Julie Holcomb ; introduction by Steven E. Woodworth.
p.   cm.
Includes bibliographical references (p.) and index.
ISBN 0-87580-319-9 (alk. paper)
1. Remley, George A., b. 1841—Correspondence. 2. Remley, Lycurgus, b. 1840—Correspondence. 3. United States. Army. Iowa Infantry Regiment, 22nd (1862–1865) 4. Iowa—History—Civil War, 1861–1865—Personal narratives. 5. United States—History—Civil War, 1861–1865—Personal narratives. 6. Soldiers—Iowa—Correspondence. 7. Brothers—Iowa—Correspondence. 8. Remley family—Correspondence. 9. Iowa—History—Civil War, 1861–1865—Regimental histories. 10. United States—History—Civil War, 1861–1865—Regimental histories. I. Remley, Lycurgus, b. 1840. II. Holcomb, Julie. III. Woodworth, Steven E. IV. Title.
E507.522nd R46 2004
973. 7'477'0922—dc22
[B]
2003058826

Contents

Editor's Note   vii

Introduction by Steven E. Woodworth   xi
   Notes   xxxi

1. "Among the Barren Hills of Missouri"
   August 21, 1862–March 20, 1863   3

2. "He Died in Hope of a Blissful Immortality"
   March 28, 1863–June 29, 1863   51

3. "A Bright and Glorious 'Fourth'"
   July 4, 1863–September 19, 1863   81

4. "Our Grand Expedition . . . into Texas"
   September 26, 1863–November 11, 1863   92

5. "Into Texas Proper"
   December 8, 1863–March 8, 1864   106

6. "To Bid His <u>Dulcina</u> Farewell"
   March 24, 1864–June 12, 1864   131

7. "We Will Have Some Fighting to Do"
   July 24, 1864–September 15, 1864   151

   Epilogue   161

   Biographical Directory   167

   Notes   169

   Index   179

Editor's Note

★ In 1997, the Pearce Civil War Collection at Navarro College acquired George and Lycurgus Remley's Civil War letters and the correspondence of other family members. Charles and Peggy Pearce purchased the documents from a historical manuscript dealer, who had bought the documents from a member of the Remley family. Internal evidence suggests Clara Remley, George and Lycurgus's youngest sister, was probably the last direct descendent of family patriarch James Remley to possess the collection. As the documents were handed down through the generations, the tie to James Remley and his children became less distinct until the final owner, feeling no familial connection, chose to sell the collection. Often when large document groups such as the Remley papers come on the market, dealers and collectors break up the collections, selling off the better items for large sums and either discarding the lesser items or selling them elsewhere. For archivists and historians this action is heartbreaking because the context and the provenance of the collection, as well as the documents, are lost to history. Fortunately, the entire collection of the Remley letters now has a permanent home at Navarro College in Corsicana, Texas.

When I began work with the Pearce Civil War Collection in 2001, the Remley papers was one of the first collections I processed. As I worked on the collection, I found myself living each day of the war through Lycurgus and George. In particular I was moved by George's transformation from a young man often overshadowed by his exemplary older brother into an experienced, well-regarded soldier. I approached Martin Johnson, history editor at Northern Illinois University Press, about publishing letters from the Pearce Collection. When Johnson, whom I had met via the Civil War H-List, suggested the Remley letters, I knew I had found my project. Collections of Civil War soldiers' letters are common, but after several months working nights and weekends transcribing and researching Lycurgus and George Remley's letters, I am more convinced than ever the Remley brothers' story deserves a wider audience.

Editor's Note

★ ★ ★

The Remley letters have been transcribed with very few changes. Spelling, capitalization, and style generally remain unaltered, with two exceptions. In the nineteenth century, dashes were often used in place of periods, commas, and semicolons; most of those dashes have been replaced by modern punctuation. Rarely, commas and periods have been inserted as needed for clarity. Similarly, spelling is corrected only when necessary for clarity, and all spelling changes are indicated with brackets. Both brothers used parenthetical statements on occasion. These should not be confused with editorial notations, which are in brackets. Lycurgus and George often added postscripts to each other's letters resulting in long, multidate documents. Bracketed editorial notations have been added to these dual-authored letters for the reader's ease. Finally, the date and place lines have been standardized for each letter, and missing information supplied by the editor is enclosed in brackets. Date and place lines *within* individual letters have not been standardized. In late 1863, George Remley began numbering his letters home. Any gaps in the numbering sequence occur because the letters are no longer extant.

Letters from other members of the Remley family have been included to give a greater sense of the ongoing familial dialogue. The letters written by members of the Remley family other than George and Lycurgus have not always been included in their entirety; only the most relevant portions are included in the text. All extant wartime letters written by George and Lycurgus Remley are reprinted without omission or changes except as noted above.

★ ★ ★

No project of this scope happens without the assistance of others, and it is a pleasure to thank those people. Without Charles and Peggy Pearce, not only would there be no Pearce Civil War Collection at Navarro College, there would be no archivist. The Pearces' initial donation of thirty-eight documents to Navarro in 1996 has grown to an impressive collection of more than seven thousand items, and a new museum and archives facility will open in October 2003. I owe a special debt of gratitude to Darrell Beauchamp, Dean of Learning Resources and Special Collections at Navarro College, whose guidance and, more important, sense of humor helped me survive my first year as a professional archivist. I am grateful to Lawrence Lipin and Alex Toth, both of whom reinforced my growing interest in history and encouraged me to make what seemed at the time an awesome change of direction in my academic career, and to David B. Gracy II, who propelled me even farther down that new path.

Martin Johnson of Northern Illinois University Press has remained supportive of this project and patient with its inexperienced editor. Howard Remley, a direct descendant of James Remley, transcribed many of the Remley letters from the 1850s and generously shared his knowledge of Remley

Editor's Note

family history. Denise Anderson of the University of Iowa Archives patiently and thoroughly answered every question I posed.

My biggest debts of gratitude are to my daughter, Jennifer, who was my first mentor, and especially to my husband, Stan, who provided financial and moral support, cooked, cleaned, and even packed everything we owned in a U-Haul and moved twenty-five hundred miles to support my dreams. Without their unstinting faith, this book would not have been possible. Any errors, however, remain my own.

Julie Holcomb
Waxahachie, Texas

George A. Remley

Introduction

Steven E. Woodworth

★   The letters of Lycurgus and George Remley reveal a family caught up in the Civil War. Their correspondence, a useful source of information about the service of the regiment in which the brothers served, the 22nd Iowa, also presents a valuable glimpse of the people of the region from which these two young men enlisted, an area less heavily studied than others in Civil War America.

What Americans now call the Midwest was known as the Northwest during the Civil War era. The region played a distinct role in the sectional balance of the United States in the nineteenth century. The first states in the region had been closed to slavery by the terms of the Northwest Ordinance of 1787. Subsequent states were free by virtue of the Missouri Compromise. Early settlers to the Midwest had flowed in along the Ohio Valley, and their Virginia and Kentucky roots had given the lower Midwest a proslavery tinge. Later waves of settlers sweeping across the prairies of the upper Midwest had by midcentury placed the region fairly firmly in the free-soil camp. The great railroad expansion of the 1850s linked the economy and interests of the Midwest to the Northeast, rivaling and ultimately surpassing the section's traditional orientation toward the Mississippi as the great highway of commerce and gateway to the world.

Midwesterners had their own views on the sectional crisis. The majority view in the region was free soil, the belief that slavery should not be allowed to spread so that new territories in the West could be reserved for free white labor. Yet the region's political culture was far from monolithic. The Ohio Valley continued to harbor much sympathy for slavery while the upper Midwest, including Iowa, contained many whose free-soil principles shaded over into out-and-out abolitionism. Evangelical Christians made Oberlin College, in Oberlin, Ohio, a hotbed of abolitionist thought and activity. The Underground Railroad operated throughout the region, spiriting escaped slaves northward to safety in Canada. In Iowa, the staunchly abolitionist Quaker town of Springdale harbored the notorious John Brown before his famous 1859 raid on the U.S. arsenal at Harpers Ferry, Virginia.

Introduction

From being a bastion of the Democratic party during the age of Andrew Jackson, the Midwest had become by 1860 sharply divided between Democrats and the new Republican party, with its free-soil and partially abolitionist ideology. Predictably, the political battle lines followed the patterns of settlement. The Ohio Valley remained solidly Democratic while the upper Midwest was enthusiastically Republican.

The region played an important role in the eventual Union victory in the Civil War. Besides the output of its farms and factories, the section also provided a major portion of the North's military leadership and manpower. It was the birthplace of the Union's best generals and the adopted home of President Abraham Lincoln. Several of the older and more populous midwestern states—Illinois, Indiana, and Ohio—each contributed more than a hundred regiments to the Union army. Iowa, though much newer and less densely settled, also contributed its share of soldiers, all of whom spent at least the majority of their service fighting west of the Appalachians, where Union armies made up primarily of midwesterners—or just "westerners," in the parlance of the time—fought the battles that ultimately decided the war's outcome.

The territory that would one day become the state of Iowa drew a steady stream of pioneers during the quarter century after Indian claims were settled. From a negligible white population in 1817, Iowa grew to nearly 200,000 inhabitants by 1850. Along the way, in 1845, it achieved statehood. The rapid growth continued right up to the Civil War, and in the 1860 census the state could boast a population of some 675,000. Once the deep, black, incredibly fertile prairie soil of Illinois had all been claimed, Iowa was the place for those who sought similar farming opportunities where the prairies stretched westward from the Mississippi. The new Iowans came predominantly from the five states of the Old Northwest—Wisconsin, Illinois, Indiana, Michigan, and Ohio. The second-largest cohort of immigrants to the Iowa prairies were those born in the states of the border, or upper, South—Kentucky, Virginia (including what is today West Virginia), and Maryland—and members of this group often came by way of temporary residence in one or more of the states of the Old Northwest.[1]

The James Remley family was among those who came to Iowa from the border South, migrating directly from their home near Lewisburg, Virginia (now West Virginia), to a farm near Oxford in 1855. Their new home was in Johnson County, Iowa, only about fifteen miles from Iowa City. The town of Iowa City was the seat of the University of Iowa and, until 1857, the capital of the state.[2] The proximity of the university was important to James Remley, a Baptist minister as well as a schoolteacher eager to assure a good education for his growing family. Between 1840 and 1857 James and his wife, Jane Alderson Remley, had eleven children.

By 1855 Virginia was becoming an inhospitable place for a man like James Remley to educate his offspring—or do anything else. The problem was that Remley believed that chattel slavery was not compatible with

Christianity, and he had the courage to say so, repeatedly. He would not have gotten away with that in the Deep South, nor yet in the more easterly, slave-populated areas of Virginia, but even in what is today West Virginia the voicing of such ideas brought consequences. When the oldest of the Remley children, fifteen-year-old Lycurgus, expressed his own antislavery views at a large student gathering at the Loudon Technical Institute where he was enrolled, a controversy arose that led ultimately to the young man's dismissal from the school in December 1855. By that time, the rest of the Remley family had already been several months on their new Iowa farm, and James had made arrangements for his son to enter the University of Iowa in January 1856. Several years later, Lycurgus's younger brother George (born September 7, 1841) also attended the university.

The outbreak of the Civil War interrupted the peaceful course of the Remley family's life. When Southerners styling themselves the Confederate States of America fired on U.S. troops and the U.S. flag at Fort Sumter, South Carolina, in April 1861, President Abraham Lincoln, following the example of George Washington when faced with the Whiskey Rebellion, issued a call for 75,000 state militia to serve for ninety days. That summer Union forces in eastern Virginia suffered a severe setback at the first battle of Bull Run. Even before that defeat, however, it had become clear that the Union was going to need far more than 75,000 men and for much longer than ninety days. On May 3 Lincoln issued his first call for three-year volunteers, 42,000 of them. By late summer he had issued an additional call for 500,000 men, and a number of subsequent calls for troops followed, each addressed to the governors of the various states.

The most famous of the additional appeals for volunteers was Lincoln's July 1, 1862, request to state governors for 300,000 men. The spring 1862 campaigns, begun with much promise for the Union, had developed poorly, especially in Virginia. More troops would clearly be needed to finish the war. Lincoln's midsummer appeal was celebrated by James Sloan Gibbons's song, "We Are Coming, Father Abra'am, Three Hundred Thousand More." Lincoln's appeal called forth a final great surge of patriotic enlistment in the North. Many who responded to his call were married men who had hesitated to enlist the previous year because of concerns for their families. Others among the "Three Hundred Thousand More" were youths below the age of twenty-one whose parents had refused them permission to go in 1861. Still others were men who had simply hoped to sit the war out but now, either because of the greater need of their country or because there appeared to be no choice, reluctantly faced the necessity of putting on the uniform. The reason military service might seem inescapable in the summer of 1862 was that Congress had recently approved conscription legislation. The looming specter of the draft gave Northern men an extra motivation to volunteer. The law provided that, if a state did not meet its enlistment quota by August 15, a draft would be imposed in that state to make up the difference. Considering it a great disgrace to be drafted, many men hastened to volunteer.

Introduction

At the beginning of the war, Iowans responded enthusiastically to Lincoln's initial calls for troops. A full regiment enlisted as part of the first 75,000. As the war continued, a total of more than 76,000 Iowans eventually served, which was more than a tenth of the total population and almost half the state's total number of men ages 18–45. Of those who served, 13,001 died—3,540 of wounds received in battle, 515 as prisoners of war, 448 in accidents, and the remaining 8,498 of disease. As in all wars before the twentieth century, microbes proved far more efficient killers than bullets, shells, and blades. This age-old feature of warfare was magnified in the case of the Iowa and other midwestern troops. Much of their service was to be in the lower Mississippi Valley, an extremely disease-rich environment.[3]

For reasons that are not clear today, Lycurgus and George Remley did not respond to any of the appeals for volunteers in 1861. This might seem strange for two single young men from a staunchly antislavery family. A possible clue to their thinking is found in the reminiscences of a fellow Iowan who also waited until 1862 before deciding to enlist, like the Remleys, in the 22nd Iowa Volunteer Infantry. Samuel Jones recalled after the war that, before the summer of 1862, many people had not considered the country's situation to be truly serious. Until the well-publicized Union military setbacks of that summer and Lincoln's call for additional enlistments, Jones wrote, "I had not thought it necessary that I should go. I had had a feeling that those who were enlisting were doing it because they delighted in the public display of the soldier life." The situation in the summer of 1862 forced him to reconsider. "A feeling came over me at this time," he later recalled, "that I was needed in the defense of my country. . . . I made up my mind to be a soldier and fight for my country."[4] The Remley brothers may well have reasoned similarly. In 1861 one might suppose that the crisis could be handled by those who fancied the quest for military glory. By the following year, thinking men could see that the country needed every healthy young man who was willing to serve.

Whatever their reasons, in August 1862 Lycurgus and George enlisted as part of Iowa's quota of the "Three Hundred Thousand More." Initial response to Lincoln's July 1 appeal was not strong in Iowa, but by early August— whether by virtue of time for reflection or the looming specter of the draft— recruits began to flock to the colors. Iowa's much-relieved governor, Samuel Kirkwood, reported, "Our whole state appears to be volunteering." During a single month, 24,438 Iowans enlisted, forming twenty-two new infantry regiments and furnishing a handful of replacements for the old.[5]

The Remley brothers enlisted in a new regiment, the 22nd Iowa. It was meant to be an all–Johnson County unit, and the county and its chief town, Iowa City, showed great enthusiasm for raising it. "Hardly a family in Iowa City and adjoining country but was represented in this Regiment," recalled one member. In the end, however, Johnson County could scrape together only seven companies, so the regiment's other three companies had to be taken from nearby Monroe, Wapello, and Jasper Counties.[6] The 22nd assembled at Camp Pope, just southeast of Iowa City on what one recruit described as "a beautiful green." Laborers were still working on the barracks that state authorities had hastily ordered to house the new regiment.[7] Bedding for the new barracks was provided by donations from the citizens of Iowa City. The 22nd's colonel was William M. Stone, a veteran of the 3rd Iowa who had been captured at the April 1862 battle of Shiloh and was still on parole (a common practice during the first half of the war) while his new regiment was organizing and training. In the colonel's absence, immediate command was the task of Lt. Col. Harvey Graham, who had started out as captain of Company A, the Wapello County company.

Graham and the regiment's company officers drilled the new recruits diligently. Battalion, company, and squad drill filled five hours each day.[8] Lycurgus had apparently gained some experience in military drill while in Chicago, possibly with a volunteer company such as that trained by well-known drillmaster Elmer Elsworth or perhaps with the "Wide-Awakes," a sort of pro-Lincoln drill team that staged campaign parades during the 1860 election. Because of his experience, Lycurgus was promoted to sergeant and helped drill his fellow recruits. Initially the men of the 22nd went through their drills, as well as regular camp guard duty, wearing civilian clothes and carrying wooden rifles, swords, and bayonets that they had made themselves because the real things were not yet available. The new soldiers were proud of their toy equipment.[9]

Real uniforms, arms, and accoutrements finally arrived early in September. Recruit Sam Jones recalled that the shipment also included "leather collars, epaulets," and all the regulation paraphernalia. Still, he considered himself and his fellow soldiers "a motley looking crowd." "Our uniforms," he explained, "were mostly ridiculous misfits. Some had to give their pants two or three rolls at the heels; others had shirts much too large which were, therefore, baggy, while others had to place paper in their hats so they would not slip down over their ears." The hats Jones mentioned were the U.S. Army's standard dress uniform headgear, the "Hardee Hat," a high-crowned, stiff, black hat with a broad, round rim pinned up on one side. The epaulets and leather collars were meant to accompany the regulation dress frock coat, but Jones noted that those accessories "were never worn."[10] Such informality about matters of uniform was typical of a western regiment. Those units put much less emphasis on "spit and polish," and they tended to sneer at eastern regiments, "paper collar" troops whom the westerners held to be slower on the march and less effective in battle. Notwithstanding the men's regional penchant for informality, the regiment cut a fine figure in Iowa City, drilling and parading frequently in front of Governor Kirkwood's house. Large numbers of local civilians turned out to see the spectacle and admire the regiment's growing proficiency in parade-ground maneuvers.[11]

On September 13 Lieutenant Colonel Graham received orders to have his regiment ready to march on short notice. After an impressive final parade through Iowa City, the column moved out of Camp Pope and marched away from its home town on the beginning of what was to become an unusually long and varied odyssey for a Civil War regiment.[12] The first march was a short one and took them to the Iowa City railroad station, where they boarded "boxcars, cattle cars and open coal cars" for the trip to Davenport, Iowa, on the Mississippi River. From Davenport the regiment traveled by steamboat, with several stops and interruptions, down the river to St. Louis and, five miles outside the city, the army's chief western facility, Benton Barracks. A week later the regiment once again piled onto a train for the ride to Rolla, Missouri, a little more than one hundred miles southwest of St. Louis and about halfway between that city and Springfield. "Rolla is a small place but I believe it is improving," wrote George Remley. "There is plenty of room for it." The soil in the region roundabout he considered "the poorest that I ever saw any where," and he wondered how anyone could make a living in the area.[13]

For the next four and a half months, the 22nd Iowa performed relatively mundane garrison duty in and around this little central Missouri town. The state's population was divided in its loyalties, and Union forces had to take precautions against pro-Confederate guerrillas and bushwhackers. "It is almost impossible to know who are and who are not Union," wrote Sam Jones.[14] The 22nd guarded commissary stores and the railroad and escorted wagon trains full of supplies on their way to Union forces operating farther south.[15] During their time in Rolla, the men of the 22nd experienced largely what most soldiers experience in war: boredom and discomfort. They lived first in wedge tents, then moved to larger Sibley tents when the weather got colder. The conical Sibley tents could accommodate more than a dozen men and had a small stove in the center for warmth. "Uncle Sam wants us to keep warm through the winter," noted Sam Jones.[16] Of this part of the war, George Remley later wrote, "While in Missouri we 'played soldier.'"

Nonetheless, the months in Rolla were important for the maturing of the 22nd into a seasoned unit. The men learned to live with military discipline. On November 17 a soldier of the Remleys' own Company F got into some kind of trouble, and the officers had him strung up by his thumbs. This was a painful and humiliating punishment that involved tying the culprit's thumbs to ropes suspended from an overhanging tree limb in such a way that he had to remain on his toes to avoid pulling his thumbs out of joint. It had been a common method of punishment in the prewar army, but it aroused so much murmuring in the regiment that the officers decided to use "milder forms of punishment" in the future. The regiment also continued to drill, both at Benton Barracks and, when other duties permitted, at Rolla.[17] "We drill both morning and evening, in the company and battalion drills, almost every day," wrote George, "and this together with the guard duty we have to perform occupies nearly all of our time."

A number of the Iowans suffered illness that first winter, which for any regiment was often a time of higher than usual rates of illness, as men were exposed to some diseases for the first time in the crowded communal environment. The 22nd experienced cases of measles, mumps, and even one case of smallpox.[18] Among the sick that winter was Lycurgus Remley, who diagnosed himself as having suffered an attack of "bilious intermittent fever." There were also lighter moments during the months of garrison duty in Rolla. Late one night Colonel Stone, who by then had been exchanged and joined the regiment, ordered the drummer to beat the long roll, summoning the regiment into line, and then proceeded to show the men an eclipse of the moon. On another occasion, after a snowstorm, the colonel divided the regiment into two sides and staged a massive snowball battle.[19]

In February 1863 the 22nd received orders to join a Union force under Brig. Gen. John W. Davidson on an uneventful campaign to Iron Mountain, Missouri, about one hundred miles southeast of Rolla by tortuous hill-country roads. "This long march through a mountainous region, at an inclement season of the year, with insufficient rations, was a severe test of the fortitude of the men," recalled a member of the regiment.[20] George Remley noted that they had passed over a spur of the Ozark Mountains, adding, "The road runs all the way through a heavily timbered country and some parts of it is very rough & hilly."

The trip brought one more rite of passage for the Iowans in their gradual transition from civilians to soldiers. On February 15 they saw their first dead Rebel—indeed, the first man living or dead whom the Iowans knew for certain to have been a Rebel. The Confederate guerrilla, killed in action against a Union cavalry patrol, lay dead in the middle of a byway that meandered through a forest. Apparently, Colonel Stone decided his men ought to see the corpse, so he marched them some distance off the main road to get to the place where the fallen bushwhacker lay, a tall red-haired fellow in butternut-colored clothing. The regiment was marching in column-of-twos, and the right file passed to one side of the body while the left passed on the other. The man's wife and children stood nearby, crying. Notwithstanding the fact that this fellow, had he lived, might have tried to kill any one of them from ambush, the Iowans were deeply touched by the grief of his family, some of them even shedding tears of sympathy. "We had not as yet been active in that part of war which makes widows and orphans," wrote Sam Jones.[21]

For the Remleys and the other men of the 22nd Iowa, as for most midwestern men who enlisted in the first two years of the war, the central event of the conflict, even the chief purpose of going to war, was restoring national control of the Mississippi River, the great highway of commerce on which the economy of their region had depended for half a century. The struggle for control of the Father of Waters came to focus on the campaign to take the Confederate bastion at Vicksburg, Mississippi. By the fall of 1862 the heavily fortified hilltop town of Vicksburg was the last remaining major Confederate stronghold on the Mississippi River. The Rebels held a smaller fortified outpost at Port Hudson, Louisiana, some miles to the south, but, as Lincoln remarked, "Vicksburg is the key." Lincoln's southern antagonist, Confederate President Jefferson Davis, agreed. Vicksburg, he opined, was "the Gibraltar of the West" and the nail that held the two halves of the Confederacy together. Control of Vicksburg meant control of the Mississippi River, and every well-informed midwesterner had known since the days of the Louisiana Purchase and before that the Mississippi River was the chief artery to America's heartland.

So it was that the 22nd Iowa's six months of relatively uneventful duty in Missouri came to an end March 9, 1863, with the arrival of orders to march from Iron Mountain to St. Genevieve, Missouri, on the Mississippi River, and there stand ready to board a steamboat for the trip down river to join Ulysses S. Grant's army operating against Vicksburg. Before the month was out, the regiment was encamped with much of the rest of Grant's forces at Milliken's Bend, Louisiana, a few miles above Vicksburg. Incorporated into the Army of the Tennessee, the 22nd Iowa became part of Brig. Gen. Michael K. Lawler's 2nd Brigade of Brig. Gen. Eugene A. Carr's 4th Division of Maj. Gen. John A. McClernand's 13th Corps.[22]

The encampment at Milliken's Bend lay on muddy river bottomland in the midst of "a vast stretch of level country, with some cotton and corn stalks standing" from the previous year's crops. It was out of sight of Vicksburg, some twenty river miles downstream, and its purpose was to serve as a supply base and a holding area for Grant's army until he could find a way to get his troops onto solid ground, accessible to Vicksburg, on the east bank of the river. Getting there had been the problem throughout the campaign. The swamps of the Yazoo River and Chickasaw Bayou, backed by the fortified Walnut Hills, blocked access to the Confederate bastion from the north. The broad Mississippi flowed by Vicksburg on the west, and the heavy Confederate batteries there prevented Grant from getting his boats below Vicksburg so as to cross the river there. While Grant tried one solution after another for this problem, his troops, including the 22nd Iowa, waited at Milliken's Bend and other camps on the west bank. They made occasional small-scale probes into the interior or up one of the tributaries of the Mississippi, and they also handled more mundane duties. Sam Jones wrote of helping unload mules, wagons, and other supplies from steamboats. Frequent rain kept the ground muddy.[23]

The 22nd had less than two weeks to wait, however, before Grant arrived at a solution. His transports, along with a naval flotilla under Rear Adm. David Dixon Porter, would boldly dash past the Vicksburg batteries some dark mid-April night. His army would march southward through the maze of bayous and backwaters on the Louisiana shore, link up with the fleet below Vicksburg, and cross to solid ground on the east bank. The 13th Corps would take the lead in this march, and Lawler's Brigade, including the 22nd Iowa, would lead the 13th Corps. They moved out on April 12, reached Richmond, Louisiana, and there drove off a small force of Confederate cavalry.[24] Pressing on, they reached New Carthage, Louisiana, by April 16. The march was a strange experience for the Iowans, as they tramped along the levee with the Mississippi close on one side and a flooded swamp on the other.

"The whole country is a water waste," wrote Sam Jones. "The houses are built on stilts or posts, so that the water can flow through beneath the living apartment."[25] Their trek ended at Perkins' Plantation, the immediate staging area for Grant's river crossing. Riverboat transports, having successfully run the Vicksburg batteries, embarked the 22nd and other Union troops, carried them down the river, and on the morning of April 30, 1863, landed them on the eastern bank at Bruinsburg. They were at last on Mississippi soil in the rear of Vicksburg, where Grant had wanted to put his army for the past four months.

Grant's plan for the coming campaign called for the army to march far from its sources of supply with only a tenuous string of shuttling wagons carrying a minimum of food, forage, and ammunition. It was therefore essential for the troops to carry a maximum of food with them on the march. Three days' rations, the normal issue, was almost enough to fill the soldiers' haversacks, the usual place for carrying food. No sooner had the first Union troops landed on the Mississippi shore than the commissaries began issuing five days' rations. The problem for the soldiers was how to carry this sudden abundance. Members of the 22nd Iowa came up with a solution that other regiments quickly copied. Two soldiers from each company walked one behind the other, carrying their rifles between them, one across their right shoulders and the other across their left. Atop these horizontal rifles they carried an entire box of hardtack between them. Throughout the morning the men took turns toting the cracker box. The soldiers carried their extra meat individually impaled on the ends of their fixed bayonets swaying above the column as the men marched along at right-shoulder shift. The day's consumption of food reduced the surplus enough that by evening the men could stow all of their remaining food in more conventional ways.[26]

Lawler's brigade had the lead, with the 22nd regiment marching second in the column, right behind their fellow Iowans of the 21st. Throughout the day they marched across the flat river bottoms. About nine o'clock that evening their road led up into "broken and hilly country," a plateau cut by innumerable winding, steep-sided ravines. General McClernand kept his corps on the march, and shortly thereafter the head of the column made contact with the first Rebel pickets. Their brigade commander deployed a company or two of skirmishers in front of his column and pressed on. The Rebels fell back, now and then taking potshots at the advancing Federals. The Iowans tramped through the darkness in cautious silence. All speaking was done in a whisper, and otherwise the only sounds came from the frogs and crickets—punctuated at irregular intervals by the startling sound of a shot up ahead.[27]

Between midnight and 1:00 A.M., May 1, Confederate resistance stiffened. The Iowa troops were approaching the town of Port Gibson, Mississippi, and it was plain that a significant Rebel force barred their way. The whole 21st Iowa deployed in skirmish line and drove the Rebel skirmishers back onto their main line. The 22nd followed in column, occasionally stepping over or around the bodies of dead Iowans of their sister regiment. Then they deployed to the left of the 21st. Two guns of the 1st Iowa Battery came up and opened on the Confederate line. The Rebels answered with guns of their own, and a short range artillery duel lit the night with its flashes. The artillerists and their horses took casualties, but the men of the 22nd Iowa, sheltered behind a fold of ground, suffered little. The firing died down an hour or two before dawn. Some of the Iowans dozed while others waited uneasily for daylight and their first battle.[28]

Those who had slept were awake before dawn. It was quiet at first, so quiet it seemed almost unnatural to the nervous, waiting soldiers. Then about 7:00 A.M. scattered shots marked the opening of the battle. Firing gradually increased along the line of battle until both infantry and artillery were heavily engaged. Additional Union troops came up and moved into line. Around ten o'clock Lawler's Iowa brigade, including the 22nd, formed up to make an assault, but the Confederates withdrew a mile farther back toward Port Gibson. Other Union troops took the lead in the next phase of the fighting, but twice during the afternoon the 22nd Iowa obeyed orders to move up to the firing line and engage the enemy, much of the time fighting in thick woods and canebrakes. As darkness began to gather, the outnumbered Confederates fled, leaving the Federals in control of the battlefield, the town of Port Gibson, and the important bridges over nearby Bayou Pierre. "Thus ended our first great battle," wrote Sam Jones. "We went into camp on the battlefield, weary and hungry."[29]

The Remley brothers came through the battle unscathed. "It is needless to tell how many narrow escapes we had and how the balls flew around us like hail," wrote George to his family back in Iowa a few days later, "yet in the midst of this storm of lead and iron we were kept from harm and came out unscathed. A Heavenly Father was kindly watching over us and shielding us from the deadly bullets. This thought comforted and cheered me more than any thing else could have done." Two members of the regiment died at the battle of Port Gibson, and twenty-one others were wounded.

As the troops that had seen some of the toughest fighting in the battle just concluded, the 22nd Iowa, along with the rest of its brigade, was for several days assigned to occupy the captured town of Port Gibson and the nearby railroad bridge over Bayou Pierre, gather abandoned equipment from the battlefield, and guard prisoners. Orders were strict that there should be no foraging—gathering supplies of food from the civilian population—and Major Atherton, now temporarily commanding the 22nd while Colonel Stone was on detached duty, held roll calls every three hours to make sure the men stayed in camp. During the ten days after the battle of Port Gibson the regiment marched only twice, and then only moderate distances.[30]

On May 12 the pace of the 22nd Iowa's campaign picked up again. Orders had them on their feet at 3:00 A.M. and on the move by sunrise. The following day they pushed on through the town of Raymond, viewing the wrecked wagons and guns and scarred trees left by a battle fought there the day before, in which other troops of Grant's army had been victorious. Their march was taking them in the direction of Jackson, Mississippi, the state capital, but on May 14 they learned that Maj. Gen. William T. Sherman's 15th Corps, now marching ahead of McClernand's 13th Corps, had taken the city that day. Accordingly, the 13th Corps, including the 22nd Iowa, turned the next morning, on Grant's orders, and marched due west, toward Vicksburg itself. By taking Jackson, Grant had struck a blow against the most likely conduit for any Confederate attempt to aid Vicksburg's defenders. Approaching the Gibraltar of the West directly from the rear, Grant now had leverage on the defending Confederate army of Gen. John C. Pemberton.[31]

On May 16 Pemberton's Confederates met Grant's Federals at a place called Champion's Hill, between Jackson and Vicksburg. That morning the 22nd Iowa marched six miles to reach the battlefield. They stacked their knapsacks, posted a guard over them, and moved forward to form line of battle along the edge of a woodland, looking out toward the open fields held by Pemberton's Confederates. Along with most of the 13th Corps, they were on the left of the Union line. The fighting that day took place almost entirely on the Union right while McClernand, confused about his orders, hung back and failed to commit his corps to battle. A couple of shells sailing over their position constituted all the battle that raged around the 22nd that day. With the Union forces on the right victorious, the 22nd and the rest of the army marched after the fleeing Confederates.[32]

This time, however, as troops who had not been heavily engaged in the battle, the 22nd's division, that of Brig. Gen. Eugene Carr, had the lead. They gathered up some 200 prisoners near the battlefield and later skirmished with the Confederates at Edward's Station, several miles farther west. The Iowans drove the Rebels out of the town, capturing more prisoners, and extinguished fires the Confederates had set in several trains full of provisions there. Their officers directed the Iowans to help themselves to the salvaged provisions, and the men, who for the past two weeks had been living primarily on what they could scrounge off the countryside—field peas, parched corn, and small amounts of fresh beef—needed no urging. The regiment bedded down near Edward's Station about eleven o'clock that night.[33]

May 17 was to be the most glorious day of the war for the 22nd Iowa, but George and Lycurgus Remley, along with their comrades in Company F, had no part in it. Detailed as provost guards after the battle of Champion's Hill, their chief duty on May 17 was guarding the numerous Rebel prisoners of war. While Company F herded its throng of disconsolate wards along the road well to the rear, the rest of the regiment experienced one of the most exhilarating victories of the war. Called into line early that morning, they marched a short distance before encountering a strong Confederate position. Pemberton had turned at bay on the east bank of the Big Black River, covering the bridges that led from Jackson to Vicksburg. McClernand deployed his corps facing the Confederate position while skirmishers and artillerymen dueled across no-man's-land. Soon after the lines were drawn up,

Lawler's brigade, including the 22nd Iowa, launched a furious bayonet assault against heavy Confederate entrenchments and successfully broke the Rebel line. This proved to be the key to Union victory at the battle of Big Black Bridge, resulting in the taking of hundreds of Confederate prisoners and sending Pemberton's badly beaten army fleeing all the way back into the Vicksburg entrenchments.[34]

Company F, including the Remley brothers, rejoined the regiment on May 22, in time to witness but not take part in the 22nd Iowa's second greatest moment of glory, a moment also mixed with tragedy. In the great assault on the Confederate lines that took place that day, the 22nd was one of a few Union regiments that managed to make small lodgments in the Confederate fortifications. The 22nd's target was the Railroad Redoubt, one of nine major Confederate forts guarding the city. During the desperate fight, the regiment's national flag flew over the Confederate parapet for nine hours. The 22nd's Sgt. Joseph E. Griffith and Sgt. Nicholas G. Messenger led a party of eleven men through a breach in the parapet and into the Confederate redoubt. For more than an hour they fought there, sometimes hand-to-hand. Only Griffith and one other man came out alive, but they brought with them thirteen Rebel prisoners.[35] The Iowans and the rest of Grant's troops finally had to give up their assault and retreat back to their starting positions that evening. Seventy members of the regiment had died that day, and many others were wounded. In all, 83 percent of those 22nd Iowa members who made the charge became casualties. During the night that followed, many of the wounded "were still lying on the slope near the fort calling for water." Their comrades rescued as many as they could reach.[36] George Remley, who had watched the fight from a distance along with the others who had just returned from guarding prisoners, wrote in a letter home a few days later, "When the regiment made that charge it seemed very hard to see them fight so bravely and not be allowed to give them that assistance they so much needed."

After the failed assault of May 22, the Army of the Tennessee settled down to lay siege to Vicksburg. For the next six weeks the routine was much the same. Each day Union snipers played a deadly game with their Confederate counterparts and generally succeeded in making the defenders keep their heads down. Taylor Peirce thought the sound of constant firing along the siege lines sounded like a lot of men busy chopping wood.[37] Each night Union work details dug their trenches closer and closer to the Confederate fortifications, in some places finally advancing to within scarcely a dozen yards of the enemy. Day and night the Union artillery, both on land and on the navy's gun and mortar boats out in the river, pounded the town and the Confederate fortifications around it. Union troops took their turns in the rifle pits, the work parties, and resting in more or less sheltered ravines a few score yards to the rear. Occasionally, while a work party of the 22nd Iowa dug its zigzag trenches forward through no-man's-land, an artillery duel would erupt between the Confederates and the Sixteenth Ohio Battery, posted near the 22nd's position. Then the Iowans would crouch a bit lower, not only in respect for the Confederate fire but also in fear of infrequent but deadly short rounds from the Union battery. At other times the Iowans met their Confederate counterparts at night in informal truces between the lines. There they swapped stories, tobacco, coffee, and other commodities. Then they returned to their trenches and went back to shooting at each other. It was that kind of war.[38]

Heat and humidity were extreme, and often the locations where Union regiments had to make their camps—in order to be at least moderately safe from Confederate fire—seemed designed to roast the soldiers in the sun. Disease made slow but steady subtractions from Grant's troop strength, and yet his army did not suffer the wholesale plague of illness that he had feared and his enemies had hoped. Blackberries were plump and plentiful in the many bramble-choked ravines around Vicksburg, and some soldiers maintained that the tangy black fruits were healthful. Mainly, though, Grant's army by this time must have been fairly tough.

The 22nd Iowa's camp was 700–1,000 yards from the Confederate fortifications, sheltered by intervening high ground. Iowa soldier Jacob Switzer described it as being located "in the head of a short ravine, formed in a [semi]circle with the convex side to the enemy, around the brow of a hill at the foot of which was a spring from which we and many other Regiments in the vicinity obtained our supply of drinking water."[39] On June 19, perhaps by luck, the Confederates succeeded in bursting several shells directly over the 22nd's camp. The Union artillery, however, replied with a vengeance and beat down the Confederate guns in short order. No more was heard from the Rebel cannon in that quarter.[40]

On July 2, 1863, the 22nd Iowa was ordered to march to a place called Red Bone Chapel, some miles to the rear of Vicksburg. The soldiers never understood just why they had to make that weary tramp, for the men were unused to marching after six weeks in the siege lines, the heat was oppressive, and a number of men suffered heat exhaustion. The next day they had an even hotter and more wearisome march right back to their old position, where they arrived in time to learn that Pemberton had sent out a flag of truce to ask Grant for terms of surrender.[41]

While the generals negotiated, troops from both sides climbed out of their trenches to gaze for the first time, in broad daylight, at the whole panorama of siege works around them. For the previous six weeks, showing one's head above the parapet even for a moment had been an invitation for an enemy sharpshooter to try his skill. Now the men savored the strange feeling of standing in the open with complete impunity. Where the lines were close enough—and the 22nd Iowa's line was only fifty yards from the Rebel parapet—the opposing sides engaged in conversation. "It was singular," recalled the 22nd Iowa's Jacob Switzer, "to hear deadly enemies chatting with each other, joking, laughing and talking, apparently as socially as if they were best of friends."[42]

Introduction

Grant and Pemberton finished their negotiations. At 10:00 A.M., July 4, 1863, the Confederate troops in Vicksburg marched out of their trenches, stacked their arms, and surrendered, all 31,600 of them. From their position on the Union left, the men of the 22nd Iowa could see Maj. Gen. John A. Logan's division of the Seventeenth Corps "marching into the city from its position with flags unfurled and waving to the breeze," a striking contrast to "the dirty white flags on the Confederate forts." More socializing followed between the lines, the Iowans engaging in friendly conversations with the Carolinians and Alabamians across the way. Sam Jones thought such sociability "the wonder of the ages." "This is surely one of the happiest days of our lives," the Iowa soldier added.[43] The tired Union soldiers celebrated exuberantly. "I now hear cheer after cheer from our men expressing their joy at this long looked for event," wrote George Remley in a letter dated 10:00 A.M., July 4.

The men of Grant's army looked forward to a period of rest after more than two solid months of vigorous campaigning, but they reckoned without the aggressiveness of their commander. No sooner had Pemberton's Confederates at Vicksburg surrendered than Grant sent the bulk of his army, including the 22nd Iowa, in hot pursuit of Confederate Gen. Joseph E. Johnston's force at Jackson, Mississippi, which the Confederates had reoccupied while Grant was busy with Vicksburg. Johnston had been hovering in central Mississippi with 25,000–30,000 men for the past several weeks with the assigned mission of raising Grant's siege of Vicksburg. He had not gotten around to striking, and now Grant determined to strike him. When word of the planned marched reached the 22nd's camp on the evening of July 4, the soldiers were dismayed. "Our men is very much out of heart this evening having to pack up and march so soon after accomplishing so much and doing so much labour," wrote the 22nd's Taylor Peirce to his wife, Catharine, that evening. Still, he added, "if by doing hard service will end this I for one will not complain."[44]

The march to Jackson the next day was a grueling one for Grant's soldiers. The roads were dusty and the weather brutally hot—up to 100 degrees.[45] Many soldiers, weakened by their previous hard service, fell out of ranks or had to report themselves sick. As the march was starting out that morning the officers of the 22nd Iowa, at least, attempted to fortify the men for the coming physical ordeal by setting out a barrel of whiskey laced with quinine and marching the men up to dip their tin cups as they went by, in accordance with medical opinion in the 1860s, which held that whiskey strengthened the body in times of particular stress or exposure to inclement weather. The whiskey certainly failed to produce the desired effect in the 22nd, and soon some of the men, having consumed their own rations and those of their nondrinking comrades, were falling out of ranks drunk. The next day's march took them through the scenes of their triumphs the preceding May, across the Black River and into camp near Edward's Station.

By July 10 they reached the Confederate fortifications around Jackson, Mississippi. For the next week they skirmished with the Confederates there, and the encounter began to take on some of the characteristics of a siege, as the Federals pushed their lines closer and closer to the Confederate works each day. Then on the morning of July 17 the Union army in the outskirts of Jackson discovered that the wily Johnston had slipped out of town with his army the preceding night, retreating eastward into the piney woods of Mississippi. This time the Union forces, commanded on the spot by Sherman, did not pursue. Before returning to Vicksburg, however, Sherman determined to damage the Confederate infrastructure in central Mississippi. Among the Union troops detailed to tear up railroad tracks, burn the ties, and bend the rails were eight companies of the 22nd Iowa. Company F, however, was one of two companies detailed to guard a battery of artillery and so missed this hard but entertaining work. The reunited regiment then marched back to Vicksburg, where they arrived July 23. At last the long campaign was over, and, for a time, the soldiers could rest.[46]

Back home in Iowa, life went on in some ways as it had before the war, and, as it had before the war, it continued to change. The state's population was growing, which was reflected in four new congressional seats awarded to the state in 1862. In Johnson County, including Iowa City, land prices continued to climb as a steady influx of newcomers more than replaced a constant out-migration of families leaving for Oregon, Nevada, California, or other western destinations. Iowa's farms continued to produce ever larger crops, as the prairie farmers more than replaced the manpower absent in the army with newfangled farming machinery. Town life also seemed to be more of the same: the *Iowa City Republican* (a newspaper) complained that the town's citizens were "devoid of literary taste and interest in educational enterprises." "A circus with a bear, dog, mule and monkey show draws thousands at fifty cents apiece," the editor scolded, while "the commencement exercises of the . . . University, free to all, are hardly noticed." Of course.[47]

The war made an impact on Iowa politics, and the state was already well on its way to becoming the one-party bastion of Republicanism it would be after the war. In the eyes of many Iowans, being a Democrat simply smacked of disloyalty. A small minority of Iowans clung to their Democratic party allegiance, and some of them were indeed disloyal—the notorious Copperheads. Their newspapers, such as the *Iowa City State Democratic Press,* raged against Lincoln, the war, and, especially, emancipation. Spitting racial epithets, the *Democratic Press* expressed the wish that some good would come of the newly announced Union policy of recruiting blacks into the army, namely that it would rid the town of African Americans. The majority of Iowans, however, would have been more in agreement with the *Democratic Press*'s rival paper, the *Iowa City Republican,* in asserting that the government should use whatever means necessary to suppress the rebellion, including, perhaps, the wholesale recruitment of black soldiers.[48] Away in Mississippi in the army, opinion was far less divided. The soldiers were all but unanimous that the war should be prosecuted aggressively to complete victory. As far as the soldiers were concerned, Copperheads were reptiles.

Introduction

★ ★ ★

Grant's army remained in and around Vicksburg for several weeks that summer after its return from the environs of Jackson. Grant was eager to undertake further offensive operations, this time against Mobile, Alabama, but the authorities in Washington had other ideas. For reasons, both political and strategic, that seemed good to the high command, much of Grant's victorious army was dispersed and, in his words, "sent where it would do the least good." Among the troops transferred away from the Army of the Tennessee was the 13th Corps, including the 22nd Iowa. In early August the corps got orders to report to Maj. Gen. Nathaniel P. Banks commanding the Department of the Gulf and headquartered at New Orleans.[49]

The orders for New Orleans arrived August 13, 1863, and the regiment boarded steamboats that same day. Company F, along with one other company of the 22nd, rode the steamboat *Autocrat*. On the evening of August 15, they arrived at Carrollton, Louisiana, a northern suburb of New Orleans. "Camp Carrollton," Sam Jones wrote, "is a beautiful camping ground on the shell road. It has every convenience and is connected with New Orleans by railroad, trains running during the day hourly." The weather, the circumstances, and even the food seemed pleasant. The soldiers thoroughly enjoyed their stay. Quite a number of them decided to avail themselves of the opportunity of attending Sunday school at a nearby church. The superintendent, however, politely asked them not to come back. The presence of Yankee soldiers offended some of the die-hard pro-Confederate members, and, besides, so many soldiers wanted to attend that they swamped the local congregation.[50]

On September 4, the 22nd Iowa was ordered out, along with the rest of the troops around New Orleans, for a grand review by their new commander, the hapless Banks, and their former commanding general, Ulysses S. Grant. The next day the 22nd, along with other troops, departed on what became known as the Bayou Teche campaign, under the immediate command of Maj. Gen. William B. Franklin. This operation took them by boat and train to Berwick Bay on the Louisiana coast. Thence they marched to Vermillionville, arriving October 10. Little of consequence took place. The expedition accomplished nothing, and only minor skirmishing occurred. Orders from Franklin strictly forbade foraging, but the soldiers proved adept at circumventing such prohibitions. They enjoyed large amounts of the chief local products—sugar, oranges (abundant but "usually of an inferior quality"), and, most of all, sweet potatoes. They did not enjoy what appeared to be the region's other chief product, very large and aggressive mosquitoes. By November 9 they were back at Berwick Bay, where they enjoyed pleasant camping for the next week before returning to New Orleans.[51]

The Lincoln administration was concerned about French intervention in Mexican politics and therefore desired to establish a Union military presence in Texas. That desire led to the 22nd's next adventure, which began on November 20 when Company F and four other companies, along with all of the 11th Wisconsin, embarked on the steamer *T. A. Scott* for the voyage to the Texas coast. After various delays and a stormy passage, they arrived off Aransas Pass, near Corpus Christi, November 25 and went ashore on Mustang Island, an overgrown sandbar just off the Texas coast. They were soon joined by the rest of their division. During the next several weeks they maneuvered along the coast and the coastal islands by boat and on foot. Light Confederate forces hovered in the vicinity, but no significant combat took place. In December the regiment crossed to Matagorda Island and went into camp at De Crow's Point. There they celebrated Christmas 1863.[52]

On January 4, 1864, the regiment was on the move again, this time crossing to the Texas mainland and camping near Indianola. The most memorable event of the Iowans' stay there was a severe winter storm that blew for a week and put a half-inch-thick layer of ice on top of all the fresh water in sight. "The soldiers suffered intensely from the keen piercing winds," wrote Jacob Switzer, "as they seemed to be much more penetrating and cutting in this climate than they are in the North."[53]

Yet spring came early on the south Texas coast, with balmy days in February. The 22nd remained in the area until late April, when they once again shipped out for New Orleans, this time headed for much different duty in a far distant part of the country. Along with several other regiments of the old 13th Corps, the 22nd was incorporated into the 19th Corps and in July embarked with that corps for Virginia. During the remainder of the war, the 22nd campaigned in the Remley brothers' native state. It became part of Maj. Gen. Philip Sheridan's Army of the Shenandoah and served with him through the series of battles that autumn culminating in the complete defeat of the Rebel army of Lt. Gen. Jubal A. Early at the battle of Cedar Creek, October 19.

At the first of those Shenandoah Valley battles, known as the third battle of Winchester (September 19, 1864), Sgt. Maj. George A. Remley was among those whom his brigade commander cited for "conspicuous gallantry."[54] It was a hard-fought battle. The 22nd Iowa, along with the rest of its brigade, started the morning at 2:00 A.M. near Berryville, Virginia. They neared Winchester, and the enemy, around ten o'clock that morning. Crossing Opequon Creek, the regiment took its place in the Union line of battle ranged over a series of low hills. The ordeal of the 22nd Iowa began at once. They were on the left of their brigade, and unlike the other regiments, which had the cover of woods, the 22nd was in full view of the enemy, who began to shell them at once. Seeing this, their brigade commander ordered their line to fall back somewhat in hopes of finding more sheltered ground for them.

At 11:30 A.M., however, the order came to charge the enemy's strongly entrenched position. Once again the 22nd Iowa came in for special attention. While the other regiments advanced through the forest, the 22nd had to cross an open field half a mile wide, torn first by shells, then by rifle fire and blasts of the canister from the enemy artillery. The latter was the most destructive type of artillery ammunition known to the era. Effective only at relatively short range, it consisted essentially of a can of lead or iron slugs. A cannon using it became, in effect, an enormous sawed-off shotgun. The blasts of canister tore gaps in the Iowans' line, but the survivors closed their ranks and pushed on.

Coming to a very slight upward slope in the ground not far from the Confederate line, the 22nd received orders to lie down and try to shelter themselves from the murderous enemy fire. The rise of the ground was very slight, and the men had to hug the dirt closely. To make matters worse, they had no sooner gained the rise than the brigade on their left broke for the rear in confusion. Confederate troops pressed forward into the void thus created and added to the punishment of the regiment by pouring a heavy enfilading fire into their left flank. After about half an hour of this, new orders came directing the regiment to fall back to its original position, as they were in imminent danger of being surrounded. The retreat covered 300 yards, and they lost men, killed and wounded, all the way.

The fight continued fiercely, and ammunition began to run low. Meanwhile, Union forces elsewhere on the battlefield had been more successful and drove the Confederates back toward the town of Winchester. Joining in the victorious effort, the 22nd Iowa and the other regiments of its brigade went over to the offensive again, advancing once more into the teeth of fierce Confederate fire and taking heavy casualties. By nightfall the enemy was in full retreat, and the victorious Army of the Shenandoah, including the battered 22nd Iowa, was in pursuit. They would fight again in the weeks to come, including the dramatic battle of Cedar Creek, just one month later, but the battle of Winchester took its place alongside the charge at Big Black Bridge and the May 22, 1863, assault at Vicksburg as one of the 22nd Iowa's most heroic and costly days of the war.[55]

★ ★ ★

The Remley brothers present in their letters an unusually good opportunity to glimpse the thoughts, motivations, and daily lives of Civil War soldiers. In some ways, George and Lycurgus experienced war much the way other Civil War soldiers did, especially those from the Midwest. They encountered the regimentation of military life and the boredom and discomfort of life in camp. They made hard marches and fought in, or at least witnessed, several battles. They also lived with the far more deadly threat of camp diseases.

On the other hand, George and Lycurgus were different from the average Civil War soldier in several ways that make their letters more valuable. They were unusually articulate, perceptive, and thoughtful, making them good observers and commentators on Civil War soldier life. Large collections of soldier letters, such as this one, are more common in the East than in the West. The Remleys were in the West. Generally, officers were more articulate and thus more likely to write full and descriptive letters than were their enlisted soldiers, and yet neither of the Remleys ever rose to commissioned rank. The Remleys had better than average education. Above all, their status as virtual refugees from the proslavery South gave them unusual insights on the war and its causes. All of these factors combine to lend special fascination to their chronicles of an odyssey that started in Iowa, led through some of the most dramatic and decisive scenes of the war, and ended in their native Virginia.

The Remleys' status as former Virginians may have influenced their perceptions of a controversy that boiled over at the University of Iowa about the time George and Lycurgus were signing up in the 22nd. University of Iowa president Silas Totten was, like the Remleys, a Virginia native. Unlike the Remleys, however, he tended to be Democratic in his politics, leading some to question his loyalty. Governor Kirkwood wanted Totten out of the university and, after a year of pressure on the board of trustees, succeeded in accomplishing his purpose. Totten resigned, and Prof. Oliver M. Spencer replaced him as interim president. Spencer had offered his resignation at the same time, apparently in sympathy with Totten. The trustees, however, rejected his resignation and elevated him to the presidency. His stated belief that a teacher's loyalty to his country should be second only to his loyalty to God was much more to Kirkwood's liking.[56] The Remleys were good enough friends of President Totten, and particularly with his son Dick, to spend a night at the Totten house while waiting in Iowa City for the 22nd regiment to organize. George Remley reported to his father the news of the change of personnel at the university, including the dismissal of another professor and yet another's conversion to Republicanism and resulting retention on the faculty. He did not express his own opinion but probably felt conflicting feelings: loyalty to a friend and fellow Virginia expatriate, on the one hand, and staunch antislavery Republicanism, on the other.

The brothers had much to say about religion. "Sunday we went to preaching twice & to Sunday School," George informed his father in August 1862, as the young men waited for the regiment to organize. The pattern continued throughout their service, as Lycurgus and George took every opportunity to attend worship and lamented that the opportunities were not more abundant. "In the Army we have next to no religious privileges," Lycurgus wrote early in 1863. "Our Chaplain, now at home, has preached only four or five times since we have been in the army. We have *no* opportunities for prayer meetings, and few, for private devotions. Add to this the contaminating influence of the example of all around us, and you have some idea of the difficulty of maintaining an upright Christian walk." George and Lycurgus frequently requested the prayers of their relatives at home. Each man carried a Bible with him, and Lycurgus purchased seven New Testaments to give out to those of his comrades who might not have a copy of the Scriptures. "I still endeavor to maintain my Christian integrity," Lycurgus wrote, "and hope by the grace of God to persevere. It is the presence & support of

Introduction

the Almighty alone that sustains me in the troubles incident to a soldier's life." George also found divine strength to sustain him. Learning that the regiment was slated to join Grant's army in the battle of Vicksburg, he wrote, "We shall be in the midst of scenes of danger and perhaps bloody strife. Though I shall be called upon to stand face to face with death—I fear it not, for I know that *he* in whom I have trusted is just as able to protect me when on the field of battle as when at home surrounded by friends."

Like most Civil War soldiers, the Remleys found themselves in a tight community of comradeship, something George alluded to when he spoke of being "enclosed within the friendly circumference of our Sibley tent" during the winter near Rolla. The army's practice of allowing men to serve in companies enlisted entirely from their own communities, in contrast to military practice in later wars, meant that the sense of community went with the soldiers into the field. The tent of which George wrote accommodated eighteen men, who had apparently chosen to tent together because they shared the same affinities. Six of them were professed Christians. Other tents were the scene of card playing and coarse language, but not the Remleys'. Later in the war, the soldiers had to give up their Sibley tents and make do with the small two-man shelter (or "pup") tents, which they hated, in part because the small tents did not allow the fellowship and camaraderie of the larger Sibleys. Beyond the circle of even the largest tent, however, the Remleys, like other Civil War soldiers, felt a strong community attachment to those they called "the boys," the men of their company.

The soldiers of the Civil War were mostly highly literate, reading fairly extensively and producing a massive volume of letters. The Remleys were even more so. Their literary interests come through frequently in the letters. At one point George mentioned that they were subscribing to two periodicals, the *Iowa City Republican* and the *Christian Times*. They also managed to obtain copies of *Harper's Weekly,* the leading periodical of the era. They were familiar with the classics too. Lycurgus referred to Vicksburg as "this modern Troy," and spoke of following "the example of Virgil in the Aeniad," in his manner of telling a story in the letter he was writing. George revealed, "I have a volume of Plutarch's Lives with which I spend my leisure moments that I happen to have." George also read his Virgil, at least enough to joke, "I saw a quotation from Virgil the other day and I want Howard to let me know whether the translation is correct or not. It is this— 'illi Lao-Coonta petunt' and may be found in the Æneid Book 2nd 212 verse. The translation is *'they all went a coon hunting.'*" Such classical scholarship was far from unique in the Civil War armies, but it does mark the Remleys as being better educated than the average enlisted men.

Yet, contrary to the prevailing conventional view regarding supposedly squeamish Victorians, they could speak very plainly about the horrors of war. During the siege of Vicksburg, George volunteered to work briefly in a field hospital and afterward graphically described the experience in a letter to his family:

I hope that I may never again be called upon to witness such scenes of suffering and horror as I looked upon that night. Were I to live a thousand years their impression could never be effaced from my memory. To hear a man deprived of an arm or a leg, beg to have those limbs covered up "that they felt cold" or to see the eager gasp of the dying man after a sip of cold water or to hear him earnestly plead to be allowed to get up that his sufferings might be alleviated, is painful in the extreme, but these things and far more than these greeted my senses as with a candle in one hand and a pail of water and a cup in the other, I picked my way *among* the wounded and *over* the *amputated limbes* that were scattered around the Hospital grounds.

Frank, articulate, thoughtful, and observant, the Remley brothers make fascinating commentators on that part of the Civil War they witnessed from the ranks of an unusually well-traveled regiment. Yet their experiences, and the scenes they observed, were representative of the Civil War careers of tens of thousands of soldiers.

NOTES

1. Joseph Frazier Wall, *Iowa: A Bicentennial History* (New York: W. W. Norton, 1978), 48–64.
2. Ibid., 100.
3. Steve Meyer, *Iowans Called to Valor* (Garrison, Iowa: Meyer, 1993), 9.
4. Samuel Calvin Jones, *Reminiscences of the Twenty-Second Iowa Volunteer Infantry* ... (1907; rpt., Iowa City, Iowa: Camp Pope Bookshop, 1993), 5–6.
5. Meyer, *Iowans Called to Valor,* 74.
6. Jones, *Reminiscences,* 7.
7. Ibid., 7.
8. Richard L. Kiper, ed., *Dear Catharine, Dear Taylor: The Civil War Letters of a Union Soldier and His Wife* (Lawrence: University Press of Kansas, 2002), 25.
9. Jones, *Reminiscences,* 8; Tony Klingensmith, *Samuel Day of the 22nd Iowa,* <www.iowa-counties.com/civilwar/SamuelDay/index.htm>, chap. 1; Meyer, *Iowans Called to Valor,* 21–22, 67.
10. Jones, *Reminiscences,* 8.
11. Klingensmith, *Samuel Day of the 22nd Iowa,* chap. 1.
12. Kiper, *Dear Catharine, Dear Taylor,* 27, 29; Jones, *Reminiscences,* vii.
13. Klingensmith, *Samuel Day of the 22nd Iowa,* chap. 1.
14. Jones, *Reminiscences,* 12.
15. Klingensmith, *Samuel Day of the 22nd Iowa,* chap. 1.
16. Jones, *Reminiscences,* 11.
17. Ibid., 10–11.
18. Ibid., 11.
19. Klingensmith, *Samuel Day of the 22nd Iowa,* chap. 1.
20. Ibid.
21. Jones, *Reminiscences,* 19–20; Klingensmith, *Samuel Day of the 22nd Iowa,* chap. 1.

Introduction

22. Jones, *Reminiscences,* 25.
23. Ibid., 25–26.
24. Klingensmith, *Samuel Day of the 22nd Iowa,* chap. 3.
25. Jones, *Reminiscences,* 27.
26. Ibid., 29–30.
27. Ibid., 30.
28. Kiper, *Dear Catharine, Dear Taylor,* 106; Jones, *Reminiscences,* 30–31.
29. Jones, *Reminiscences,* 31–32.
30. Ibid., 32–33.
31. Ibid., 33.
32. Ibid., 33–34.
33. Ibid., 34.
34. Ibid., 34–36.
35. *The War of the Rebellion: A Compilation of the Official Records of the Union and Confederate Armies,* 128 vols. (Washington, D.C.: Government Printing Office, 1880–1901), ser. 1, 24(pt. 1):154–55 (hereafter cited as *OR*); Edwin C. Bearss, *The Campaign for Vicksburg,* vol. 3, *Unvexed to the Sea* (Dayton, Ohio: Morningside, 1986), 825–27.
36. Jones, *Reminiscences,* 39–40.
37. Kiper, *Dear Catharine, Dear Taylor,* 115.
38. Jones, *Reminiscences,* 40; Klingensmith, *Samuel Day of the 22nd Iowa,* chap. 9.
39. Klingensmith, *Samuel Day of the 22nd Iowa,* chap. 9.
40. Jones, *Reminiscences,* 41.
41. Ibid., 42.
42. Klingensmith, *Samuel Day of the 22nd Iowa,* chap. 9.
43. Jones, *Reminiscences,* 42.
44. Kiper, *Dear Catharine, Dear Taylor,* 124.
45. Thomas H. Bringhurst and Frank Swigart, *History of the Forty-sixth Regiment Indiana Volunteer Infantry, September, 1861–September, 1865* (Logansport, Ind.: Wilson, Humphreys, 1888), 66.
46. Jones, *Reminiscences,* 44–46.
47. Wall, *Iowa,* 111, 129; Hubert H. Wubben, *Civil War Iowa and the Copperhead Movement* (Ames: Iowa State University Press, 1980), 136, 191.
48. Wubben, *Civil War Iowa,* 130.
49. Ulysses S. Grant, *Personal Memoirs of U. S. Grant,* 2 vols. (New York: Charles L. Webster, 1885), 1:579–81.
50. Jones, *Reminiscences,* 47–48.
51. Klingensmith, *Samuel Day of the 22nd Iowa,* chap. 11; Jones, *Reminiscences,* 49, 53.
52. Klingensmith, *Samuel Day of the 22nd Iowa,* chap. 12; Jones, *Reminiscences,* 53–55.
53. Klingensmith, *Samuel Day of the 22nd Iowa,* chap. 12.
54. *OR,* ser. 1, 34(pt. 1):281, 37(pt. 1):285, 43(pt. 1):331.
55. *OR,* ser. 1, 43(pt. 1):329–31, 337–38; Jones, *Reminiscences,* 86–87.
56. Wubben, *Civil War Iowa,* 41, 71.

Southern SONS, *Northern* SOLDIERS

★ ★ ★

Chapter One

"Among the Barren Hills of Missouri"

— IN CAMP —

Thursday, August 21, 1862 — Iowa City
Dear Pa,
Having learned that nothing would be done before Monday, we had concluded to walk home and spend the time there, but upon farther consideration, and in view of the showery weather, we have determined to remain. We lost our barrack, and are boarded at the American House. Fare is better than I expected.

The Captain has appointed Geo. W. Handy Ord. Sergeant. Wm. Schell 2nd & myself 3rd Sergeant as I have been informed. Lewis Logan & Rutter have some offices. Corporals perhaps.[1]

The object of this note is to save you a trip Saturday if you or the boys had any intention of coming to see us mustered in.[2]

George has no office. My wages will be $17.00 per month.

Yours affectionately, L. Remley

Tuesday, August 26, 1862 — Iowa City
Dear Pa,
Having obtained leave of absence from the camp for an hour or two, I came over here (Mr. Oak's) to let you know how we are getting along. When we first came to town, we were quartered in the American House kept by Dan Smith. Not liking the fare we removed to the Burlington House (a private boarding house kept by Mrs. Bay) on College Street near Harts. We staid there until Monday morning (yesterday). We had there very good fare and Lycurgus & I had the best room in the house. Sunday we went to preaching twice & to Sunday School. We took tea at Mr. Mordoff's one evening & I staid one night at Dr. Totten's. I don't suppose you have heard what the Trustees did with the University. Doctor Totten resigned ? his place in the University.[3] Spencer did likewise & his resignation was not accepted. He then gave the trustees to understand that he wouldn't stay unless he could be President. They complied and he is president for one year only.[4] Griffin is dispensed with & his place will be supplied by the other proffessors.[5] Parvin (they say) has turned republican and keeps his place.[6] Mitchel's wages is reduced from $25 per month to $15 & he is going to leave.[7] I have not heard whether the salary of the Professors is cut down or not.[8] Now for our camp experience.

We went into camp yesterday morning. When the dinner hour arrived we were armed with a plate, knife & fork, 1 spoon & a tin cup; were then formed into line & marched to Smith's establishment (on the grounds) & each one received his cup full of coffee (sweetened) and his plate full of boiled beef, potatoes & soup all mixed together & on top of that a great slice of bread. That was our dinner. Supper & breakfast were like it except at breakfast we had no potatoes nor soup. We carry our meals to our barracks where there is a long board, with hinges, fastened on each side which serves as a table. There is no blessing asked at meals but plenty of the opposite thing. I have heard more swearing since I have been in camp than for the last two or three years all put together. As soon as we can get camp kettles, etc. we will do our own cooking. Last night we did not get to sleep much. There was a crowd of nearly one hundred men all together for the first time & you may be sure that there was not much chance for sleep. Our barracks hold just 96 men. Each bunk is 6 1/2 ft by 4 or 5. There are 16 bunks in each tier & three tiers. Each bunk contains two men. Lycurgus & I have a very good bunk in the upper tier & next to one end where there are two windows. We have a very quiet set in our part of the house. Lewis Logan & Lewis Yenter sleep just at our feet.[9] We have a place there to put our dishes & hang up clothes, etc. By the way we have to wash & take care of our own dishes. For our bed last night we had some straw in our bunk & 2 quilts or comforts which we slept between. I had for my pillow an overcoat & Lycurgus had a carpet sack. The bed clothes were furnished by citizens of Iowa City. We have been mustered into the United States service but have not been furnished with blankets, guns, uniform, etc. yet. Expect them today. The paymaster is also expected today or tomorrow. The Governor [Samuel J. Kirkwood] & all the captains here held a caucus yesterday & decided to put all of Johnson Co. men into one regiment (the 22nd). We expect to leave here about the first of next week for Benton barracks [St. Louis, Missouri]. No matter when we leave we intend to go home to see you all before we start. We will probably be there next Saturday. We are both well & in good spirits & think we can stand camp life as well as any of the rest of the boys. I write this with a pencil because I have not any pen of my own & Mr. Oaks has all of his locked up & has not come home yet.

[Lycurgus continues:] **Aug 26th** — Camp Pope, Remley's Bunk
I will add a little to George's letter.

George is mistaken as to the number of Johnson Co. companies in the 22nd Reg. Stewart's (North Bend) Co. & George Clark's Co. will be left out.

We will commence cooking our own rations day after tomorrow when we will have better fare and can save our surplus and exchange for vegetables, etc. As it is great pieces of good bread & meat, sometimes half we get has to be thrown away, can't eat it all. In the (uncooked) regular rations we will get beans, rice, potatoes, salt, sugar, coffee, etc. Our mess I presume will consist of the following persons[10]

August 21, 1862–March 20, 1863

1 L Remley	2 G.A. Remley	3 Lewis Logan
4 Lewis Yenter	5 Geo. Kibler	6 Jas Johns[t]on
7 Simeon Pool	8 Jas. Montgomery	

You know all these except Pool & Montgomery. Pool (Lewis Logan says) is a clever fellow and (Lewis believes) a member of the church (but he don't know certainly). He is our drummer. Montgomery is Packard's brother in law, a good steady fellow 29 years old.

I have to drill three hours this PM (one as serg't). In a short while I will have to drill others. My Chicago drilling comes in good place now.[11]

There are some good fellows in our Co. and many profane, some the most vulgar, obscene, profane fellows you ever saw.

We are liable to be called to march any day but I don't much expect we will go this week. If not, we will go home Saturday on the cars and return Monday.

Remember us in your prayers.

Yours Affectionately, L. Remley

Tuesday, September 16, 1862 — Camp Pope, Iowa City
Dear Pa,
Camp Pope is all excitement this evening. At dress parade the captains were all ordered to have their men in readiness to march at an hour warning. We have all our things packed ready to go at any time and the sooner that time comes the better most of the Regiment will like it. Cap't [Alfred B.] Cree says that he expects to go tomorrow. We are certain (at least as certain as things generally are these last days) to start from here tomorrow or next day. If you wish to see the Regiment take its leave, you had better come tomorrow (Friday), for "its hour is near at hand."[12] I have left a shirt and pair of socks at Mr. Oak's and intend to leave my Bible there if I can get it sent over. I have bought a good polyglot reference Bible about half as large as my old one for which I paid twenty five cents.[13] A little boy (son of the sexton at the Baptist Church) gave it to Lycurgus at Sunday school last Sunday, thinking I suppose that he was supplying a soldier who had none. Lycurgus bought 7 good second hand testaments of the Methodist Sunday school for 30 cts. and let me have the Bible for a quarter. He is going to give the testaments to those who have none. Lycurgus subscribed to the [Iowa City] Republican for six months and W. H. Harrison and I have subscribed for the Christian Times & so we three will have two papers sent regularly to us. The Christian Times is sent to soldiers for one dollar per year. We subscribed for six months which costs twenty five cents apiece. We received the first copy today. There are more in our company that talk of sending for it.

Last Sunday was the first one that I ever spent in Camp. The Captain gave a great many of the boys passes to go to preaching. Lycurgus & I, Lewis Yenter & some others went to Sunday school & preaching at the Baptist Church. After service, the Lord's Supper was administered. It is not likely that we will have another opportunity of enjoying that privilege again for some time. We took dinner at Dr. Lillie's Sunday.

Mr. Westover took supper with us one evening this week. We have had several good dinners brought in for us by the friends of our mess mates.

I am now writing on an old box in the upper story of our barrack surrounded by a crowd of men talking, smoking, reading, etc. There is so much noise that I can't even hear myself think. The men keep running about & climbing up and down so much that it is hard work to write.

Give my love to Ma & all the rest of the family. I will write again when we get some where.

Your Affectionate Son, Geo A Remley

Sunday Night, September 21, 1862, 9 o'clock — Benton Barracks — [St. Louis, Missouri]
Dear Pa & Ma,
I wrote you Sept. 17 & 18th a long account of our trip from Iowa City here to this place, which I suppose you have received.[14]

George, our mess captain, is now in the cookhouse, cooking bacon, drawing rations, and packing up provisions, kettles, etc. and I am writing to inform you that our Regiment has orders to be ready to march to the depot at a moment's notice. We expect to start to Rolla & Springfield [Missouri] tomorrow morning. This last is not official, but all things indicate that region as our destination.

Our neighbor boys are all well and in good spirits. We had a hard time marching from the landing out here and again today, at "grand review." Today we were out, with our knapsacks on our backs, about 3 hours.

When we make another halt I (or George) will write again, but if you have not yet written do not wait, as it will be safe enough to direct merely to us, "Co. F. 22nd Iowa, St. Louis, Mo." The letters will follow us.

If you should see the Eds. of the Republican soon, please inquire why my paper didn't come with the others. I received this morning ten copies of the Chris. Times for my subscribers, etc. I had previously sent the money. The papers came via Iowa City.

About half a dozen of us had very pleasant prayer meeting tonight (the first meeting) at which was present one of my old Chicago schoolmates (or rather pupils) a paroled prisoner, whom I unexpectedly met this evening.

Give my love to all the family and write soon.

Yours Affectionately, Lycurgus Remley

Wednesday, September 24, 1862 — Camp Sigel — [Rolla, Missouri]
Dear Pa,
Supposing that you would like to know something of our whereabouts I take the first opportunity to write to you. We are now at the very place that I didn't want to go to. Our camp is situated on a ridge about three miles southwest of Rolla. We left Benton Barracks last Monday evening about

August 21, 1862–March 20, 1863

three o'clock and marched at a quick pace to the depot of the Pacific railroad, or at least a branch of it, at St. Louis. The sun was hot, the road was very dusty and our knapsacks heavy and I can assure you that to a good many of us the road seemed pretty long though the depot is not more than four miles from the barracks. My load seemed pretty heavy but I did not get very tired. I can stand a march as well as any of the rest of the boys. When we got to the depot, we had to wait until 10 o'clock at night for the train to come from Rolla. When the train came, we were all stretched out on the ground in every direction. Then there was a general bustle & hurry; men strapping on knapsacks, looking for friends, calling rolls, etc., all tended to make a rather lively scene, viewed as it was by candle (lamp) light. We were crowded into cattle cars fixed up with rough board seats. I regretted very much that we had to travel in the night. We had a very long train and a powerful engine and we rolled along over that road faster than I ever traveled before. The country was pretty rough and one moment we would be on a high embankment & the next we would dash through a deep cut with solid rock on each side standing up like a wall. We had not gone more than thirty five miles when for some cause, I don't know what, five cars were left behind. I suppose that the load was too heavy for the iron horse. Two and a half companies were left, among which was ours (Co. F). The main part of the train went on to Rolla taking with it the officers, who were in a first class passenger car. They arrived there in the morning & our captain got out of the car to look up his company & form them into line and lo and behold they had come up missing.

We staid all night at a small place called Franklin. None of us got out of the cars until morning. I did not get to sleep any that night, but I dozed a little in the morning. About 6 o'clock a train came along from St. Louis and we hitched on and we soon were on our way at the rate of forty miles an hour. We had to stop several times and wait for trains to pass. At one small town a few of the boys & I went to an orchard & got as many apples as we could carry. We didn't "confisticate" them. We had the consent of the owner. The country through which we passed in the day time is mostly covered with forests of white & black oak, walnut, elm, and a kind of oak called the "black jack," extending as far as I could see on both sides of the road.[15] There are not many improvements except at the railroad stations, and even the towns and villages have a deserted appearance. We arrived at Rolla about noon and found the rest of the regiment there waiting for us rather impatiently. Rolla is a small place but I believe it is improving. There is plenty of room for it. There is an earthen fortification there called Fort — something I don't know what. It is mounted with can[n]on & is garrisoned by 80 men and I heard that they have about three hundred prisoners there.

After resting at Rolla until three o'clock, we started for this place. The sun shone very hot and the dust was so thick in the air that we could hardly breathe at times. When we had marched about three miles, we came to an old camping ground of Sigel. We halted on a hill or rather a ridge that slopes towards the South and was at one time covered with small black oak and hickory trees, but they have nearly all been cut down for fuel. There is a small creek running along at the foot of the hill. We get our water from a splendid spring about three hundred yards from the camp. On every side as far as the eye can reach nothing meets the gaze but a barren tract of country covered with trees of a stinted growth. On looking towards Rolla a mound can be seen, on a slight elevation, with some dark looking objects on the top; this is the fort whose morning and evening guns come booming across the hills & vallies to remind us that we are soldiers and must not forget our duties. I don't see how any one can live in such a country as this part of the state seems to be and judging from appearances I don't think many do live here. Excepting a small patch of ground that has been cultivated at some former time on the camp ground, there is not the least seen of a farm or any kind of improvement to be seen from here. The soil is the poorest that I ever saw any where (not excepting old Mr. Kerr's land in Va.). It is a mixture of sand, gravel, etc. and on the bluffs there are plenty of stones, some places so thick that you can not see any thing else. All along the railroad between here & St. Louis I noticed that about three feet below the surface there was stone in horizontal layers, extending down into the ground to considerable depth. About here where I have had a chance to examine it, it seems to be a kind of sand stone.

There are plenty of small hazel bushes growing all over our camp ground. I found some wild plums here, but they were rather out of date. Some of the boys found wild grapes. There is "right smart" sassafras all over the hills around here. We had tea of it once and I thought it was first rate. I noticed also a great many small huckleberry bushes in this vicinity. Small I say because this soil is not able to produce any thing on a large scale.

Thursday Sept 25th
This is the second day that we have spent at Camp Sigel. The first night we all slept on the ground. I slept very well with nothing but a blanket over me; but I did not undress, not even pull off my boots. Yesterday we got our tents but there was one lacking and, as I was cooking at the time they came, I did not secure one and the rest of our mess all look to me for nearly every thing. Last night six or eight of us slept in the open air again. The days are very warm here and the nights quite cool as you will know when I tell you that we had a heavy frost last night. Every thing looks dry & parched up here, the grass, what little there was, is dry as hay. In the roads the dust is three or four inches thick. It don't look like there had been any rain here for six months.

Rumors of all kinds are afloat throughout the camp. 10,000 rebels are reported to be within thirty miles of here. The people at Rolla sleep on their arms every night. Cavalry pickets are posted about three miles out all around. They have taken several prisoners since we have been here. Yesterday it was reported & the report confirmed that one of the pickets was killed by the bush-whackers. Last night one of our guards, supposing that the rebels were coming, shot at a bush or some dark object and raised the alarm. When we left Iowa City, we brought with us 20,000 rounds of cartridges and though we have been in places where there was danger and have passed through & are now in semi-rebel country and are liable to be attacked at any time, yet none of our Co. except the guards, have had a single cartridge given to them.[16]

My health has been very good since I wrote last. Our rations here consist of crackers (hard bread), bacon, coffee, sugar and then rice, cracked corn, beans & potatoes on successive days.[17] We have to sit on the ground and eat our meals. I have washed once and I think I did it very well. I only washed a shirt and a pair of socks.

I think of home very often and wish I could just step in some evening and see you all. But I must stop as another tent has come and I have to help fix it. Remember me in your prayers for I feel that I need Divine grace here more than ever before.

Give my love to Ma & all the rest of the family.

Lycurgus said perhaps he would write some. Write as soon as you can for I have not heard a word from home since I left town.

Your Affectionate Son, Geo A Remley

P.S. Direct your letters to Co. F 22nd Iowa, St. Louis, Mo   GA Remley

[Lycurgus continues:]

George has said every thing so completely that there is scarcely any thing for me to add. Missouri is the land of mules. Mules in drays, mules in wagons, mules in drove, everywhere mules. As we are on the Springfield Road we see constantly long trains of six mule government wagons nearly all with bales of pressed hay (for this desolate country couldn't support the teams). There are perhaps six or seven other regiments in this vicinity. [Francis J.] Herron's brigade. How long we shall stay here or whither we shall go is uncertain.

Among familiar vegetables I have seen persimmon trees, polk berries in abundance, etc.

I have been suffering with the toothache for the last three or four days, otherwise am pretty well.

Write to us soon

Your son, Lycurgus R

Friday, October 17, 1862 — Camp near Rolla, Missouri
Dear Ma,
Howard's, Mit's & your letter (or letters) dated Oct. 10 & 11 was received last Tuesday the 14th. I had that same evening mailed one to you & Pa.[18]

Since that date (14th) I have been on the sick list. This matter with me is biliary derrangement, accompanied with diarrhoea. This doctor gives me morphine to check my diarrhea, salts to purge me, quinine solution &

whiskey as a tonic and proposes to give me blue mass pills to rouse my liver.[19] I have pains in my bowels & uneasiness in my stomach and feel very weak, but as yet nothing serious is the matter with me. So much for my health. George is all right. Lewis Logan is still in the hospital. His measeles are is (?) as yet undeveloped. His complaint is of bilious character too. Lewis Yenter is moping about though not yet on the sick list. Lewis Gohen (who may perhaps be included among "our neighbor boys") has been on the sick list some time. John Klenk also, for the last two or three days. Nothing much very serious, however, ails these two. Such is a catalogue of the sick of our acquaintance.

It has been pretty well settled that we are to remain about Rolla this winter. We shall probably remove there, or near there, in a day or two. Lt. Col. [Harvey] Graham is Post Commander and our Adjutant [Joseph B.] Atherton, Post Adjutant. Lieut. J. W. Porter is our Acting Adjutant. I guess, however, that "Jeff" keeps you all posted.[20]

The weather here is very fine during the day but frosty at night. We have made a fire place in our tent, with a flue under ground and a chimney of stone, sticks & mud away off outside a very nice arrangement, keeping our tent warm and comfortable and enabling us to cook occasionally for ourselves, fry bread, etc. [see drawing of tent] The fire place is a square hole in the ground nicely lined & arched with stone.

Last night after going to bed I received a letter from Uncle Wm. & Aunt S. M. Zoll which I send for your perusal.[21]

Give my love to all the family and believe me
your Affectionate Son, Lycurgus

Did you receive a letter from George dated Sep 25?[22]

Please excuse pencil. My ink is dry.

October 22, 1862 — Oxford, Iowa

My Dear Boys,

Your letter of the 13th inst., was rec'd last Saturday and we were all, as we always are, much gratified to hear from you. In a strange land as you are, and leading a new and untried life, you will necessarily have much more to tell us, than we at home where all things move on in their wonted course can possibly have to interest you. Besides your time hangs heavily upon your hands, while every moment of ours is or ought to be actively employed "er go", you should not expect us to write so much nor so often as you do.

For the last three or four weeks we have been making molasses. Sorgum is a rare institution. A very large quantity has been manufactured this season and the whole country is flooded in "liquid sweetness long drawn out." We have made considerably over 500 Gal. but I cannot at this moment give you the exact amount, and am still at it, though we expect to close today. Until this week I have all along attended to the boiling & my working clothes have got so saturated with the viscid material that light substances such as beds, lounges and chairs, when I come in contact with them stick to me, and this same viscidity, about my person is supposed to be the reason why I have <u>stuck</u> so closely to the business that I could not for three week[s] get off long enough to write a letter. You want to know what we are doing on the farm. It is all told in one word — 'lasses.

I hope you will bear with christian fortitude whatever may befall you, and that amidst all the pernicious influences of a Camp life you will not forget your duty to God nor lose the spirit of devotion. If the war should continue you will become used to it and I doubt not be more contented and happy than you can be now. If it should please God [to] preserve your health you can bear as much as any body else.

Your Ma rec'd a letter from Sister S.M. Zoll. William is a union man & has been a refugee at Sedalie but was at home again when she wrote.

I am much pleased to hear of your prayer meetings & I hope you will persevere. You may be the means of much good to your fellow soldiers. May God bless you my dear boys & bring you safe back again. We do not forget to pray for you everyday. Remember me kindly to all our neighbors & acquaintances in your Camp.

Your affectionate Father, James Remley

Tuesday, November 11, 1862 — Camp near Rolla, Missouri
Dear Pa,
Howard's letter, dated the 31st Oct. was rec'd just a week ago; but as we had already sent two or three letters, to which we were daily expecting answers, we have been in no particular hurry about writing again. Today, however, having but little to do, and thinking another letter might be opportune, I concluded I would give you another "benefit." As I write the rain is pouring down, and sixteen of us are enclosed within the friendly circumference of our Sibley tent, sitting and lying around our comfortable stove, variously occupied: some "snoozing," some talking, some reading, (myself) writing, others toasting bread, eating, sewing, etc.[23] Four of the poor fellows will have to go out pretty soon to stand guard. By the way, we have got in our tent a first rate set of "boys" taken as an aggregate. The number is eighteen, and among them six professors of religion & six non-commissioned officers (2 sergts & 4 corpls). We have no card playing, and but little swearing in this tent. I regret to say, however, that Lewis Yenter seems to be departing from the path we once hoped he would pursue. He is morose, sometimes uses bad language, and is frequently absent at night, playing cards in another tent.

I am as well, I believe, as before taken sick, on full duty, was on guard last Saturday & company & battalion drill yesterday. George is as well as ever, eats <u>"orful"</u> and has become <u>pretty</u> fat. Lewis Logan is nearly well again, eats nearly as much as anybody. Lewis Yenter is somewhat "under the weather" on the sick list, and marked "ex" (exempt from duty). I don't know exactly what ails him. Dr. [William H.] White kept me in the hospital nearly a week longer than was necessary, chiefly to do some writing, but partly I believe for the purpose of diverting my rations into the hospital store. The requisitions being for a week or so of course, the greater the number of patients in the hospital at the time it is made, the greater the number of rations drawn and the better the dinners the doctors can have. It was, at least, certainly curious to see the number of convalescents, suddenly returned to quarters, when the requisitions had been made. This, though a digression, gives a little insight into the way things are conducted around here.

It was the <u>writing</u>, I was going to speak about. Dr. White had a report to make to the Post Surgeon I believe. He merely scribbled it down with a pencil in the most uncouth angular style imaginable, making innumerable interlineations & blunders, which it would sometimes fuzzle a Philadelphia lawyer to decipher.[24] The task assigned to me, was to re-write this report, in a fair hand and in my own language, merely preserving the <u>ideas</u>. I would sometimes cut down three or four lines to about <u>one or two</u>. Well, one evening, before it was quite finished, Dr. White carried it over and read it to Dr. Taylor, the Post Surgeon, and came back in the best of humor, making the most enthusiastic professions of friendship, and promises of his influence, etc. The style was highly complimented by the Post Surgeon for its flowing ease, etc. under the supposition that it was Dr. White's. The Dr. no doubt, laughed in his sleeve, and appropriated it all to himself. In fact I know he did. He promised me pecuniary reward, and to bring my name prominently before Gov. Kirkwood, neither of which, so far as I know, has been fulfilled. If disposed to do the latter, he would now have a good opportunity in this wise. Our adjutant J. B. Atherton has been appointed Major of our Regiment, and it is highly probably that John W. Porter, who is our <u>acting</u> Adjutant, will receive the permanent appointment.[25] This, with the promotion of 2nd Lieut. Haddock, would leave the 2nd Lieutenancy vacant, to be filled from our company.[26] I believe the Governor has the appointing power, and why mightn't I receive it as well as any body else? If some kind friend, would be so kind as to "bring my name prominently before Gov. Kirkwood," it might do some good. If I should be so lucky as to get an appointment of this kind, I should be "might" glad of it; if not, I will try not to die of despair.

Our Regiment has a little more to do now than formerly, escorting wagon train going to Springfield, as far as Waynesville. "Jeff" has told of the expedition of Co. "B." At one time last week as many as four companies were absent, escorting as many trains. Co. F started last Tuesday about six o'clock A.M. and returned Friday about noon. While gone they feasted on the fat of the land "confiscating" or jayhawking one beef and numerous hogs.[27] Geo. will tell you the whole story when he writes. I was too weak to stand the march, and was left with about 15 others, sick, etc. The boys came home as ravenous as bears, pitching into the cold beans, etc. as if they hadn't "tasted food for twenty four hours." George, however, brought in his haversack a little confiscated beef and offered me some, which I, at first, received but afterwards threw away.

There seems to be a good deal of game in this country: deer, wild turkeys, foxes, coons, rabbits, squirrels, quails, pigeons, etc. Our captain's family had a "possum," cooked up a day or so ago.

Butter is scarce here, and poor in quality. John W. Porter had a keg of 100 lbs. sent here, by express, from Iowa City. It cost there 14 cents per lb., the express charge was 4 1/2 cents, making the total cost 18 1/2 cents per lb. It is worth here from 20 to 25.

Howard's letter was very satisfactory and did us "lots of good." He should be encouraged and try, try again.

Your molasses speculation seems to have been very profitable. You can now have all the plum & crab apple pies, puddings, cakes, etc. you want. I wish I was there to help you lick your "lasses" a while. I am glad to hear of the rise in the prices of farm produce. I hope you will be more reconciled to the hog, if he remunerates you fairly this year, though doubtless sheep raising is the best business an Iowa farmer can go at.[28]

We are getting along first rate, but I wish the war was over so that I can go at something else than lounging around. Although we are in comparatively comfortable circumstances, yet the time seems to me as almost absolutely wasted.

The purpose of my life seems but little further by the months spent in the Army. We must endure it, however, as a necessary evil. And, upon the whole, I don't see how we could better spend our lives than in endeavoring to preserve our government and institutions. But then the needlessness of it!

Write "early and often." Your kind letter was rec'd and almost immediately answered (my answer was dated the 26th ult. and George wrote a week ago last Saturday). To neither of these have answers been received.[29]

The paymaster hasn't come yet, though we expect him daily. My cash on hand is just 15 cents.

Give my love to Ma, Allie, Clara & the boys[30]

Your Affectionate Son, Lycurgus

P.S. Geo emphasized the word "pretty" on the first page.

P.P.S. Lycurgus says that "Geo eats 'orful.'" I don't know how that is but I do know that the Government does not furnish any of that article with our rations. Those who are on half duty are so hearty that it has become a proverb in this company, instead of saying that one has been put on half rations, to say that he is on double rations. Lycurgus is no exception. Geo Lycurgus isn't on half duty and besides "double rations" means double duty standing guard, etc. L

Tuesday, November 11, 1862 — Oxford, Iowa
Dear Lycurgus,
George informs us that you were honorably discharged from the hospital fully recovered from your illness, etc. I am very glad that your fever was not more serious and hope that as you have now gone through your seasoning or acclimation with safety you will here after enjoy good health.

I see from the tenor of your letter that Doctor White has been practicing some of his art upon you. The caution I would give you may be thus stated: <u>Beware</u> <u>of</u> <u>soft</u> <u>soap</u>. I have no doubt the Doctor is a good physician. That's all. I shall be much pleased to see in your next a full account of your hospital experience. You never say anything about your Chaplain. Have you not made his acquaintance yet? If he is a good christian man and at his post I think it would be very pleasant & profitable for you & George to approach him, make yourselves known and thus secure an interest in his sympathies and kind offices. I hope to hear of your promotion amid the many changes which are taking place. I have all along expected that you or George would advance. You must learn to push <u>yourselves</u> a <u>little</u> forward. While I hate the whole business of war, I would if engaged in it like to be a <u>Captain</u>.

Nov. 15th — I wrote the above on Thursday while it was raining, but as Howard was sending his letter to you that same day, I thought I would retain what I had written and finish it some other day. We are now ready to commence building our barn but I am afraid our good weather is past and we will have cold work. We have seen your communication in the Christian Times. It is well written and gives me much pleasure, but to an impartial critic perhaps it would seem to lack point. It would have the impression that the writer[']s aim was rather to <u>make</u> a <u>communication</u> than to communicate anything of importance. In writing for a newspaper one should aim to express his ideas in as few words as possible, so as to make the sense clear, presupposing always, that he has ideas to express. You will doubtless appreciate my motives in writing this, which is, not to discourage your attempts to write, but to save you from the common fault of newspaper correspondents, too much diffusiveness. Everybody is too busy to sift a bushel of chaff for a grain or two of wheat.

I think there is a prospect of greater activity in the prosecution of the war and I hope it will soon be brought to a close. I would be so glad to hear of an honorable peace and to see you all returning home to enjoy it. Sometimes I think that perhaps as a nation we have become already ripe for destruction, and that God designs now to bring it to pass. The war does not seem to improve the public morals in the slightest degree, but statesmen and generals seem as much as ever to be false, selfish and unjust. Thousands of private citizens are even now speculating in the public misery and trying to make money out of the blood and dying groans of innocent people. The war I fear is being prolonged on purpose to give more time for these traders in human wars to carry on their fiendish business. How much of this the Almighty will suffer before he destroys a nation I cannot tell. Surely we can claim nothing on the score of justice, but I know his mercy is great.

As ever Your affectionate Father, James Remley

August 21, 1862–March 20, 1863

Tuesday, November 18, 1862 — Camp near Rolla, Missouri
Dear Pa,
Your very welcome letter of the 11th & 15th inst. was last night rec'd, and although George wrote to Howard only a day or two ago, I concluded to write again thinking that this rainy day was the best opportunity I might soon have, and that I had matter sufficient for a letter. I know I run the risk of being considered a too frequent correspondent, but I hope you will be so kind as to give me timely warning before I make myself too much of a bore. But to commence.

You ask me to give you a full account of my hospital experience. Omitting the first two or three days spent in the tent hospital at the old camp, our hospital at Rolla was a room formerly used as a dry goods' store-room. On each side was a row of cots, leaving an aisle (about four feet wide) in the middle, in which was a stove, nearly obstructing the travel. There lay the sick, about 28 in number. There were four nurses — detailed soldiers — who served two at a time in two "reliefs" of twelve hours each. All this seems well enough, but let's look a little further. The floor shook awfully whenever anybody walked over it; and there was an almost continual commotion, nurses and innumerable others, running in and out with heavy tread, which with the loud talking, the incessant coughing & the intolerable smell, sometimes disguised with burnt coffee, made that room a very desirable place for a sick man to lie. Our meals which consisted for the most part of tea & coffee, boiled rice, bread (sometimes toasted), molasses and sometimes soup, the specific gravity of which, as I remarked to the Colonel, was 0.6, came two or three hours behind the proper time, say breakfast 8 1/2 or 9 o'clock, dinner 2 or 2 1/2 sometimes about 3, and supper about seven or half past. It was interesting to see the sick waiting for their meals and to hear them "growling." The room in which the steward prepared the prescriptions and the kitchen were so arranged that all communication between the latter and the hospital must be through the former, which added greatly to the order of the institution. There were two "matrons," dissolute women, whose chief business seemed to be to carry the food from the kitchen to the patients. I believe they nominally prepared the food for the sick. I don't know how many "matrons" have been introduced and presently discharged. The doctors had a room upstairs where, especially at night, they would have fine times, drinking their toddy (?) and playing "euchre" with the Col., Lieut. Col., Captains, Lieutenants, etc. Well, I endured this state of things until well enough to be discharged, except I was quite weak. The doctor then, as I have already told, kept me nearly a week to write for him. I then fared "first rate," ate with the doctors, had a good bed upstairs, walked out when and where I pleased, etc. After the day for making the requisitions had passed (having finished my writing) I was discharged. They say a great change for the better has been lately made in the hospital arrangement, and that things are now carried on about as they should be. I don't know how this is. So much for my hospital experience. What do you think of it?

As to Dr. White's "soft soap." It was of the transparent kind, as transparent to me as to you, but then I didn't know but that he might do something, and in fact he has since manifested some interest in me, so that I don't think much harm has been done. I will, of course, keep as clear of his lubrications as possible.

As to our chaplain, I formed his acquaintance long ago. He used to preach nearly every Sunday, but as preaching in a tent would be an impossibility and bad weather seems to have set in, I don't know when there will be any more preaching. The truth is our chaplain seems to be almost a cipher and is so regarded by most of the regiment, so that when he does preach, but few attend. He seems to about as unable to devise ways and means (secure a tent, etc.) for holding prayer meetings, as any private. He appears to be a good man, but very inefficient.

The question of the Adjutancy is as yet undecided. There are several candidates, among others Dr. [William M.] DeCamp and his chances are said to be pretty good.

A day or two since there came near being a row in camp. A man wasn't in the ranks at roll call for which our orderly put him on extra (guard) duty. He flatly refused to go on guard. From this it went on until finally the Major gave him his choice to be tied to a tree in the rain for 24 hours, or to go on guard. He chose the former. An excited crowd soon gathered around him, and he was presently cut loose, released. He was then sent to the Fort. The crowd, his partisans, who had by this time got their guns, talked strongly of going to bring him back, but they lacked a leader of sufficient influence. At length Lieut. J. W. Porter came and demanded and obtained their arms. The crowd soon dispersed and the excitement subsided.

It is now raining and has been more or less since Saturday night. George was on guard yesterday and last night in town and came in this morning dripping like a drow[n]ing rat. He was, however, well protected by my rubber blanket. I was on guard last Saturday night & Sunday morning and got a taste of the rainy weather. This was in town. About midnight we made a pretty good haul, arrested five Irish from an adjoining shanty, who were becoming rather too obstreperous over their beer (or whiskey) and cards. Turned them into a little wedge tent, wet & nasty, without blankets, overcoats or fire, where they huddled down like hogs and soon went to sleep, although at first they expressed great fear of the "grey-backs" (body lice).[31] The guards in town don't have a very hard time. They have a good Sibley tent, with a stove (and two or three other small tents); and outside a large log fire around which they can sit and at which they can roast their potatoes, toast their bread, etc. four hours out of every six.

It is certainly funny trying to write in such circumstances as these, a gloomy day, huge dripping overcoats sometimes dragging over my paper, etc. Every now and then a scuffle occurs among some of the more rude of the inmates of our crowded tent, breaking up stools, kicking up a dust, and deranging things generally. But all this we must get used to, though it does seem rather uncivilized.

Your mention of my communication to the Christian Times was the first I had heard of its fate since I mailed it, our last week's papers not having made their appearance. I suppose its apparent pointlessness was in part owing to the fact that the news therein contained was to you, like "twice told tale,["] not news, having been previously made the matter of our letters home. Its objects was, in fact, not to bring before the public some great central idea, but to give an idea of matters and things with the 22nd Iowa, in general; which, I hope, was with those not previously acquainted with them partially at least accomplished. I am, certainly, myself, no great admirer of a very diffuse style. I didn't rush at random into print having, before we left Iowa City, received an invitation from the publishers of the Christian Times, occasionally to furnish articles for their columns. Let it go for what it is worth, no more.

While at the hospital I drew a sketch of Fort Wyman as it appeared from the hospital steps. Upon the request of Serg't Major [Franklin] Hobart, I drew a nice duplicate for him to send to "Harper's Weekly," which he has no doubt done. If it has good luck, it will make its appearance in two or three weeks. It attracted some attention, and I have a great many applications for copies, more than I could draw in two or three months. I have promised Major Atherton a copy.

By the way Hobart is the regular correspondent of the Davenport Gazette from our Regiment. His nom de plume is "Frank Forest."

I notice from your letters that there is a remarkable coincidence between the weather you have up in Iowa and that of this part of Mo., when you have rain, so do we, etc. While you were writing last Saturday I was on guard in town and the weather was just about such as you described, only yours was perhaps a little colder.

Have you heard any thing from Uncle Wm. Zoll lately? I wrote him a long letter Oct. 24th to which I have not yet received an answer.

How [are matters] with your sheep project? Has it proved impracticable and "fallen through?" Please give us some information on this point, if not inconsistent with the public interest. If you have the "wherewithal" I wouldn't think it would take long to put up your barn. I am glad that you are making one and that you are gathering about you more stock, colts, calves, etc.

Although we have been mustered for pay, I don't know when payday will come. I haven't a cent "to my name," but suppose I shall get along some way, though I don't exactly see how. By the way, what about that order on the Township Treasury? Has it ever been cashed? If so, was interest paid? I left a memorandum of the Am't due, etc.

What about Mr. Christopher's ten acres of corn? Is it yet husked, and if so what was your share?

Your letters "do us lots good." Let them come! I repeat it, let them come!!

Post us well on farm affairs. Has Allie forgotten how to use a pen?

George's weight is now 138 lbs. My weight was Oct. 28th 129 lbs. I suppose I have gained somewhat since that time.

Give my love to all and write again soon.

Your Affectionate son, Lycurgus

The health of our neighbor boys is about as usual.   L.

Tuesday, November 25, 1862 — Nemora, Oxford, Iowa
My dear Boys,
Lycurgus' letter to me dated the 11 inst. & George's to Howard of the 17 were both duly rec'd. I am fully convinced your "life in camp" would have nothing in it at all agreeable to my tastes & feelings and that it must be a severe trial to you to endure it, but still it is necessary in the present unhappy condition of our country and as a <u>duty</u> I hope you will bear it with proper fortitude and hope. If the war shall be conducted to a successful issue & you are so fortunate as to survive, the scenes through which you are now passing will be the most cherished source of pleasant and grateful reflections & patriotic pride. You will be honored by your fellow countrymen for the self sacrifice & devotion you are now making. Though appearances may indicate to you that you are to winter at Rolla, I have no idea that such will be the case. I think it far more likely that you will be sent down the Mississippi with Gen. McClernand and that you will see New Orleans before spring. Staying there among the barren hills of Missouri is just what I would not desire although I might do so with perfect safety. Far rather encounter the dangers of a military expedition into the enemy's country and keep the blood in circulation by action than to rust, (not to say rot) in camp. Life consists of emotions & actions and should be measured, not by days & years but by what one feels & does. Three or four months in camp would be a blank, a gap, a lost link in the chain of existence more than equivalent to so much cut off from life. A little modification of the adage "A short life and a merry one" will express my idea. A short life and a useful one. I have strong faith that you will be preserved by our Heavenly Father through all the danger and trials of this war, that you will acquit yourselves like men, will come home with untarnished honor & unblemished character and realize th[r]ough life the proud satisfaction of knowing that in our country's greatest danger you did what you could to avert that danger, and contribute to her glory & prosperity. Heaven and your country will smile upon you then.

Our barn has not made much progress yet. We have most of the framing timbers on the ground and the foundation post planted, but have not time to work on it.

Freddy wants me to write a little for him to Lycurgus & George which I promised to do it he would tell me what to write. Here it is:

Pa bought a colt for me from Mr. Pine named Leona and then sold to Mr. Mead & gave me five cents of the money. I will save it till Christmas to buy candy. I am growing finely & in three weeks will be four years old. I want to see you very much. I want you to write me a little letter, and put it in a little envelope with a picture on it. Your little brother Freddy.

Sidney also wants to dictate a few lines thus:

Dear Lycurgus & George, I wish you were here to help us eat taffy. We have it very often & sweet cakes. Your brother Sidney.

I will now close by assuring you that you are constantly remembered by us at the throne of grace & we pray God to take care of and keep you in all your ways.

Your affectionate Father, James Remley

Wednesday, December 3, 1862 — Camp near Rolla, Missouri
Dear Pa,
Your letter dated Nov 25th was received last Monday evening. We had been expecting a letter for some time, having been about two weeks since we heard from home. We are still here at the same old place "among the barren hills of Missouri." When I wrote last I supposed that we would change our camp ground in a few days, but the rain that fell about that time made the ground so wet that it would not be good for the health of the regiment to move the tents to a new place and by filling up the springs (holes dug in the ground) that we have here, obviated the necessity for such a move.

We have more to do now than we had some time ago. We drill both morning and evening, in the company and battalion drills, almost every day and this together with the guard duty we have to perform occupies nearly all of our time. Every few days some of our companies have to go to Waynesville to escort supply-trains on their way to Springfield. We have gone only once, but expect to go again before long. Co. A started this morning. Company D returned last Monday evening bringing into camp three deer and twelve wild turkeys that they had killed on their way back. They report game very plenty.

Col. [William M.] Stone arrived here last Sunday, but not having been very well since, he did not take command of the regiment until yesterday evening at dress parade. He was greeted, by the regiment, with three "rousing cheers" and afterwards through J. W. Porter, acting adjutant delivered a very good address to the men, pledging himself to the best he could for their comfort and welfare and asking their sympathy, earnest support and co-operation. Among other things he said that "we are now about to take an active part in this bloody strike etc." Whether this has any peculiar significance respecting the destiny of this regiment or is merely rhetorical flourish, I know not.

It is generally supposed that John Porter will be appointed to the adjutancy. I shall be very sorry if such is the case, for he is one of our best officer[s] and in my opinion the only one who is well fitted to command a company.

We are now having very fine weather for winter, very different from what I expected. I had supposed, from what I heard here, that we would have rain, mud or snow all the time. Four or five successive rainy days some time ago is all the really bad weather we have had. During the night it is cold enough to freeze the ground a little and sometimes bottles of ink that are left too close [to] the outside of the tent.

Never before did time seem to me to pass away more rapidly than it does now. Days and weeks fly away so swiftly that I can hardly keep track of them. Sometimes, however, when there is no preaching, Sunday drags a little. Lycurgus and I are both well and so are all of our neighbor boys, except Lewis Gohen who is troubled with the rheumatism in his back. I now weigh 138 pounds having gained 18 pounds since I left home. The health of the regiment is as good as could be expected, there having been but four deaths, including that of J. W. Dunlap who died at Iowa City, in it since we came here.[32]

At the Post Hospital, where are collected the sick from all regiments that have been near here for a long time, the deaths are very frequent. Almost every day some of our men are detailed as a funeral escort.

There is a strong probability that Col. Stone will take command of Post Rolla and that Lt. Col. [Harvey] Graham will then be commander of the regiment. If so, it will be a pretty good sign that we will remain here all winter or for some time at least. There is a camp rumor, however, that Stone will return to St. Louis in a few days with the intention of forming a brigade and becoming a brigadier general. If it seems good to the "powers that be" to keep the 22nd regiment here, buried in obscurity and deny them the privilege of distinguishing themselves in battle I will try and be as contented as possible under the circumstances but I would much rather go down the Mississippi to Vicksburg or further still to Texas. I might then possibly get a chance to see some of our relatives.[33] However much I desire to be at home and enjoy the privileges and advantages of home I would not for a moment entertain the thought of returning before the rebellion shall be crushed, the war brought to a close and peace established upon terms, honorable to the government and upon a basis firm and lasting.

That all of Dr. White's talk to Lycurgus was nothing but "soft soap" you will know by the following. Not long ago he by his influence with Graham had an order issued detailing "private Lycurgus Remley of Co. F" as a nurse in the regimental hospital, but as there was no person in the company of that description, the order was of course disregarded. It seems that he wanted to have Lycurgus nominally as a nurse but really as a private secretary, he not being allowed by the "regulations" any clerks at government expense. White, finding that the said "private" did not in due time make his appearance, came to Lycurgus to see about it. He threw aside all claims to his services on account of the "special order," for he was well aware of its illegality and his own duplicity in having it issued, and tried to get him to do a job of writing for him first by persuasion and the assurance that he would be well paid, afterwards by threats and hints that he would use his influence against him. Lycurgus, however, resisted all these conflicting influences, having determined not to become the mere tool of White for any consideration, and finally White took his leave in no very good humor.

August 21, 1862–March 20, 1863

Not long since I had my first experience in that, so much dreaded and so much talked about, business of guarding property in the South. It happened on this wise. It seems that some persons, supposed to be soldiers, had been committing depredations on the property, hen roosts, etc., and threatening the person of a good union man named Perry, who lives in this vicinity. There were four of us to whom this business was intrusted. It was in the evening, and as we approached the house, we were greeted by the savage barking of a large dog but he did not prove at all dangerous. Mr. Perry very cordially welcomed us and invited us into the house leaving the dog outside to give warning of the approach of any intruders. The house is a small balloon framed, story & a half house, the lower part being all in one room.[34] This room is furnished with a nice cottage bedstead, half a dozen chairs, a stand, table, cooking stove and a book-case well filled with books, mostly of a legal character. The furniture is of the plainest kind, but still the interior of the room wears an appearance of neatness and comfort that is not usually found in this region. The family consisting of Mr. Perry himself, a young man and his wife, who seem to be the housekeepers, and a small child, was at supper when we came and we were kindly invited to sit down with them, but having already eaten we of course declined.

Mr. Perry is a middle aged man, tall and rather slim, is a member of the Missouri Legislature, which meets sometime this month and seems to be a very intelligent, well informed man and well versed in the current news of the day. He is a Con[n]ecticut Yankee, a true Union man and a thorough emancipationist and endorser of the President[']s emancipation proclamation. He has travelled pretty extensively in this country both north & south and seems to have formed a very sensible opinion of slavery, its relation to the Government and its bearing upon the political and social interests of this people. He was very free and sociable in his manners and it gave me real pleasure to listen to his interesting conversation and amusing anecdotes. It was the richest intellectual treat that I have had for some time. Mr. Perry offered us the best sleeping accommodations his house afforded but we thinking that perhaps we might become spoiled by sleeping on a bed, chose rather to lie on the floor. In the morning we were pressed to stay for breakfast, but not wishing to put them to so much trouble, we thanked them for their kindness and returned to camp without having seen or heard any thing of the expected depradators, they doubtless having had some intimation that the place would be guarded. This is the first time I have crossed the threshold of a dwelling house since I left Iowa.

You say that your letter paper was all gone. I don't consider that any misfortune, to us at least, but rather a benefit for we received a long letter on fools-cap on that account.[35] I have plenty of paper yet and if you desire it I can send you some by express. The paymaster has not been around yet and most of the "boys" are about out of cash and sutler tickets are as plenty as shin plasters in Iowa City. The sutler instead of being unpopular as it was at first supposed he would be, is patronized by a majority of the men in the regiment. I have had nothing to do with him yet, except that I bought one lead pencil, nor do I expect to have any of his tickets.[36] I have drawn a pair of shoes for the purpose of saving my boots for muddy weather. I made a requisition a day or so ago for two shirts, one pair of drawers and two pair of socks.

Thanksgiving day was celebrated in camp by having no drill. We had no turkey or good dinner. The day was windy and cool and I staid in my tent all day not having the liberty of going outside of the lines. It would have done one good to have had a regular, old-fashioned thanksgiving dinner, but such things are not to be thought of. Wait till the wars are all over, then.

About two weeks ago 250 recruits for the 1st Iowa Cavalry arrived here enroute for Springfield where their regiment now is. They remained here, encamped near us, for a few days waiting for a train which they were to escort to get ready. While here one of their number died.[37]

Some time ago nearly all of our teams were sent to Springfield with provisions and will not return for 2 weeks. Last Sunday there was a grand review and inspection of this regiment and cavalry stationed near here. This is something that has to be gone through with the last day of every month and if that day happens to be sunday, all the better, it saves one week day for drill or some thing else. Military necessity overrules all claims of the men to that as a day of rest.

Today about 50 secesh prisoners, guarded by some of the 18th Iowa, passed through Rolla on their way from Springfield to St. Louis.[38] They are a very wretched looking set of men and are said to be miserably clad. I didn't see them myself.

Every few days there are sales on confiscated property. Mr. Perry of whom I spoke bought a cow, one that would "come in" before long, for six dollars. In Iowa she would have sold for at least $20.

The government price of sugar is 11 cts. per pound and the price of coffee is 28 cts. per pound but in Rolla it retails for 40 cts. Our mess of 25 men saves about one dollar's worth of coffee every week. This goes to pay the cook.

I learned from Mr. Perry that, in this county (Phelps) which is pretty large one I believe, there are only thirty slaves. I don't think I have seen more than a half a dozen since I have been here.

I suppose from what I saw in the last Republican that Johnathan Lengle & Wm. Morton will have to return to the army very soon or be treated as deserters.[39]

Did you get cash for the colt you sold to Mr. Mead? If so, that was a good way of selling corn to Mr. Pine and getting paid for it in a reasonable time.[40]

Tell Clara, Sidney & Freddy that I will write to them when I get the right kind of envelopes.

I asked Howard several questions in my last. I would like it if he would answer them in his next letter.

I sent to Chicago for a copy of S. S. song book called the "Golden Shower," a sequel to the "Golden Chain" and I think a very good book. I will send it to you as soon as I get a one cent stamp to pay the postage.

August 21, 1862–March 20, 1863

We have the "Golden Chain" here. L. Yenter sent for it.

Give my love to Ma, Clara, Sidney & Freddy and all the boys. Whenever the "spirit moves you" write again and tell us all the news

        Your Affectionate Son, George A Remley

Saturday, December 13, 1862 — Georgetown, Halton Co., Canada West
Dear George,
When your letter came to me we were just beginning to move out of the university house, and consequently I was exceedingly busy for the next ten days; immediately afterwards, I received a letter from Canada telling me to come on as soon as possible, and the preparation for coming, and the business after I arrived here have taken up all my time. Georgetown is a place of about twelve hundred inhabitants: the people are very pleasant and seem more like the people in Virginia than those of Iowa. I have come on here to take charge of a school and think that I will find it quite pleasant. The people are so much more orderly than those of Iowa that they can not fail to bring up their children orderly too.

I hope that you are getting on well in the army. I do not know whether you have had any fighting to do or not but have watched the news to find out. And if you have, I hope that you came out safely. Give my regards to your brother and all of my friends that are with you. And George write again and let me know how you are all getting on.

May the God of us all bless you and keep you from all harm.

    Write soon and remember me as your aff. friend, Richard Totten

Thursday, December 25, 1862 — Salem, Dent County, Missouri
Dear Ma,
I have been writing to Sidney & Fred and I thought I would enclose in the same envelope a few lines to you.[41] It has been a little more than a week since we heard from home. The last letter we received was a long one from Howard directed to Lycurgus. There was in it a note from Pa enclosing $2.00. The money though unasked and unhinted for was very acceptable for we, especially Lycurgus, were nearly out of writing material, and we are proportionately thankful for it. I spent all of mine for stamped envelopes and papers. I have on hand now a pretty good stock of the wherewithal to write, enough to last me for a good while. My stock consists of 29 stamped and 7 common envelopes and also 5 postage stamps, and 1 1/4 quires of large and one half quire of small letter papers.[42] So you can see that I am fully well supplied. I had to pay twenty-five cents for a quire of large letter paper. I bought stamped envelopes because it was considerably cheaper to do so. Gave 50 cents for 16 stamped envelopes, thereby getting 16 envelopes for two cents. If I had bought them separately, they would have cost one cent a piece. So much for that subject. Let it rest.

Now about our health. Lycurgus is well and has been ever since he came from the hospital. I am well now but have not been for about three weeks.

Dr. [Joseph] Ledlie the Post surgeon here tells me that I came very near having an attack of a kind of Typhoid fever usually called "camp fever."[43] I was not at any time very sick, never confined to bed, but every afternoon I had a very severe headache accompanied by a light fever. I felt miserably dull & stupid all the time.

We left Rolla on Tuesday the 19th of Dec and I was taken sick the Thursday before. The "regulations" are such that a person must either be on duty or on the "sick-list" and report himself to the Doctor. There is no half way watch to rest in when one does not feel very well and yet would rather not have any thing to do with the Doctor. Such was my case and I continued to maintain a position between duty and the "sick-list" for several days but had at last to have my name put on the "sick-list" and go along with the rest of the afflicted of the company, on a short visit to Dr. [Oren] Peabody, who attends to the sick here at the regiment. He pronounced my disease to be "Portal congestion" and prescribed for it a large dose of calomel, mixed with a little rheubarb & aloes, I believe, giving the whole mixture the euphonious title of "Cathartic Powders." I presume he thought by so doing he would deceive me in regard to the true character of the medicine. Instead of taking the "Cathartic Powders" as desired I threw them into the fire, where I thought they would do as much good and less harm than if I had taken them, and took in place a dose of "Ayers Cathartic Pills" which had the desired effect. When the order for our company to go to Salem came to camp, I thought that I could not go along as all the "boys" had to carry their own knapsacks; but Capt. Cree kindly promised to have mine hauled on the wagon, so I concluded that I would try it. The first day I walked all the way and was not so tired as I was the day before. The whole distance is 25 miles. For the first few days after we arrived here my health remained "in status quo" and I considered myself very fortunate in having escaped from the clutches of Drs. White & Peabody. Lycurgus, having described my symptoms to Capt. [Timothy M.] Wilcox, who is an old physician of 10 years experience, he said that they indicated an attack of typhoid fever and gave Lycurgus a prescription which he got filled at the Post Hospital to relieve my headache.[44] It was a few drops of the tincture of achonite on a little refined sugar. The next day I went to Doctor Ledlie, the Post Surgeon, and he continued the medicine prescribed by Capt. Wilcox. This relieved my headache some. The Doctor told me the next morning that my headache was beginning to assume a neuralgia form and gave me a few powders, containing about equal portions of quinine, opium and ipecac, which he thought would relieve me. I went to the Hospital several times after this, but did not get any more medicine, except a dose of castor oil. The Dr. says that all that is required to make me all right is good beef, chicken and other wholesome food. I feel as well now as I did before I was taken sick, only I am not quite as strong but am getting better in that respect every day. Capt. Wilcox said that throwing Peabody's medicine in the fire was the best thing I could have done with it and thought that if I had staid at Rolla, White would have had me in the hospital, sick with a fever. Enough and too much about myself. Now for a few other things.

Our company is very pleasantly situated here at Salem. We have houses to live in, very little drilling or guard duty to do and no guard line to keep us from going about just where we please. All the "boys" and the captain unite in hoping that we will stay here all winter. We have been here more than two weeks, but whether we will remain much longer is a question of doubt.

It was reported here about a week ago that the 22nd had been placed in Gen. Fitz Henry Warren's brigade and that we would all have to go to Houston [Missouri] where he is now stationed, but that report seems to be false for we are not yet under the command of that "paper General" nor is it very likely that we will be soon.

Colonel Stone has been appointed commander of Rolla District, which includes Houston, Salem, etc., in place of Col. [John] Glover of the 3 Mo. Cavalry, who was relieved at his own request. Lt. J. W. Porter has been permanently appointed adjutant of the regiment. Thus we lose our best company officer with not even the slightest hopes of filling his place with another half so good. The vacancy, however, will have to be filled, but by whom? is a question that has caused a great deal of speculation lately. It surely ought not to be by the orderly G. W. Handy for there have been, not long since, two petitions for his removal from the office he now holds signed by nearly the whole company, the one presented to the major and the other to the Colonel; but through the influence of Capt. Cree neither of them had the desired effect.[45]

The first 10 days that we were here the only kind of bread we had was hard crackers. Then having the privilege of drawing flour if we preferred it, our mess drew flour and got the Post bakers to bake it for us, giving us one pound of bread for one pound of flour. I was opposed to this movement, but the majority ruled and so I had to be contented. When I tasted the bread, such stuff I hardly ever saw thick hard crusts, sour not light and not at all good. I could hardly eat at first. Most of the "boys" think that it will do pretty well, but for my part I would much rather prefer the hard crackers that we have had.

Lycurgus & I and three others, five in all, have made "entirely different arrangements" about our cooking, eating, etc., which are to continue in force as long as we remain here. We have engaged a very respectable looking woman, named Mrs. Powers (not an Irish woman) to take our rations and cook them for us. We are to eat at her table, just as if we belonged to the family, and she is to furnish any thing extra that is needed, such as, beef steak, sausage, pies, etc. As a compensation for all her trouble & expense she is to have the extra rations, if there are any, and in addition we engage to pay her one dollar per month, that much apiece.

The face of the country in this vicinity is much smoother and the soil much better and more productive than about Rolla. The greater part of the country seems to have been not very long ago destitute of trees and I think was a prairie country. Now it is covered for the most part with a dense growth of young, straight white & black oak trees. The rocky roads, native of the country, climate, houses & character of the people very frequently remind of Old Virginia.

A short distance from town there are two hills composed almost entire[ly] of iron ore. I picked up some stones that looked just like cast iron and seemed equally as heavy as [a] piece of casting of the same size. This State needs more than any thing else the enterprising genius of the Yankees to develop its rich resources.

The people here are nearly all "secesh," or have been at one time but have now taken the oath of allegiance to the Federal Government. Such men can not be trusted very far. "Bushwhackers" are plenty about 10 miles from here and they are frequently killed by our cavalry scouts.[46] The rebel captain I spoke of in my letter to Sid had some very interesting correspondence on his person when killed, by which certain government officials in St. Louis are implicated.

We are having the warmest winter weather that I ever saw. For the past few days the wind has been blowing from the South and the weather rather inclined to be showery but the wind has now changed and it has cleared off warm & pleasant. We do not very often have fire in our room for it is not needed. The nights are warm without frost. This is more like the weather we usually have in September than December weather.

A few days ago I drew from the Government 1 pair of pants, 1 pair of drawers, 2 woolen shirts & 2 pr. of socks. None of my old clothes are worn out, but as we do not always have a chance to draw when we want to, I thought I had better get them while I had an opportunity. The new pants are not like the first ones we got. They are fine black casinett and not at all suitable for a soldier.[47] The materiel for making the old kind is exhausted I believe. I washed my old pants a good while ago and they shrunk up so much that I had to let out the hem, and whip it over at the end to keep it from r[a]veling, in order to make them long enough. The first 2 pairs of sock I drew are not worn out yet but they have to be darned several times. I expect it would make you laugh to see me darning my socks. I use Lycurgus' needle & yarn for I did not bring any myself. I have never yet regretted that I brought my waistcoat along with me. I find it of great service to me and very comfortable. A great many of the "boys" either bought waistcoats here or sent home for them.

Tell Howard that I received a letter from Dick Totten a few days ago. He is now at Georgetown, Halton County, Canada [W]est teaching school. He did not say one word about his father's family. I don't know where they are now. They are not in Canada with him. He thinks he will like it there the people are so different from those of Iowa City and so much like those of Va. where he used to live.

I also received a letter from Ira Johnson since we have been here. He says that you had staid all night at their house a few days before he wrote.

There is a church (meeting house) here with its sides pierced full of bullet holes. There is preaching in it once every month. Sunday after next is the next time for preaching and I expect to attend if we stay here long enough.

December 26th
Drew our rations this morning and took our share to Mrs. Powers for her to dispose of as she sees fit. Have just returned from our dinner at Mrs. Powers, the first time I have set down to a table and eaten a regular meal since I left home. Had a first rate dinner, roast goose, sausage, good salt-rising bread, like yours, and biscuits, rice, stewed peaches, molasses, doughnuts and peach pie, of course there was coffee with cream & sugar in it. Now don't you think that was a pretty good dinner for a soldier to get hold of? I thought so at any rate and did full justice to it. Let me tell you a secret. Mr. Powers has some girls who are not very small, and that I suppose is the reason that Lycurgus, for he did all the negotiating, got such a good place for us. It may be possible that he will settle somewhere down here after the war is over.

There is a man here, even here in this little town, who has obtained license to sell whiskey, etc. Last night being Christmas night a few of our "boys" thought they would get on a regular "bust" and judging from the actions of several of them last evening I think that they succeeded pretty well. One respectable young man who lives not very far from Iowa City got drunk, so drunk that he was perfectly crazy. It was the first time, I believe, he ever did such a thing.

Day before yesterday Lycurgus trimmed my hair which was getting pretty long, not having been cut since I left home, and I in return trimmed his hair for him and did it very neatly too. Lycurgus is gradually fattening up. He now weighs 142 1/2 pounds. I lost about 12 pounds in weight when I was sick. I suppose I will gain some now. Ever since Lewis Logan came from the hospital he has been very hearty and "eats awful." He now weighs over 180 pounds and is still growing heavier. He is beginning to be a little uneasy about it. Lewis Logan received from home, by express, 2 pair of socks and a pair of woollen gloves. Lewis Yenter had 2 pr. socks sent him in the same package. Some of the "boys" have got papers, envelopes, butter and cans of molasses, plum butter, etc. in the same way. It is very pleasant to get such things, but it costs more to get them here than the things are worth.

Now for those questions that could be found. They are not of very great importance, but still it will give me some satisfaction to have them answered. One was, did you ever get my Bible from Mr. Johnson's? The next. Was Hopwood['\]s overcoat ever taken home or to John Koller as you said you would? Hopwood is here in the same room with us & I would like to know for my own satisfaction whether his coat was sent home or not. The third is Lycurgus' question. How many sheep have you; if any, if not, what caused the enterprise to fall through? Tell Howard to call on you for these questions the next time he writes.

By the last mail Lycurgus received $5.50 from J. W. Porter, the proceeds of 19 pounds of coffee that our mess had saved. Porter sold it for 33 cts. per lb. but had to take a voucher for it instead of cash, which had to be discounted in order to get cash. The extra coffee we sell does not quite pay our cook. I, [who] have done entirely without coffee for a while, received 20 cts. of this money in cash. With 10 cts. of this I bought molasses in partnership with Lycurgus. 05 cts. bought a good lead pencil and I have .05 remaining in my pocket book. Don't you think I am rich, got all I want and some money left and pay day not far off! I suppose you have more molasses than you know what to do with. You all must be a sweet set by this time. I could go on at this rate all day but I suppose I had better stop. Give my love to Pa, Allie, Clara and all the boys. Tell them to write often. I would be glad to have you write too when you have time. Direct your letters as usual.

Your Affectionate Son, George A Remley

[George continues:] **December 27th 1862, 8 o'clock PM**
Dear Pa,

It may seem strange to you that my letter has so many dates, but it can be accounted for by the fact that the mail does not go to Rolla every day. We have just received "an abundance of letters" from you, Clara, etc. We had been expecting it for some time and were truly glad to get it. It did me more good than a "Christmas dinner."

I am very glad to hear that you were expecting to have a good time Christmas and hope that you <u>did</u> enjoy yourselves to the fullest extent of your capacities. I guess Mit was "in clover" Christmas night, when he had the Luses, McCandlesses, etc. to "cut up" with. I would like very much to have been with you had such a thing been possible. I hope you did not let any thoughts of us mar your enjoyment during your festivities, for we are in a good place, have good eating now and are as well situated as a soldier could hope to be.

Write frequently.

Your Affectionate Son, Geo A Remley

Friday, January 9, 1863 — Salem, Dent County, Missouri
Dear Pa,

We received your welcome letter of Dec 22d. This is the last we have had, although we live in daily expectation of another. About Dec. 28 Geo. mailed a voluminous letter of seven or eight pages, which you have doubtless received. Thinking it about time to visit you with another epistle, I have concluded to do so without waiting for the letters due us from home.

First, as to our health: Geo. is well and fattening up wonderfully, having gained nine pounds in weight, in about as many days. For the last four or five days I have been somewhat <u>unwell</u>, having an almost constant nausea, or sickness at the stomach. I think my liver is somewhat deranged; the change of my complexion, at least, indicating this. Jaundice perhaps.

August 21, 1862–March 20, 1863

Since we last wrote, we have remained at Salem in status quo, notwithstanding the many and conflicting reports concerning our belonging to Warren's Brigade, and our immediate removal to Houston [Missouri]. The prevailing opinion now is that we do not belong to Warren's Brigade and that we shall stay here all winter. It is, however, possible, and even intimated, that we may be sent down the Mississippi. I am still Acting Post Adjutant, have become better acquainted with my duties, and "get along first rate." I receive no extra pay for my services. Our duties here, as a Company, do not amount to much: foraging, hauling wood, patrol and prisoner-guard duty. Capt. Wilcox, Co. G, 3d Mo. Cav. having gone to Houston, Capt. Cree now commands the Post. Capt. Wilcox was relieved by a Co. of the 9th Cav. Mo. State Militia, fighting stock, having participated in the Kirksville Battle at which the Guerrilla [Joseph C.] Porter and his large band were "cleaned out."[48]

Several changes have occurred, or are likely to occur, in our company. Porter, as you know, has been promoted to the Adjutancy, thus leaving the 1st Lieutenancy vacant. This is to be filled by 2d Sergeant Wm. J. Schell, to whom the Wilson's Creek Battle has given prestige.[49] Lieut. [William G.] Haddock has sent in his resignation; and it, no doubt will be accepted, which would leave the 2d Lieutenancy vacant. I think, for this, Handy, Orderly Serg't. has the "inside track." We shall know more about this by and by.

A report was circulated a week or so ago, that this Post would be evacuated; to which color was given by the removal of nearly all the Commissary Stores from this point to Houston. This emboldened the secesh to come back into the neighborhood, furnishing, thus, abundant game to the Federal scouting parties. A party of 70 or 80 cavalry, who had been (with a good many more) scouting towards Arkansas, stayed here last night en route to Rolla. They made a pretty good haul, having killed three & captured seventeen prisoners, and twenty two horses. Most of these were caught only about 30 miles from here. George told you of a scout made by some of Co. G 3d Mo. Cav.[50] I send you a piece of silk & some brass wire embroidery (for shoulder straps, etc) found in the haversack of the rebel captain who was killed. (Allie may take them in charge, and preserve them as mementoes.)

This county (Dent) has furnished about 700 or 800 recruits for the rebels, and perhaps 250 for our army, the loyalty of a majority of whom, however, may justly be suspected. The number of men who have stood for the Union, "through thick and thin" is, in this country extremely small. The presence of Union soldiers has, however, made Unionism very popular; and you rarely, if ever, meet with an avowed disunionist. The farthest they go, is to be in favor of the "Old Constitution." The state of society may be imagined, when men who were perhaps intimate friends before the war, are now mortal enemies, joining in hunting one another down; and when men who were formerly enemies embrace the present troubles as the fit opportunity to ruin one another. So much for matters in general. Now to descend a little into the minutiae.

First the weather. Has been almost as mild as October, no snow, not much rain. In fact it is some time since I have seen such winter weather. We often sit in our open upstair[s] room without feeling the need of a fire. How is it up in Iowa?

George told you about our fine boarding place. Well, they found it too much trouble to keep so many, and [we were] told we might take our rations somewhere else. Lo[a]th to leave, I went and procured a new lease for George and myself, and let the rest "slide." We are boarding there still, and "get along first rate."

While you all were revelling in the luxuries of a loaded Christmas dinner table, we repaired to desolate looking garret and dined upon our homely "grub." Christmas did not, to us, herald its approach by the ringing voices of little ones, overjoyed at finding in their stockings, the precious deposits of good old Santa Claus. The first sounds greeting our ears were (perhaps) the obscene jest, or the profane oath. Well, well perhaps it won't be so always. I may be a little "blue" today. The jaundice is apt to make one so.

We have heard of the Murfreesboro Battle, and are eagerly awaiting news from Vicksburg, which is reported taken.[51] If so, it may be that the crisis of the War is past, at least [I] hope so.

In the 9th Cav. M. S. M, stationed here, is an Alderson. He is from Randolph Co. Mo. I tried to trace out a connection with our family, but failed. His father emigrated from Kentucky to Mo. His grandfather came from Pennsylvania and was one of the first settlers of Kentucky. I believe he is still living. The family is English, so we are not the only Aldersons in America.[52]

An Artillery Lieutenant passed through here about ten days ago who knew Uncle Wm. Zoll, having done business in Warrensburg. His name is Newgent (of Cass Co. Mo.).[53]

Let me tell a little incident that happen[ed] some time ago. Some of the boys, more through fun than any thing else, were getting up a letter to Gen. [Samuel R.] Curtis, making inquiries about the modus operandi of being transferred to the gun boats. I took the job, wrote the letter & signed their names; and it was duly mailed. Well, by and by, after we had given up all hope of receiving an answer, a clerk employed at Head Quarters brought to the one whose name was first signed a circular giving some information on the point, and said that a telegram had been received at H'd Qrs. from Gen. Curtis on the subject, that this had been sent by Lt. Col. Graham (Post Comd't) to our Regimental Commander Maj. Atherton. As we never received it, he through fear of losing some of his men, must have suppressed it.

We did expect payday some time this month, but don't know when it will come. It seems as far off now as it did two month ago.

I guess I may as well close. I might spin out my mos[s]y thread indefinitely but this is as good a place to cut it off as any. Next time you happen in the Republican office, ask Jerome if he ever received my letter. If so, please obtain.

[Lycurgus]

August 21, 1862–March 20, 1863

Thursday, January 15, 1863 — Camp near Rolla, Missouri
Dear Pa,
As some changes have occurred in our circumstances since my last letter home, I embrace this, the earliest opportunity of writing again.

You see by the date where we are at present. Well, we have evacuated the Port of Salem, "pulled up the post" and skedaddled to Rolla and are now on our old stamping ground which we find very bleak and desolate nearly all the sheltering trees and brush having been cut away. Coming back yesterday evening, we pitched our tents in the mud (at least on the ground just after a rain). No straw, or hay, for bedding, could be obtained. The best we could do, was to "rake up" some old, empty grain sacks (just like coffee sacks) and spread down for the substratum; next, my India rubber blanket, which has proved itself invaluable; kept out the moisture; upon this are spread our bed and managed to sleep comfortably in spite of circumstances. Today it is snowing, for the first time, I believe since last October. George is on guard up in town. I am sick, have the jaundice, took six big cathartic pills this morning. All things taken together: uncomfortable quarters, dismal weather (comparatively), jaundice, and especially the pills, have given a decidedly blue tinge to my feelings, which is in no wise relieved by the gloomy news from the war. Thus you have a sketch of our present circumstances. But you see I have followed the example of Virgil in the Aeniad, and given the last of the story first. To go back, a little:

You have, probably, long ago seen in the Tribune accounts of the upstirring of the rebels in S.W. Mo.: the battles at Springfield, Hartsville, etc.[54] Well, they were terribly scared at Rolla (or St. Louis) and had eight or nine regiments, among them the 8th & 14th Iowa, hurried in here, the citizens enrolled and set to digging ditches and making breastworks, and were, I believe, actually thinking of moving to the fort. They thought the enemy was just going to "gobble" them up. Of course this was before the reinforcements arrived. We at Salem, although we heard of the fighting at Springfield, etc., were in blissful ignorance of any danger to ourselves, until Monday evening (12th) a messenger came dashing into town, with an order from Head Quarters, Rolla, for us to move, forthwith, to Rolla with all portable government stores, etc. A scouting party of twenty men was just on the point of starting in pursuit of some dozen secesh scoundrels who had been the night before plundering Union families, only seven or eight miles distant (or rather to intercept them; the pursuing party had started out soon after the plundering happened). This scout was of course abandoned, and men sent in every direction to impress teams to haul away the government property.[55] The night was, in good part, spent in loading the wagons as they came in, packing up, etc. and by about day light we were ready to start. Of[f] we moved, first the advance guard of cavalry, next the oxteams, then the horse teams and our Co. then the six mule teams, and lastly, the rear guard of Cavalry (in about this order), in all about a dozen wagons. Our train was considerably augmented by the Union residents, who couldn't bear the thought of being left to the mercies of the secesh. It was sad to see families packing up and starting off from their homes, to a distant town with no previous provisions made for their comfort. In <u>general</u>, only the heads of the families, who had made themselves obnoxious to the secesh, went with [their] most valuable portable property. The majority, perhaps, of the citizens, secure in their secession sympathies, remained. Just as we were about to start it commenced raining, which added to the desolate appearance of the scene, and the discomfort of all concerned. We had our knapsacks hauled this time; and as I was sick I had the additional privilege of riding. Well we marched on over roads rough & muddy till we reached that Dr. Hyer's about three o'clock PM (ox teams & all). Here we pitched our tents, and with the help of lots of straw, taken from his rick, spent the night very comfortably, notwithstanding the fact that it rained nearly all the time.

Next morning we got a pretty early start, the rain having stopped, and trudged along through the mud, up hill & down, until we reached Rolla about three o'clock PM. Today I rode three fourths of the way, on the horses of the Cavalry men, who were anxious to walk, to warm their feet the weather having grown colder. This was the first horseback riding I had had since leaving home. If at home, I would like to have a good cavalry horse, as a riding horse. They are so well trained. Coming to Camp, we found a letter from Howard, dated Jan. 2, Republican with my communication in it, Christian Times & two Harper's Weeklies from Mr. Mordoff's (for which you will give them our thanks). This brings me to the part of the story already told. The rest of this letter will be detached scraps of news, etc.

To give an idea life in this country: Last Saturday a man who had made himself rather prominent as a secesh, a well-to-do farmer, was shot dead within three quarters of a mile of Salem. A Union soldier, a neighbor of his, whose house had been burned over the heads of his sleeping family, of which deed this man was suspected of being a participant, most probably shot him. When shot he was returning home, seven or eight miles distant, with some purchases he had made in Salem. He was found next morning and taken home to his family, who were, till then, in ignorance of his death. This deed is what probably excited the secesh to commit the depredations before alluded to.

Several of our old neighbors are here, Jonathan Lengle, Wm. Morton and I suppose, Lorenzo Davis, Wm. & Allen Eddy, etc. though I have not yet seen any of them. Their camp is a mile off.

Part of the 2nd Mo. Artillery (Dutch), at the fort, became mutinous, because they were not mustered out of service, as they claimed they had a right to be and laid down their arms. They were then divided out among the companies of our Regiment, our company receiving ten, four of whom have deserted; the others are still here. As they won't take up arms, they are made to work, under guard, chop wood, etc. They do nearly all the wood chopping for one regiment. So much for the Dutch stubbornness.

All our neighbor boys are fat and thriving. Lewis Logan was Post Blacksmith at Salem, the last ten days before we left for which he gets $.40 per day extra. He had to work hard.

Did you ever have the jaundice? If so, you know how to sympathize with me. It is a <u>most wretched</u> complaint. This moment I feel scarcely able to sit up, sick at the stomach, etc. I think I have fallen off ten or twelve pounds since I have been sick. My "passages" occur only about once in three days.

This day was duly noted in my mental calendar as your birthday. I wish I could be with you a little while but that may not be till perhaps, August 1865.

I send those things I forgot to enclose when I sealed up my last letter, also a specimen of the "countersign."

Write more frequently, please. We think we ought to have a letter from home, at least, <u>every week</u>. Give our love to all the folks at home. Tell Ma to send something, sometimes in the letters from home, I mean write to us. It is useless, I suppose, to ask Allie to write to us.

Your Affectionate Son, Lycurgus

Tuesday, January 20, 1863 — Warrensburg, Missouri
Dear Lycurgus,
Since the receipt of your letter there has been some fighting, not a great distance from your Camp, when we heard of the fighting at Springfield we thought of you & George & that you might have been in the fight, we first heard the Rebels had killed & captured the entire federal force then at Springfield (we thought 1500) and were inclined to think it a fact as the Rebel force was said to be 6000 with 6 pieces of artillery. While such was the report here, the Rebel Sympathizers were exultant as far as they dared be. Their faces showed plainly the desires of their hearts. Since then, we have heard a different account & from the last reports of the fate of the daring Rebels, we can see nothing encouraging to the friends of Disunion. I can not see what object Missourians had in view when they first started out in this Rebellion, to my mind it has always been a plain case. That the institution of slavery would be injured if not destroyed in this State by the act of secession or Rebellion and now we know & the Rebels surely see they have injured the cause they pretend to espouse, but in all this there is nothing to comfort us, or them. Their failure has made them desperate & so long as the war lasts & until a Peace is made, these same men we may naturally suppose will try to get back into this State. Their families & property is here. They have nothing elsewhere. They are & will be kept out only by numbers they fear. The County Board is gathering up the property of the Secessionists who have been taxed to pay for I don't exactly know what, but think to indemnify Union men for losses sustained & the new Militia. There will be a great amount of property sold at Public Auction for Cash.

We have nothing much of importance to write at this time, have had no letter from your Father & Mother lately. Times here continue the same our Command here do some scouting & sometimes come across those they seek to catch. I am glad Troops are here, but in Justice to our Town must say that the Troops are not improving the Town either in appearance or Morals, a total disregard is paid to the interest of Citizens property by the Soldiers. There are any amount of negroes in Camp to cut & haul wood & yet they burn fencing around the Houses they occupy without regard to what a man is, or may be, now this in my opinion is not as it should be, our Town is in the woods, wood all around it, and now since we have snow, about 22 inches deep, we may expect the houses to be burnt if it don't accommodate the soldier to hunt a part of them. We have no late news from Va. not having written or received a letter from there for many months. They may have blotted us out of the Book of Remembrance because we, did not like them, go Crazy. In the last letter from my Sister on the Kanawha, she said the Ka[nawha] Valley was full of Yankees, the inference is plain that she is a Rebel, I have not since had time to answer her letter, for if men who are Loyal are Yankeys then I would glory in the name of Yankey. We still look for you & George, while you remain in this state and as the Commanders charge about to suit their convenience, why may you not, come to this land of plenty & of beauty. But if this deep snow should go off to leave mud & your Command should visit us then, I am not sure that you would be favourably impressed but then you are used to deep soil & that sort will get deep and muddy. I will direct this letter as heretofore & shall hope to hear from you soon again. Your Aunt sends her love to you & says the only reason she has not written is want of time, do you believe that.

I am as ever affectionately

your Uncle, Wm. Zoll

Friday, January 23, 1863 — [Rolla, Missouri]
Dear Pa,
I haven't much news to communicate, but I wish to mention one or two things. First I have been keeping a "private journal," my book being full was closed Dec 31st. For fear of losing it in the vicissitudes of war, I have given it to Wm. C. Luce (a painter of Iowa City) who has been discharged and is going home, to take with him. He will leave it with Mr. Turner. Please get it when it arrives. I have no objection to the family's inspecting it, provided the pencil writing is not blurred.[56]

You said you expected to get that money from the Township Treasurer some time this month, what about the interest? Was that allowed?

I feel quite unwell today. My eyes and skin are pretty yellow, and I (to use a slang phrase) "don't care whether school keeps or not."

It seems strange to us that we don't get letters from home more frequently. Three weeks (and we don't yet know how much longer) is too great an interval. Remember us in your prayers & believe me

Your Affectionate Son, Lycurgus

August 21, 1862–March 20, 1863

Sunday, January 25, 1863 — Camp near Rolla, Missouri
Dear Pa,
Considering the fact that George wrote home (to Howard) only day before yesterday, you may be somewhat surprised to receive another so soon; and that, too, written on Sunday.⁵⁷ Well the occasion of it is this: we are to start tomorrow morning to Houston [Missouri], or rather to Pocahontas, Arkansas, to over take Warren's Brigade, which marches immediately to the latter place, at least Rumor says that is Warren's destination. So it seems the long mooted question, as to whether we are to go into Warren's Brigade, or not, is at last decided. I, for one, and I suppose most of us, would much prefer to go to St. Louis and down the River, or almost any where, to marching with knapsacks over the mountains of Southern Missouri and Northern Arkansas. But military orders are imperative, and we must obey. The <u>danger</u>, as far as that is concerned, may be somewhat <u>less</u> going this direction, but the <u>glory</u> would be proportionately less, and the labor infinitely greater.

I am still jaundiced, but improving, not yet able to carry a large load very far in a day. I have fallen off some twelve or fifteen pounds in weight. I suppose my knapsack will be hauled for me, at least until I become stronger. George is well, as he usually is.

Not much relishing the idea of making pack mules of ourselves, some of us concluded to lighten our knapsacks by sending most of our clothing not absolutely necessary, home (in a box) by Express. The box is sent to Mr. Albert Westcott of the firm of Eastman & Westcott.

I have put the following articles in the box viz:

One pair black pants costing (government price)				$3.03
One dress coat	"	"		7.20
Two shirts	"	"	@88 ea	1.76
One pair Drawers	"	"		50
			Total	$12.49

The Box will be opened in Iowa City and the various articles distributed as directed. Mine are marked "care of J. T. Turner Esq. Iowa City." Lewis Yenter sent his dress coat, also in the care of Mr. Turner.

The pants are new; never were worn but three days. They are rather unsuitable for a <u>soldier</u>, but I suppose <u>cheap</u> enough.

The dress coat I have scarcely worn since leaving Iowa City. The shirts and drawers are all new; never worn but once, and sad to say, are now unwashed. The order to march coming suddenly (only last night) found me unprepared in the (clean) clothes line. The price of all kinds of clothing has risen considerably since Jan 1st. For instance shirts have risen from 88 cents to $1.30. Now if any of this clothing fits the boys and they want to wear it, they can do so by allowing me the above named prices. Otherwise please keep it, with the rest of my clothing, "till that war is over." It is so much money with me.

I have mailed a Harper's Magazine to Milton and a Harper's Weekly to

Howard, the last chiefly on account of the large central picture "Christmas Eve." Let me know whether you ever received them or not. By the way, did you ever get a Missouri Democrat containing the message of the Governor of Mo.?

This is the fourth letter sent home which is as yet unanswered, viz one by me dated Jan. 9th, one Jan. 15th, one by Geo. Jan. 23.[58] Please write more frequently. We think once a month altogether too seldom. Direct as usual. We will try to write every opportunity to let you know our whereabouts, and of our welfare.

I wrote to Uncle Wm. Zoll sometime near the middle of Dec and ha[ve] as yet received no answer. That letter Aunt S. M. Z. wrote to us never arrived. Wonder what's the matter.

Our Adjutant J. W. Porter has sent in his resignation and only waits to see whether it is accepted before he starts home. His father's ill health is the cause. We are very sorry, would rather seen any other officer (almost) in the Regiment resign than him.[59]

There is a good deal of other news I might communicate, but will defer it, though it isn't of much importance at any rate. I must close by asking you to give my love to all at home. Ma, Allie, Clara, Fred, Sidney & the other boys.

Your Affectionate Son, L. Remley

Monday, January 26, 1863 — Camp near Rolla, Missouri
Dear Pa,
You will probably be surprised at receiving three letters from us in such quick succession, but the contents of this will explain the reason. Yesterday (Sunday) Lycurgus and some others in our tent packed up some of their clothes to send home. I was not in the tent at the time and did not know any thing of Lycurgus' intention until I came back and as the box was then full I could not get any of my things in it.

I had not, until this morning, intended to send any thing home as I did not draw any more clothes than I thought was necessary; but when I packed my knapsack, it was so full that I could not buckle it and so heavy that I knew I could never stand it to carry such a load. This morning I procured a box and packed in it the following articles:

1 Dress Coat
1 Pr (Blue) Pants
1 Woollen shirt
1 Cap

I sent the Box by express directed to Mr. Mordoff and requested him to pay the charges and keep the clothes until you called for them. Four others are interested in the box and I suppose the expense will be divided among them. If you will get the clothes and pay Mordoff my share of the freight, I will bear the expense and "make it all right" when I get home. The things I have sent are all new and I would like to have them kept for me till I come back. They are soldiers clothes and are very unsuitable for the boys to wear. I don't suppose that they would want to do it, at least I don't want them to. In the pocket of my dress coat is a small copy of [illegible] that Dr. Lillie presented to me just as we were leaving Iowa City. You may think that it was not very wise in me to draw so many clothes. My inexperience in the marching part of a soldier's life may partly account for it. Enough on this subject.

We are still here at "Camp near Rolla." This morning was the time set for our departure South, but on account of the rain, which has been falling most of the time for the last twenty four hours, and the almost impassable state of the roads, it was postponed until tomorrow or next day. If we have to march over land nearly 200 miles through the mud and sleep on the wet ground, it will be pretty hard on us, especially if (as is the case) the knapsacks have to be carried. There is some talk of taking us to St. Louis, down the river and up the Arkansas river thus avoiding the necessity of a tedious march.

The paymaster has not made his appearance yet, but according to Rumor is coming every day. But day after day, passes and he [doesn't come].

The weather is warm, rainy & and the roads are in a miserable condition as bad if not worse than Iowa roads.

My health continues good. Lycurgus is nearly as well as usual.

Have not heard from home since the 2nd of Jan. Would like to get a letter very much. Write soon & oftener

Your Aff Son, G A Remley

P.S. The Box weighs 27 pounds. Enclosed you will find the receipt given by the express Co. My love to all G A Remley

Please pay my express charges as indicated by Geo. The notion to send seized me suddenly yesterday. L.R.

5 o'clock AM, January 27th 1863

Dear Pa,

Got up at four o'clock this morning, have had roll call and have eaten breakfast. Are ready to start for Houston by 8 o'clock. Turned cold last night and the ground is frozen hard. Roads are very rough.

It is rumored in camp that Gen. Warren is placed under arrest and Col. Stone has been promoted to his position.[60] Our Brigade belongs to Gen. [John Wynn] Davidson's division which has been in S. E. Missouri for some time.

Excuse the scribbling of this letter. While I was writing last night there was a fiddle going at a rapid rate in the tent and the first thing I would know my pencil would be keeping time with the music.

Direct your letters to St. Louis

Good Bye

Your Son, G A Remley

Wednesday, February 4, 186[3] — West Plains, Missouri
Dear Pa,
Started from Rolla a week ago yesterday and after a six days march arrived at this little village called West Plains, one hundred & twenty miles from Rolla. The road runs all the way through a heavily timbered country and some parts of it is very rough & hilly. We passed over a spur of the Ozark Mountains. A good part of the road is covered with fine, sharp, flinty gravel, which made it very hard on boots. I carried my knapsack all the way through. Lycurgus had his hauled part of the way for him. He was not very well part of the time. We are both well now. It is reported that the 21st, 22nd, & 23rd regiments Iowa infantry and the third Iowa Cavalry are to be formed into a brigade and will be commanded by Col. Stone. These troops had a brigade drill yesterday and a sham battle. Shot five rounds. Had also six or eight pieces of artillery. They will be in our brigade I believe. We are in Gen. Davidson's Division and will probably move upon Batesville on the White river in Arkansas about 80 miles from here where a force of rebels is said to [be] concentrating. Are now only 12 miles from the State line.

There is no regular mail route between here & Rolla & it is very hard to get a letter through. I don't [know] when this will start.

Last night after we were in bed we received orders to be ready to move at 7 o'clock this morning, with two day's rations in our haversacks. Our destination is unknown to any but the higher powers. I don't know how many troops are going, but, rumour says, only five companies of this regiment.

While writing, I hear it said among the boys that we are to guard and run a mill about 25 miles south of here.

Ever since I wrote last the weather has been pretty cold and the ground frozen hard. It is very sharp this morning.

We have not had a line from home since the 3rd of last month and it is impossible to tell when a letter will reach us now. I would like to know whether our clothes got through safely or not. I have not time to write any more but must get ready to start. Lycurgus is on guard and can not attend to his things, so I suppose I must do it for him. My love to all. Write soon.

Your Aff Son, Geo A Remley

Friday, February 6, 1863 — West Plains, Missouri
Dear Pa,
George, in his letter of a day or two ago, doubtless told you of our long march from Rolla to this place (120 miles distant) performed in six days, or an average of 20 miles per day. I don't know what he wrote, as I was out on picket guard at the time, but will say (at a venture) that the trip was pretty hard upon me. I carried my knapsack four of the six days when I was taken with what [I] suppose was the bilious intermittent fever, as I had chills & fever alternately, two of each. I then had my knapsack and sometimes myself & gun hauled. I never knew <u>before</u> what soreness of limbs, galled shoulders, etc. meant. If it results in permanently hardening me, it will not be in

vain but this seems to have "used me up" in four days. Perhaps, however, I can stand the next trip better.

We reached this place, some 12 or 15 miles from the Arkansas line, last Tuesday Feb 2nd. The weather was first rate for marching, clear & bright, nights cool, roads frozen during nearly half the day. Since we have been here, however, we have had a sample of Iowa winter weather, it having snowed Wednesday night about eight inches. Tuesday evening I and six others of our company were sent out on picket guard. While out, Co. F packed up and started back to Rolla, leaving us, and six others (invalids, etc.) behind (13 in all). I didn't much care when I found I was left; as my jaded limbs remonstrated strongly against taking another tramp of 240 miles so soon. While the company is gone, I have command of what is left of it: attend to the sick, make morning reports, draw rations, detail guards, etc.

The concentration of so large a force here seems to have been a blunder, as it is so far out of the world that subsistence can not be obtained in sufficient quantities. Yesterday instead of full rations, we drew only half rations. We accordingly start tomorrow to Pilot Knob (or Ironton) contrary to our expectations, which were that we would go to Batesville on the navigable waters of White River. Batesville is only about 70 miles off. I am tired of such "tomfoolery," marching, now advancing, now retrograding.

Gen. Davidson's whole Division, with the exception of one brigade, which moved last Monday to Salem, Ark., is here, some ten or twelve thousand men. Col. Stone commands an Iowa Brigade consisting of the 22d, 21st, & 23d Iowa Regts. and the 3d Iowa Cav. and some Artillery. I don't know whether the whole Division, or only our Brigade will go to Ironton or not; but tomorrow we set out again. When we get there, we can get our mails regularly. By the way it is very strange that we can't get any news from home. You don't know how anxious we are to receive a letter from home; and how often we have been disappointed.

This letter can not go far into details concerning any thing but can give only the summary. When we become settled, we will try to give you full accounts of our travels & adventures. Meanwhile we will anxiously await some news from home. Give my love to all and believe me
your Affectionate Son, Lycurgus

Wednesday, February 11, 1863 — Rolla, Missouri
Dear Pa,
Here we are at the very same place which, two weeks ago, we hoped and expected never to see again. I suppose that you know before this time that the 22nd left Rolla the 27th of last month for the southern part of the State and expected after joining Davidson's Division to continue its course southward until Arkansas was cleared of the rebels.

Well, we did start at that time and after a six day's march through the forests and over the mountains of southern Missouri we reached a small village, nearly south of this place and only twelve miles from the Arkansas line, called West Plains. Here about 17 thousand troops had been collected for the purpose of marching against Batesville, on the White river. A few days before we reached West Plains one brigade composed entirely of cavalry and artillery started out towards Batesville on a reconnoitering expedition. We found Gen. Warren's Brigade, now commanded by Col. Stone, at West Plains and with it the three Co's that belong to this regiment. We arrived there Monday, the second of this month, staid there Tuesday and early Wednesday morning just a week ago. We, company F, were ordered back to Rolla as a train escort. Just as we were packing up to start and before any of us, not excepting the captain, knew where we were going, I wrote a short, hasty letter to you and left it there to be sent to Rolla by the first mail, but as we came directly through to this place I suppose you will get this one first. Lycurgus and about a dozen others of our company were on guard at the time and not having been relieved they could not come with us. If it had been known where we were going, they would not have been left.

We left West Plains with two days rations expecting to draw more at Houston, but when we reached that place four days after we started, we found that all the troops excepting some sick and convalescent had left there and that all the commissary stores had been removed to West Plains. We were greatly disappointed, for we had been on half rations for the last three days and the idea of going all the way to Rolla, 60 or 65 miles, with nothing, but a little hominy and a few beans that we succeeded in obtaining at Houston, to eat would under ordinary circumstances have been any thing but pleasant. But we, remembering that we were surrounded by disloyal people, for the most part, determined to make the best of it and live on the fat of the land. We did too, mostly hog fat, however. Hogs, sheep, chickens, geese and sorghum molasses suffered considerably.

The first night after we left West Plains company F confiscated about 1000 pounds of fresh meat, one beef and the rest pork. We laid over there the next day on account of a snow storm and the meat was about all consumed before we left, fifty teamsters helping us.

Our road southward did not go by Houston but left that village about ten miles to the right. On our return we passed through Houston, coming almost the entire way on a different road and thus we had an opportunity of seeing more of the country. The soil is of the poorest kind and a great part of the country is covered with small, sharp, flinty gravel, in some places so thick that it is impossible to see <u>any</u> soil. The people who live here correspond, in their circumstances very well with country. I can not see how they make a living. A small log hut, a small field, a horse or two, a few cattle, pigs & chickens and almost invariably a half dozen ragged dirty children constitute their all. This is not always the case, however. Sometimes in a deep valley, between two steep rugged hills, a comfortable looking farm house and a small, fertile piece of land can be found. The mountain streams which are numerous are of the clearest, purest water I ever saw.

August 21, 1862–March 20, 1863

We arrived here yesterday having been gone two weeks and on the march just twelve days. The sum of the whole matter is this: started south, marched 240 miles and at the end of two weeks found ourselves exactly at the same place we started from.

It is a little doubtful whether we will ever return again to West Plains, though that was the intention when we left there. The expedition that went to Batesville found the enemy there, attacked them and drove them into the river killing or capturing almost the entire force.[61] It was also ascertained that there was not forage enough in that region to support an army; and that together with the fact that it is an impossibility to obtain supplies from this point at this season of the year, made it advisable to move the whole army this way. I suppose that it will then start down the river to Vicksburg. The train that we came with will start back in a few days, loaded with supplies to feed the army which has been on half rations for some time. We will have to escort it back through the mud I suppose.

The paymaster has not found company F yet. He arrived at West Plains the day before we left and was paying the troops two months wages. I suppose the rest of the regiment has been paid some by this time. There is now a paymaster here at Rolla, and Capt. Cree says that we will get two months pay tomorrow. If I can, I will send some of it home.

My health is still good. Lycurgus was well when we left West Plains. When our regiment started from here 24 sick were left in the hospital, but not one of these was from company F.

The weather for the past two weeks has been variable, very cold and stormy, rainy, snowy and clear & pleasant. The night after we left West Plains about five inches of snow fell and the next day & night was as cold as almost any Iowa weather. The snow all disappeared in a few days and since then it has been raining most of the time.

The roads are in a miserable condition. Mud in Rolla is nearly knee deep.

I have not heard a word from home since the 2nd or 3rd of January more than a month ago! Our mail comes here every day, but we can not get our[s] until the regiment comes here or we go to the regiment.

While on the march, though we pitched our tent on the frozen ground in the mud and had sometimes to shovel away the snow, yet I always managed to have a good bed. No one in our tent had, as a general thing, as good a bed as I had. Some times I would go more than a mile for hay or straw and sometimes gather a large blanket full of leaves and this after I had been carrying my knapsack all day. I always had the bed to prepare. Lycurgus was either too tired or too inef[f]icient to do any thing towards it. I suppose my love for a good bed is hereditary.

We spent two Sundays on the march but there was no difference between Sunday and any other day.

Coming back to Rolla seemed almost like coming home.

J. W. Porter, our adjutant, has resigned & returned home. I hope you will write to us more frequently, it seems so long since we heard from home. Continue directing your letters to St. Louis. We may be in Vicksburg in two weeks.

Give my love to Ma and all the rest of the family.

Your Affectionate Son, George A Remley

Sunday, March 8, 1863 — Iron Mountain, Missouri
Dear Ma,

It is Sunday, but as we expect to leave this place tomorrow morning for Farmington and St. Genevieve, and it is uncertain when I can [find] another so good opportunity of writing home, I have concluded to embrace the present.

As you have doubtless been informed before this by our letters, we reached this place Feb. 25, having a day or two previously, received a number of letters from home & elsewhere. The date of the last one from home, however, was Feb. 15th, since which we have received no intelligence from you all. We were glad to find among the other letters (from home), two or three short ones, written by you, a rather unusual occurrence, as you must confess. We are "thankful for small favors, and larger ones in proportion." The date of our last, home was Feb. 26th & 27th.[62]

Since our last, we have been lying quietly on the side of Iron Mountain, eating Uncle Sam's rations, drilling (company & battalion), guarding, etc. Nothing of any special importance has occurred since the date of our last. Our health (with the exception of my few days' sickness a week ago) has been good. On the last day of Feb. we were mustered again for pay. How soon pay will come, I can't say. As you are aware I have as yet, not received one cent of pay. Well, the pile will be the bigger, when it does come, about a hundred dollars (my own pay). Some little camp excitement was occasioned by the 32d section of the Conscription Act, which grants furloughs for thirty days to twenty per cent of the soldiers, at a time.[63] At this rate it would be nearly two years before the last could obtain their furloughs. I believe Col. Stone is going to commence issuing furloughs. What plan of rotation will be adopted, I can't yet say. Pay will, of course, run on, while only half fare on the railroads, will (most probably) be charged.

The guard down in town, lately seized some contraband whiskey, which was brought to Col. Stone's headquarters. The Colonel had the companies march, one at a time, to the front of his Quarters, and every man treated to a glass of whiskey. There are fifteen or twenty in our Company who didn't take any. I never knew until I came into the army that so many of the young men were so fond of whiskey.

George and I intended to send our overcoats, and some other things home, but our March weather thus far has proved so cool and unpleasant that we have conclude[d] to keep them a while longer. We have no idea, however, of carrying heavy overcoats all summer.

Two of our Company, Charles Able, whose father lives on the Marengo road about half a mile from the brick tavern (3 mile house), and Smith Purcell, son of old Isaiah Purcell, have deserted, been gone 11 days, and not heard from.[64]

The health of our Co. is good, only two on the sick list.

I am glad to hear of the revivals of religion among the churches at home. It is an indication that our country is not <u>entirely</u> deserted by Heaven. In the Army we have next to no religious privileges. Our Chaplain, now at home, has preached only four or five times since we have been in the army. We have <u>no</u> opportunities for prayer meetings, and few for private devotions. Add to this the contaminating influence of the example of all around us, and you have some idea of the difficulty of maintaining an upright Christian walk. I still endeavor to maintain my Christian integrity, and hope by the grace of God to persevere. It is the presence & support of the Almighty alone that sustains me in the troubles incident to a soldier's life. I am glad, too, to remember that there are friends at home who pray for me. Let us still have an interest in your prayers.

As I have (as I stated at the start) but little news to communicate, and as George wants to write some, I will bring my letter to a close. Please write again Ma, as soon as convenient. Give my love to all the family and believe me,

Your Affectionate Son, Lycurgus

[George continues:]
Dear Ma,
I send in this letter a specimen of literature written in <u>genuine southern style</u> Allie may have to keep as a "memento." It was found on a secesh, who was killed by our scouts. You will also find enclosed a few cotton seeds, all that came from a pod which I got on a farm about five miles from Rolla. If any of you would like to experiment in cotton raising, you can have an opportunity.

Your Son, Geo A Remley

[written on verso]
March 8th 3 o'clock PM
Dear Allie,
As Lycurgus has left room for me to write, though he has told all the <u>news</u>, I suppose it is necessary for me to say something and I know of no one to whom I would rather address it than you. We have heard but very little from you since we left home and but for a short letter that you wrote not long ago in connection with Mit, we would have no visible evidence of your existence. But I hope this state of things will continue no longer. The "ier is now broken" or at least cracked and I trust that you will use pen, ink, and paper a little more freely than heretofore and let us know that you still think of us sometimes.

Since Lycurgus wrote we received a letter from home written by Milton, dated March 3rd, the first one since the 24th of last month.

I am very glad indeed to hear, that while there is so much sickness prevalent in your part of Iowa, you have all been permitted to enjoy good health. That this may continue is my most earnest wish.

Lycurgus has already told you that we expect to leave here tomorrow morning. It is also expected that we will have to leave our comfortable stoves and Sibley tents and put up hereafter with small "shelter tents." We do not much relish the idea, but it being a "military necessity" we must submit and it is a matter of policy as well as duty to do it cheerfully.[65]

After considerable personal experience in the matter, I can now most heartily endorse the sentiments of the poet when he says that "Lugging knapsack, box and gun is harder work than farming."

Last Monday I paid a visit to the famous Pilot Knob of Missouri and enjoyed the satisfaction of standing on the very highest rock and looking over the surrounding country. Three small towns, Arcadia, Ironton & Pilot Knob, lay around the base of the mountain, spread out below like a map.

I procured some specimens of ion ore from the top of the "Knob" which I would like to send home if I had an opportunity. Pilot Knob is only six miles from here so I had a nice little walk in the bargain.

Tell Pa that I have no desire whatever to "go on the gunboats."

You may also tell Mit that his reasons for not catching prairie chickens are very satisfactory.

Hoping that you will continue to favor us with the productions of your pen, since you have now begun, I subscribe myself

Your Affectionate Brother, Geo A Remley

P.S. Send me a copy of the "Nemora Recreator" and I shall be under great obligations to its editress. GAR

Saturday, March 14, 1863 — Camp near St. Genevieve, [Missouri]
Dear Howard,
Your favor of the 8th inst. was last night received. I need not say that we were very glad to receive your "benefit," and hope you will "benefit" us often, the oftener the better. Our last, home was also dated the 8th. You have no doubt rec'd it before this time.

We started next morning (the 9th), as we expected, on the march to this place. The road was excellent, a delapidated plank road, gradually being transformed into a turnpike. We performed the march of about 42 miles in three days, reaching camp the last day (the 11th) 20 min. before 1 o'clock, having marched about 17 miles. Nothing of importance occurred on the trip except that there was a good deal of straggling and marauding or robbing in the neighborhood of camp. Soldiers, and those too, who at home would scorn the name "thief," would go to the houses of the citizens at night, and demand whatever "took their fancy," or tempted their appetites, insulting the owners not caring whether they were Union or Secesh. Sometimes, to prevent such things, a guard would be posted and this is what certain newspapers in the north grumble so about "guarding rebel property." The country through which we passed is an old-settled country, with well improved farms, old apple and peach orchards, fields of fine looking fall wheat, large barns, etc. and a pretty good sprinkling of rather white looking darkies. George and I carried our knapsacks, blankets, overcoats, and all. We stood the march "first rate." I didn't get sore and stiff, as I did on the trip from Rolla to West Plains, felt a great deal better. So much for our trip.

We are now encamped about half way between the town and the steamboat landing, half or three fourths of a mile from each, on a commanding hill (overlooking the river) covered with a beautiful grove. The owner (said to be a secesh) prizes the grove very highly, having, as they say, once had a man fined $50.00 for cutting a tree. If this is so, he now "comes to grief," as many a tall tree now lies low, used for the ignoble purpose of cooking! The 23d Iowa (of our brigade) left yesterday for New Madrid [Missouri]. How long we shall stay here, is uncertain. Col. Stone is of the opinion, however, that we shall be paid before leaving. Let it come. Five transports laden with troops passed down the river yesterday. Soldiers seem to [be] abundant every where.

The weather is splendid, spring like, in fact quite warm. I am now writing in our tent, with my blowse off, and sweating at that. Blue birds, larks, etc. are about and have been for a month. A couple of radishes, three or four inches in diameter, have just come into our tent. People are making gardens, selling "greens," etc.

As we intimated in our last letter, we have packed up our overcoats, and some other things (a list of which will be enclosed) in a box and expect to start them home today. Lewis Yenter, Lewis Logan & Wm. D. Hopwood, also have articles in our box. The box is directed to Pa, care of J. P. Wood and will be forwarded by the U. S. Postal Express Co. Of course the others will pay their proportion of the express charges. By the way what was our share of the expense of sending those other boxes?

I spoke in our last about furloughs. Two of our company (John Lenderman & Michael Ruppert) started home last Monday on furloughs of 15 or 20 days, and I presume some went from all the companies. When the next will go, I can't say. It will probably take over a year to give all in the company furloughs. Of course it is somewhat uncertain when our turn will come, as all the married men must have a chance first.

"Father" Emonds (Catholic priest) of Iowa City is here. He had service in the Catholic Church this morning to which all Catholics in our Regiment had permission to [attend]. Dr. White has just got back from a visit to Iowa City.

I am glad to learn that the barn is so near completion, that it was no failure this time. About what did it cost?[66]

I would like to have heard Allie & Co's Recreator read. From the specimens of the contents given, I would infer that Milton has been guilty of sparking; also that the Recreator was written impromptu.[67]

My journal was taken to Iowa City by Wm. C. Luce a painter. He spent two or three weeks in Illinois after leaving Rolla but has arrived at Iowa City before this.

Yenter, Logan, Klenk & co. are pretty well, as is the company & regiment generally. Well I believe I have nothing more of interest to write and unless

Geo. wishes to say something I will close. Don't let Ma to whom my last letter was addressed, and Pa, forget that letters are expected from them. Give my love to all.

Your brother, L. Remley

P.S. When our clothes come, you can see a specimen of my tailoring, the pockets of my overcoat. Ma will [you] please take care of those specimens of Iron ore. I have in my trunk some lead ore. Who knows but that this may be the foundation of a mineralogical cabinet? L.R.

[George continues:]
Dear Ma,
At dress parade this evening we received positive assurance that our entire Division is ordered to join the forces under Gen U. S. Grant, now before Vicksburg and that, as soon as the requisite number of transports arrive, we will start for that great center of attraction. We are to have with us three days (cooked) rations which will be issued tomorrow. All of our wagons and teams will be left here, except the ambulances and hospital wagons. It is probable that before this reaches you, we will be on our way to the land of "Dixie."

Well the time, though long delayed, has at last come when we shall be in the midst of scenes of danger and perhaps bloody strife. Though I shall be called upon to stand face to face with death, I fear it not, for I know that <u>he</u> in whom I have trusted is just as able to protect me when on the field of battle as when at home surrounded by friends.

I feel a kind of an inward assurance that, whatever we have to pass through, I shall come out all right.

I took the box containing our clothes to the steamboat landing this afternoon, and placed it into the hands of an agent, who will ship it to St. Louis and from there it will go through by express.

I sent with some of my clothes specimens of iron ore from Pilot Knob & Iron Mountain and also some specimens of the kind of bread we soldiers mostly live on.

We are having "splendid" weather now. I have been sitting on the ground in the open air while writing this.

We will try to keep you fully posted in regard to our whereabouts, health, etc. and hope that you will let us hear from home as often as possible.

My love to all & tell Clara, Sidney & Fred that I will write them another letter before long.

Your Affectionate Son, Geo A Remley

Thursday, March 19, 1863 — Camp near St. Genevieve, Missouri
Dear Howard,
Your last letter dated March 8th was received on the 13th and, though it was immediately answered, nevertheless, as it has been nearly a week since that time, I have concluded to write again.[68] Though this town <u>is</u> on the river, yet the mail reaches us only twice a week. And when the mail <u>does</u>

come, one would naturally suppose, that, on account of coming so seldom, there would be more of it; but such is not the case for the company does not get as many letters at a time now as we did when the mail came very day. Yesterday evening only three letters and a few papers came for the whole regiment! I don't know where they all go to, but am sure that they do not show themselves very often. I hope, in writing, you will make all due allowance for miscarriage.

When we wrote last, we had just received orders to join Grant's forces as soon as the necessary transports should arrive; and, though nearly a month has passed away since then, we are still here. Every day some of our troops have been starting down the river, but as the largest and best boats are in the service of the Government further down the river, the embarkation has been necessarily slow. Nearly all the regiments, except those of our brigade, have already left and I have no doubt but that our turn will come in a day or two.

That Vicksburg will be our immediate destination seems to be a matter of considerable doubt. That we must "join Grant's forces" does not necessarily imply that we must go to Vicksburg, for we may be at Memphis [Tennessee] or Helena [Arkansas] and still be under the command of Gen. Grant. The chaplain thinks we will [go] to Memphis. There is a tract of country, lying between the troops under Grant and those under Rosecrans, not at present occupied by any part of the Union army. This place being subject to frequent guerilla raids, it may be the intention to transfer the tramping ground of this army to that region.

There is an infinate variety of rumors in circulation through the camp in regard to going up North to fight the "tories," Indians, etc., etc., but of course I place no confidence in any such reports. There has been no call for more men yet that I have heard of, Congress having merely authorized the President to draft 600,000 of the militia should he consider it necessary, but should a draft be made and resistance offered as would probably be the case in certain parts of the North, I think there are certainly enough loyal men left to put down any such disturbance. But if circumstances render it necessary, I would just as soon shoot a northern traitor, who openly avows his sympathy with the rebellion and does all in his power to discourage union men and bring disgrace upon the union cause, as a southern rebel, who has the courage to take up arms and does nothing more than carry out in practice the infamous sentiments of their northern brethren.

I think the season here is about a month in advance of your latitude. The grass is beginning to look green and certain kinds of trees are putting forth leaves. I saw, the other day, some peach blossoms just beginning to burst from the bier.

While at Iron Mountain the weather was cloudy and rainy all the time, but since we have been here we have had a spell of uninterrupted, pleasant, springlike weather. The air is warm, the sky soft and hazy and all things combined have a great tendency to bring on an attack of the disease commonly known as "spring fever." I have not been troubled with it yet and hope that I may not be.

Our camping ground here is the best one we have yet had. It is a high bluff covered with a beautiful grove of trees. A short distance to the right is the ancient town of St. Genevieve, a little farther to the left is the steamboat landing known as "Little Rock"; while in front is the broad Mississippi, dotted with islands, whose waters are daily plowed by the numerous government steamers that are constantly passing, loaded with troops, provisions and all kinds of army supplies. This would be a splendid place for a residence.

The operation of the law, passed by Congress, giving soldiers the privilege of obtaining furloughs, has been suspended, for the present at least, by the order of some general who has command of this Division. I hope this will not continue long.

In the last "Republican" I noticed a list of deserters from this regiment from the time of its organization to the 1st of this month. There were about twenty I believe, four of whom were from Company "F." Since the 1st of March, four more have deserted from our company and 16 from other companies of the regiment making about forty in all.[69]

Two of these were caught in St. Louis and returned to the authorities here last Sunday. Since that time they have had the pleasure of carrying, what in camp parlance, is called "wooden knapsacks," that is a piece of wood, weighing about 50 pounds. This is tied on their backs with small cords and has to be worn all the time.[70]

The river has fallen about two & a half feet since we have been here and is still falling.

St. Genevieve is an old town, older than St. Louis, I believe. It was first settled by the French and even yet a large proportion of the inhabitants is French with a slight mixture of Spaniards and Negroes. The streets & pavements are very narrow.

The health of the regiment is very good. The 22nd has been greatly favored in this respect.

All "our neighbor boys" are well, (Lewis Yenter of course included). Lewis Gohen has lost the use of his voice so that he is unable to speak above a whisper. He is in other respects as well as ever.

I believe Lycurgus wants to write some. I will therefore leave the rest of this page for him to fill.

My love to all

Your Aff brother, Geo A Remley

[Lycurgus continues:] **March 20th 1863**
George has told all the news, but I have one thing [to] mention. Lewis Yenter's friends (his mother I suppose) told him in a letter that I had written home that it took him half an hour to wash the federal soil off his face. I recollect that I did write something of the kind from Eminence and it is a literal fact, but still it isn't flattering to his friends to hear about it, I would therefore ask that some caution be used with respect to the persons before

August 21, 1862–March 20, 1863

whom such things in our letters are mentioned. I never dreamed that that remark would come back to me.[71]

The mail agent reports 18 bags of <u>letters</u> on the road to this Brigade (or Division, I don't know which) and that they will be here today.

Since George wrote the above there are serious symptoms of our starting at last. The Quarter Master's stores are being packed and the boats to take us away are momentarily expected. We will be on the boat about three days.

A funeral procession from the 21st Iowa passed just a little while ago. This is, I believe, the second death in that Reg. since we arrived here.

This Division consists of two Brigades and is commanded by our Col. Stone. Our Brigade is commanded by Col. [Samuel] Merrill of the 21st.[72]

Write soon and frequently

Your Brother, L. Remley

Friday, March 20, 1863 — St. Genevieve, Missouri
Dear Sid & Fred,
Knowing how much it will please you and how it will make your eyes sparkle to receive a letter, I thought I would write you a little one this morning. This is a beautiful Spring morning. The Sun is just above the horizon and the birds are singing sweetly in the grove around me. Spring comes sooner here than it does in Iowa. People around here are making their gardens and fruit trees are beginning to bloom, while you are having cold weather yet.

Ma says that when she writes you trouble her by asking her to write some for you; now, boys, you must not trouble Ma <u>too</u> much; but whenever you can I want you to get Ma or Allie to write for you; for I like very much to get little letters from you. I hope you both will learn to read and write as fast as you can so that you need not depend on others to do such things for you. I know you would not like to be, when you grow up, like some people down here who can neither read nor write. I will tell you a little story about one of them. Some of our men were out a scouting expedition not far from Houston in this State, and happening to stop at a house they very naturally entered into a conversation with the <u>lady</u> of the house, the man, as is very generally the case, not being at home, and among other things asked if she had ever heard of Lincoln. "I don't know," said she. "I know most every body around here, but the other day a stranger passed by here. I expect that was him." She was then asked if she got any mail. "Mail! I don't know what that is" said the woman. "Do you get any letters?" was asked by way of explanation. "Well, yes," said she "we did get one from Indiana about eight years ago, but we don't get any now." There are a great many such people here and that is one reason that they are secessionists, they do not know any better.

Some of the soldiers are very much given to stealing. Sometimes when they are placed as guards over goods they will break open boxes, etc. and take apples, oysters or any thing they may happen to fancy. This propensity is so great that they often take things that can be of no use to them whatever. I met a soldier the other day with a pair of skates in his hand and heard him saying to his companion "I couldn't find any thing else to steal so I thought I would take these.["]

One evening at dress parade an old woman was seen putting onion set[s] in the ground and that night they all mysteriously disappeared and some of the boys were seen eating small onions.

I hope <u>you</u> will never have to be a soldier.

I have been vaccinated and my arm is just beginning to get sore.

I weigh 142 pounds now, more than Lycurgus.

Give my love to Allie & Clara.

Your Brother, Geo A Remley

Chapter Two

"He Died in Hope of a Blissful Immortality"

— THE BATTLE FOR VICKSBURG —

Saturday, March 28, 1863 — On board steamer "Fred Lorenz," Memphis, Tenn.
Dear Pa,
We left St. Genevieve about noon day before yesterday, the 26th, and have got this far on our way into "Dixie."[1] Our destination is said to be Yazoo City [Mississippi]. We are stopping here to take on coal and will go on down the river as soon as that is done.

We go in company with three or four other boats loaded with Iowa & Illinois troops. Only three companies of the 22nd are on this boat, the rest having started down the river several days before we did.

Saw our paymaster Penn Clark this morning. He will accompany us on our way southward, I believe.

After this, I think it will be better to direct your letters to Cairo [Illinois]. Will write again whenever I have a chance to send the letter. We are both well.

My love to all the family

Your Son, George A Remley

P. S. There are two "decks of cards" in operation on the same table that I am writing on, one on each side. They shake the table and jostle me so that I can hardly write.   GAR

Wednesday, April 1, 1863 — Milliken's Bend, Louisiana
Dear Pa,
Howard's letter of March 19th was duly received before we left St. Genevieve. We have had no mail since.

Since we last wrote (at St. Genevieve), we have made a considerable trip, and are now pretty far down in Dixie, within 8 or 10 miles of Vicksburg (in a direct line). But to commence "al ir itis."

Friday, March 20th the bugle sounded <u>"strike tents,"</u> and in about half an hour, the tents were all down, and every thing packed ready to move. But no orders came to "fall in," and after waiting till near night we <u>pitched</u> our tents again and conclude[d] to stay awhile longer. Next day, however, about 5 o'clock PM a steamboat having at last arrived, seven companies — all but Cos A, F & D — were again ordered to strike tents. They embarked some time during the night, leaving us in daily expectation of being ordered to <u>follow suit.</u> But no orders came, and there we lingered, in suspense, day after day, until Thursday, March 26th when our three companies, and three Cos. of the 21st Iowa, embarked bona fide on the steamer Fred Lorenz, an old stern-wheeler. We then bid adieu to St. Genevieve, recommended by the Provost Marshal to steal Vicksburg, some of our boys having distinguished themselves in that line at St. Genevieve.

We reached Cape Girardeau, about dark, a much larger place than I had supposed, and stopping only an hour or so, continued our journey down the river passing Cairo in the night. At daylight we found ourselves run ashore, between Cairo & Columbus, an accident caused by the drunkenness of the pilot. Becoming extricated at length, we soon were at Columbus, the once famed rebel strong hold. The battle ground of Belmont is nearly opposite.[2] The bluffs at Columbus are quite high and are crowned by some pretty extensive fortifications. We saw several pieces of Artillery and large quantities of shot & shell, which had been buried by the rebels in a gulch and were but lately unearthed. Continuing our course we passed the famous Island No. Ten, which with its peach orchard in bloom, corresponded very nearly with the published descriptions of it, at the time of its capture.[3] We "lay to," this night (the 27th) at Fort Wright, formerly Fort Pillow, but as our arrival & departure were both in the dark, I saw nothing of it. Next day, almost noon, we reached Memphis. As we had to take in coal, etc. we had time to pay the City a short visit. We saw some beautiful residences, adorned with cedars, magnolias, flowers, etc. I saw here some old fashioned poplar trees, the first I have seen in the West. They were nearly in full leaf. There are a great many soldiers, 40,000 I was told, quarter[ed] at Memphis.

Having taken in coal, etc. we started off again about noon next day, Sunday 29th, and reached Helena [Arkansas], without any incidents worth[y] of note, about dark. George went out to see some of his friends (Bivens, DeWitt, Holmes, etc. in the 24th Iowa) and most unexpectedly met with Cousin E. F. Remley of Marion [Iowa].[4] He is in Co. G, 24th Iowa. Geo. stayed all night with him, and not knowing that 28th Iowa was there also, returned to the boat without seeing Cousin John Remley.[5] I was very desirous to go out next morning to see John, and my other acquaintances in the 28th, but finding some difficulty in getting a pass, and not knowing when the boat would start, I was obliged to forego the pleasure. Having exchanged the Steamer "Fred Lorenze" for the larger "John H. Groesbeck," we moved off again about noon, Monday (30th); and, traveling all afternoon & night, we reached Milliken's Bend [Louisiana] about 10 o'clock AM.

The Mississippi is very high at present, twenty or thirty feet higher than it was last Fall, nearly filling its channels, and in some places overflowing the low bottom land. It looked almost like an inland sea. The shores, and the islands, are covered with a dense growth of soft wooded trees, cotton woods, sycamores, willows, etc. which are now becoming green. We could notice very plainly that the further South we traveled, the greener the trees became. As we approached Mississippi and Louisiana, plantations with their villages of negro quarters, steam cotton ginning establishments, levees, etc. became more common. Although, when the river is not rampant, this must be a fine country, at present, partially submerged, it seems rather too watery, to suit my notions.

March 28, 1863–June 29, 1863

At first glance, one would perhaps think that this trip down the river was, to us, only a pleasure excursion, but such was by no means the case. In the first place the weather was uncommonly cold, windy and rainy, and you know our overcoats had gone <u>North</u> in search of cold weather. Next the <u>sleeping arrangements</u> were not particularly convenient & comfortable. Once, we slept in the Caboose on the upper deck, a rather airy place. Next, in the cabin, where the floor was literally carpeted with supine soldiers and the air very confined. Having been nearly smothered in this place, we concluded to try it next on the guards, where, with one blanket over us, we came nigh freezing. The last night on board was spent in the <u>hold.</u> The <u>cooking</u> arrangements too were rather imperfect. Stumbling on piles of boxes, baggage, coal, wood, etc. in the dark lower deck, to the stern of the boat, we come to a small space occupied by a stove, and a crowd of struggling soldiers with their coffee kettles, frying pans, etc. trying to prepare their meals. We could rarely cook anything but coffee, in which, after our knick-knacks were gone, we could soften our hard bread (of which, I hope you have before this, received a specimen). Cabin fare on a steamboat is pretty good, but soldiers' fare, wretched. So much for our trip.

A few words concerning our present situation. Milliken's Landing was once a little village, but is now mostly in ashes. Our camp is about half a mile from the river, on the plantation of a Mr. Morancie. Some of us visited the grounds of his fine mansion, yesterday, and learned from one of his ex-slaves, a shrewd negro man, some particulars of his masters estates, etc. This plantation consists of 1000 acres of land under cultivation, and untold acres of uncleared land. He owns about 160 <u>hands</u> and other negroes in proportion in all, perhaps four or five hundred. His average cotton crop is about 1000 bales, which at present prices could be worth nearly a quarter of a million dollars. The old man left his home here, only about a week ago, the federals coming too near. Some dozen or so guerillas having fired upon one of our boats, from this neighborhood, sundry cannon balls, hurled rather carefully about the house, admonished them of the consequences. One chimney was knocked off, and several holes put through the house. Besides this plantation, the old man, or rather his two sons, own two other plantations, back eight or ten miles in the country, to one of which he has retired. I haven't time to describe the beautiful grounds around his fine house with their luxuriant hedges of Cherokee Rose, etc., their Cedars, Arbor Vitae trees, branching Oaks, Box Elders, Magnolias "Spanish Dagger" plants, Roses, etc., etc.

Well, they say we are in the 2d Brigade of the 14th Division of the 13th Army Corps. Our Brigade Commander is said to be Colonel of one of the Wisconsin Regiments, whose name is [Charles Lofer] Harris. Our Divis. Comd is General [Eugene A.] Carr, while General [John A.] McClernand commands our Army Corps; and Gen. [Ulysses S.] Grant the whole "caboodle." We are encamped, along with the troops that were with us at West Plains, [Missouri] in a large very flat corn field, which furnished work to our fatigue parties, clearing off the corn stalks and digging ditches for drainage in case of a rain. Camps are stretched nearly all the way between here and Vicksburg.

How many troops are here, it is impossible to say but there are "upwards of several." I believe the superabundance of water prevents operations against Vicksburg (shouldn't it be written Vix-burg?) by land forces. When we will be needed to take some important battery I can't say, but we will doubtless be present at the Capture of this modern Troy.

Well I believe this is a summary of our experience since we last wrote. We would like very much to hear from home and learn all about Pa's school in Marengo, my old stamping ground.[6] What you get for your cord wood (& ties) and where it was chopped. How the timothy looks, etc. If I understood your account of the corn & sorghum ground, there will be only 5 or 6 acres of both, West of the orchard & South of the road to the spring. Is this correct? Write often & give all the news. If here, you might get a thousand bushes of cotton seed. We are all well at present, but it is very, very, sickly about here. My love to all, Ma, the boys & girls.

Your Affectionate Son, Lycurgus

Saturday, April 11, 1863 — Camp at Milliken's Bend, Louisiana
Dear Pa,
Our last letter from home dated Mar. 19th was received at St. Genevieve, the day we left, March 26th. But one mail has reached our Regiment since that time, which unfortunately contained no letters for us. Next day after we arrived at this place (April 1st), I wrote a long letter home, describing our trip and present location which I hope you have, before this, received; at least, I will act upon that supposition.

Since we have been here, we have been kept pretty busy drilling — company, battalion, and brigade, "passing under review," standing picket guard, etc.[7] Geo. is out "on picket" now. To go a little more into detail: Last Sunday, our whole company was out on picket in a beautiful grove, almost in full leaf. The ground was carpeted with green grass, and the large trees (some of them being about six feet in diameter) were draped with a mossy, gray, pendent parasite, called, I believe, Spanish Moss. When dried, it looks almost like horse hair, and is used as stuffing for cushions, etc. It makes a <u>splendid bed,</u> and it is this upon which we now sleep. This, by way of digression. Upon the whole this picket duty was not very onerous, and bat[t]ing the mosquitoes at night, seemed more like a pick-nick, than any thing else. At the <u>"grand review"</u> our Regiment was highly complimented by the staff officers, Gen. McClernand, etc. Our marching was said to be equal to that of the <u>regulars</u> of whom there were two companies present. There were seven or eight regiments and a battery or two of Artillery reviewed at once, making with the aid of a fine brass band, a pageant as imposing, at least, as that spoken of so much by the Iowa City Republican, the 6th Iowa Cavalry. As to the drilling, the Colonel insisted very emphatically upon the commissioned officers' coming out with their companies to drill and accordingly a much greater <u>interest</u> is now taken in the drill, and proportionate improvement made. Capt. Cree had not drilled us since leaving Camp Pope, and but once, that is, as a company. (Of course he had to come out on battalion drill.)

The weather since we have been here has [been] very fine, almost as warm as May or June, in Iowa. The health of the regiment has been, so far pretty good. Two deaths, however, have occurred in the Reg. since our arrival.[8] Typhoid Fever is the prevailing disease. So much for the past, now a little of the future.

We are now making preparations for another move, we don't know whither, cooking five days' rations, etc., expect to leave tomorrow morning. Carrying knapsacks in this warm weather will be no fun.

As to matters about Vicksburg, I have no doubt you at home who see the papers know a great deal more about what is going on here, than we do. We all feel confident, however, that the attack on Vicksburg will be made in a few days exactly when, we can't say and we are pretty confident, too, that Vicksburg will fall this time.

I believe I have no more news of importance to write. Lewis Yenter, with the exception of a cough, Lewis Logan and all the "neighbor boys" are well. I haven't had better health for a long time. Our Chaplain seems to be a little more active now, preaching every Sunday, and holding prayer meetings twice a week, when practicable.

I would like to step in some fine morning to see you all, but it may be some time before I can enjoy that privilege. I hope you are "getting along" as well us usual. What about that Marengo School, etc.? We are very anxious to hear from home again, but the mails to the army, are very irregular. Don't be saving them, of paper & ink. Rutter rec'd a letter, in which it was said that you had baptized twenty persons at Johnson's School House, is that so? If so, who were some of them?[9]

Please send us some postage stamps, as we find it impossible to procure any away down here, this land of cane brakes, alligators, mosquitoes, etc.

Give my love to all the family,

Your Affectionate Son, Lycurgus

P.S. George has some roses pressed to send home, but as he is out on picket I will enclose them. They are for Allie and Clara, I suppose.

Write to us, some of you, at least once a week. LR

P.P.S. This flowerless, black looking specimen of vegetation is a cutting from a mistletoe, a parasite very common down here. It is a wood (?) plant. Palms, from which the palm leaf fans are obtained, grow down here. Peaches are now as big as hickory nuts. L.R.

[Note at top of first page of letter:] I send this by Mr. McCartel a discharged soldier who will put it in some post office on the other side of Memphis, perhaps in Iowa City if not searched by the Authorities. GAR

Saturday, April 18, 1863 — Camp near New Carthage, Louisiana
Dear Pa,
Though we have not heard from home for nearly a month, the date of your last being March 19th, yet in order that you may have the satisfaction of

hearing from us at least once a week I have concluded to write to you this morning. Lycurgus wrote last Saturday just a week ago today. I did not see the letter, but I suppose he told you everything up the date of his letter. I will now endeavor to let you know what we have been doing since then.

The next [day] being Sunday, the day generally set apart in the army for such purposes, we left Millikens Bend with five days rations in our haversacks for parts unknown. Our route lay in a SW direction and by two o'clock in the afternoon found ourselves at Richmond, about 12 miles from our starting place. Richmond is a small town, in the county seat of Madison Parish and is situated on a bayou nearly west of Vicksburg. It was held by the rebels until about two weeks ago, our forces passing that way gave them some pretty strong hints in the shape of a few shot and shells that they had better retire. It is hardly necessary to add that they took the hint. We remained in camp at Richmond until last Thursday when we came on to our present camp about 15 miles distant. While camped at Richmond, the weather was not very propitious for "soldiering." We had some very hard rains and as the ground is nearly perfectly level the water had no chance to run off. One night many of us were driven out of our tents by the water and compelled to seek shelter elsewhere. While here we exchanged

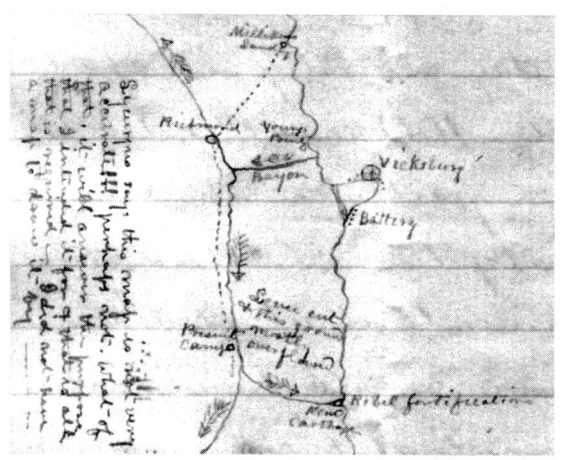

our "Sibley tents" for a kind of tent called the "Bell tent," from its shape, made to accommodate ten men. As the mud, according to our views, was not suitable for a bed, boards from certain fences, stalls, etc. in the vicinity were "confiscated" and soon converted into floors for our new tents.

The ladies of Richmond are rampant secessionists and express a perfect hatred to the "Yankees" and without the slightest hesitation openly avow and defend their sentiments.

The annexed rude map [see map] will give you some idea of our present situation. New Carthage is on the Mississippi at the mouth of a bayou. On an island near this place about 2000 rebels had entrenched themselves and had some heavy artillery to defend their position. We are now within four miles of them and if they do not "skedaddle" pretty soon it is very likely that the 22nd will have an opportunity of testing their fighting qualities before a great while. Night before last six or seven gun boats and two transports ran the blockade at Vicksburg and are prepared to operate against the rebels at Carthage.[10] The only loss on our side while passing the batteries was the sinking, or burning, of a transport.[11] The enemy did not come off quite so easily, however, for they had a regular Yankee trick played upon them. The gun boat "Benton," I believe, pretending to be disabled, stopped working the engines, let the steam off through the escape pipes and floated along down towards the shore. The rebels supposing that they were about to secure a valuable prize crowded upon the levee, many <u>patriotic</u> ladies among them, anxious to have the honor of first boarding a "Yankee gunboat" when suddenly the "Benton" righting itself, poured a full broadside into the crowd killing and wounding a great many. We heard the firing very distinctly here. Not a day passes without more or less cannonading sometimes in the direction of Vicksburg and sometimes at Carthage. I can hear it now while I am writing.

It is thought by some that the object in coming around Vicksburg with a large force, as we have done, is to drive the enemy from Carthage and then proceed down the river and assist in the capture of Port Hudson. It would be perfect folly and an unwarrantable sacrifice of human life to attempt the capture of Vicksburg by storming its almost impregnable fortification, but by cutting off their communications on all sides as we are now doing and destroying the Jackson railroad as we have already partly done, the rebels will be compelled to surrender, evacuate and fight their way out, or come out from behind their entrenchments and give us a fair fight.

The army of the Union seems to be steadily gaining ground in this part of the country. The men are in good spirits and the prospect of making some decided advancements is growing brighter every day. I do not know what is being done in Tennessee or on the Potomac, for we very rarely get any news here, but I presume that "all is quiet, etc."

Our expedition through this part of the country seems to have been entirely unexpected by the rebels, for they very recently had possession of all their region and by simply cutting the levee along the bayou they could have completely flooded the whole country and thus stopped our progress. A great many of the slaves have been taken further South & West. Yet as we pass the plantations negroes of all ages, sizes and complexion come out and gaze upon us in child like wonder. One old woman exclaimed as we passed "Lor a' marcy! Where dey go so many men." A philosophic old man when he saw how many there were of us said: "Guess de Norf ain't whipped out yet." At one place the negroes said that their master promised them "Yankee meat to eat" whenever we should come along and I suppose the only thing that hindered him from fulfilling his promise was that very urgent business demanded his attention elsewhere just a few days before we arrived!

When "massa runs away," the negroes do not pretend to put in crops or do any kind of work. The cotton crop is entirely neglected and the planters seemed to have been giving corn their undivided attention, but now even that is interrupted in this section of the country. There was a great deal of cotton raised here last year, we are camped in a cotton field now, and all of it that the rebels did not have time to burn when they left is confiscated by the government. It would grieve the hearts of the good <u>housewives</u> of Iowa could they but see how little care is taken of that precious article and how much of it is continually being wasted.

There is something peculiar about the bayous that intersect this state in almost every direction. The water does not seem to be at all particular which way it runs. Some times the bayous were separate and the two parts run in directly opposite ways, as is the case with the one we are now camped on.

They are very useful, however, as a way for transporting cannon and ammunition which is done in flat boats made for the purpose. They are deep enough for <u>steamboat</u> but so narrow that they cannot turn in them. There is one in sight now that came up from Carthage.

The weather is very warm, hot, but I suppose it will be a great deal more so two months from now and we might as well make up our minds to get used to it.

Lycurgus & I have very good health. The health of the company was never better than now. There are only three on the sick list; one of these, however, is Lewis Yenter and as he does not feel like writing today he requested me to let you know how he is, etc., which I did in a faithful manner.

When he had the measles at Rolla last October and was convalescent he "caught cold" and ever since then has had a slight cough which instead of getting better gradually grew worse. He has lately "caught more cold" and as a matter of course his lungs are somewhat affected and are sore and feels feverish. There is nothing serious the matter with him now, but he must take care of himself or there will be. He is in the same tent with us, sleeps with Lewis Logan. I forgot to say that he cannot speak above a whisper. This is the third case of the kind that we have in our company. Lewis Gohen, Peter Subbury (of the <u>3 mile</u> house Marengo road) & Lewis Yenter.

Two of our men who went home on furloughs returned yesterday, E. H. Bovie & J. Rolston. The 24th & 28th Iowa Regiments have come down the river and are now camped three or four miles north of us. Some of the "boys" went up there today. I would have gone too if I had not been writing. Cousin John Remley is well.

I have been "in swimming" several times since we have been here. I am told that alligators will put a veto on that pleasure when the water becomes warmer but we will see about that when the time comes.

Tell Ma that I can drink coffee now as well as anybody without sugar, too, sometimes. Often a cup of coffee & a cracker constitute a whole meal, but even that seems good.

I wish one could get some letters for it seems <u>so</u> long since we heard from home. Tell us how you are getting along on the farm, about the weather, our overcoats, <u>Express charges,</u> and whether you made the "dicker" with the Marengo Directors or not and also about the Nemora Sunday School. Give my love to Ma, Allie, Clara.

Your Affectionate Son, George

Write often for we don't get all you write.

P.S. I am more healthy than at any time last winter. I weigh near 150 lbs. now, more than for a long time. We are all in better spirits and more hopeful by far — although in the face of the enemy — than we were at Rolla, out of danger lying at ease.

P.P.S. If you have never seen a confederate note the inclosed one may serve as a curiosity. G.A Remley

Also a Reb postage stamp which I found at Richmond

P.P.S. continued April 20th

I have just now heard that no mail will be allowed to leave camp for some time, after a Battle that is to come off one of these days. Troops are being transported over the river as fast as possible and our time will come soon.

Wednesday, April 22, 1863 — Camp near New Carthage, Louisiana
Dear Pa,

Yesterday was payday. I received $96.90 and George $52. George having some on hand (having been paid at Rolla last Feb.) we are enabled to send home $160.00, of which $87 belongs to me, and $73 belongs to George.

In the same package is Lewis Yenter's money, $55 and Wm. D. Hopwood's $65.

The money of the Regiment will be carried to Iowa City by the Chaplain Rev. R. G. Allender and left with some reliable person there. I think that of our Co. will be left with John W. Porter or C. F. Lovelace our ex-Q.M.

George wrote to you last Saturday or Sunday (18th or 19th) and gave the letter to be carried by Mike McCordel who is discharged and going home. He starts this morning. Your last letter dated March 29 was rec'd last Monday. We will write again the first opportunity.

We have been at this camp (within three or four miles of Carthage, which is on the Mississippi away below Vicksburg) ever since last Thursday. We are to move again this morning towards Carthage, and perhaps across the [Mississippi] River.

Yesterday ten or twelve thousand troops passed us going down the same direction.

I have one request to make. As I am held responsible in Chicago for that debt, I would like to see it discharged. It is $27.25 with ten per cent interest since April 21st 1862.

If it would not interfere with your plans, I would like to have all my money invested so that it would yield something. Suppose you were to buy that Power's land for me. Let me know what you think of it.

We are well as usual. Lewis Yenter is not very well. Geo. described his case more at length in his letter before referred to.

Your Aff Son, Lycurgus Remley

Cousin J. Remley is not very well. I heard from him yesterday. Saw Wm. McKee of Marengo & Joe Kurtz yesterday.

Tuesday, April 28, 1863 — Marengo, Iowa
Dear Lycurgus,

I am teaching school here, engaged for seven months. Last Friday I went home and saw your letter. I was truly glad to hear from you. I hope that God will preserve you and restore you again to us, unscathed by the dangers & untouched by the corruptions of war.

Tell us about those things which concern you individually, for while we feel a very deep interest in the progress of the war and the success of our cause, we still have a deeper interest in you. Our country is very dear to us, but our children are dearer still. For my part I think almost every hour about you. Indeed my solicitude on your behalf is vastly increased since you have gone so much nearer that vortex which has swallowed up so many promising young men of the country.

I commenced school here on the 13th inst. so you see this is my third week. I do not like the school-house & fixtures. I think they are abominable. In fact if I had known how disagreeable the arrangements would be I would have declined to engage. I suppose things are about as they were when you taught. As to the scholars, they are like boys & girls every where, much more inclined to play than to study. However I am getting some of them pretty well "broken in" & think I shall after while have a good school.

Alice has grown considerably since you left & is much improved. She is through her Arithmetic & is studying Algebra. I found the boys at home doing remarkably well. Howard and Milton are everything I could wish and are doing their best.

It is not true that I baptized twenty persons down on clear creek or anywhere else, but I did baptize three: Miss E. Dennison, Miss M. Summerhays & John Smith. Rolla Johnson & Mrs. Johnson & several others are expected soon. A deep religious feeling pervades the whole community down there & indeed extends up into our neighborhood, & I feel confident that if proper means were used a general revival would ensue.

I want one or both of you to write to me at this place for I do not expect to be at home again for a month. I beg you to be as careful of your health as you can be. I am much more afraid of the climate than the Rebel guns. My desire is that you consider this as addressed to both of you & hope you will both receive a Father's blessing & live near to your Father in heaven.

Your Affectionate Father, James Remley

Dear Brothers,

I left home yesterday morning came up in the 10 oclock train. But I suppose Pa has told you all about it in his letter. I have only gone to school one day and a half but I think that I shall like it. The scholars talk a great deal about Lycurgus. Pa said that there was a little boy came to him most every day to ask about him and said he wished he could write to you.

We would be very glad if you write a letter to "us folks" way up here.

Your Affectionate Sister, Alice Remley

P.S. Pa wants me to say that the name of that little boy is Benjamin Cripe. He says he would like to get a letter from you. Allie

March 28, 1863–June 23, 1863

Wednesday, May 6, 1863 — Ten miles North of Port Gibson, Mississippi
Dear Pa,
The last intelligence we have had from home was a long letter written by Howard dated April 12th and received on the 27th. Lycurgus wrote home on the 26th ult. and since then it has been impossible to send letters away from camp, both on account of our situation and strict orders prohibiting it.[12] Beginning, then, where Lycurgus left off. We remained in camp at Perkins Plantation till the evening of the 27th when, leaving tents, cooking utensils, etc. behind, we got aboard the transports bound for Grand Gulf. Started about 10 o'clock the next day, the 28th, and after a few hours ride on the river were safely landed on the levee in sight of the rebel batteries at Grand Gulf [Mississippi]. At 8 o'clock the next day, 28th, our (iron clad) gunboats, seven in number commence[d] the attack on the batteries and, after dismounting or temporarily silencing, most of the enemy's guns withdrew. The transports had, in the meantime, been bringing troops down the river as fast as possible. Our loss on the guns boats, so far as I can learn was about 75 killed and wounded. A shell penetrated the plating of the "Benton," 3 1/2 inches thick, and bursting killed 7 men and wounded others. (It was a conical shell.) The "Tuscumbia" was slightly disabled and lost six men by a shell entering a port hole. The loss of the enemy in both men & <u>material</u> was much greater than ours, but I am not able to state it exactly.[13] That evening we marched along the levee about five miles further down the river and after dark the gun boats again engaged the attention of the enemy and during the action the transports, loaded with provisions, artillery, horses, etc., passed the batteries without any loss, but that of five horses killed by a single shell. Thus without any serious loss on our part, a large army and a fleet of transports & gunboats passed what [David G.] Far[r]agut calls the heaviest rebel batteries on the Mississippi. The enemy's guns were not all silence[d] but I have since learned from prisoners that if the gun boats had kept up the fire a short time longer, they would have been compelled to abandon them. It was a indeed a fortunate thing for us that this did not happen for we should then have attempted to drive the enemy from their fortifications by storm and had this been done, such is the character of the fortifications, our army would have been fearfully cut to pieces.

On the morning of the 30th we again embarked on the transports and under the protection of the gun boats went five or six miles farther down the river, landing on the Miss-side [near Bruinsburg]. About 15 miles North East of this place [Bruinsburg] is a town called "Port Gibson" where the rebels had begun to erect fortifications and had already collected a large force which they were increasing as fast as possible. Now Port Gibson is the key to Grand Gulf with which it <u>was</u> connected by railroad and the fame now about the place was to see who could hold the place. If we could take Port Gibson, G[rand] Gulf would fall without any more fighting.

But to proceed. After resting a short time at the landing we started for

"HE DIED IN HOPE OF A BLISSFUL IMMORTALITY"

Port Gibson marching slowly all afternoon and night until one o'clock when we met and drove in the enemy's pickets.[14] Here one man was severely wounded. This was but the introduction to what was about to follow. Past here commenced the "Battle of Port Gibson," or perhaps "Magnolia" from the name of a Church. [O]n the battle field, and in order that you may properly understand its description you must imagine a rough, hilly country partially covered with timber, having an undergrowth of almost impenetrable cane-brakes, the canes woven together with running briars and other vines, cane cut up with deep ravines and gullies. Such was the battle <u>field.</u> Our approach to this place was a long a narrow lane which made a sharp angle on the brow of a hill. The enemy had stationed their artillery so as to completely rake this part of the road.

After the pickets were driven in, the "1st Iowa Battery" was quickly thrown forward and the rebels then opened upon us, sending grape shot and shell hissing through the air like demons incarnate. Our own battery was soon brought into position and gave them back <u>fully</u> "as good as they sent." One of the first shells very boldly introduced himself to me by puffing his hot breath into my face. I didn't admire the manner very much & as he did not stop to apologize I concluded not to renew the acquaintance. Therefore, in obedience to the command of our officers, we all lay down on the ground and let the intruders pass over us. In a few minutes we were ordered forward to support the battery and as we neared the turn in the road, the shot & shell flew "thick and fast." While passing here I saw stretched upon the ground the body of the first one who fell. A passing shell had taken his breath. Notwithstanding the more serious scenes around me I could not help being amused at the sudden panic of the negroes who were with us. To say that they were frightened would not convey the proper idea, they were terrified. Some would cling to the ground not daring even to look up. Others would throw down whatever they were carrying and make for the rear about as fast as persons generally travel on foot. When we reached the turn in the road we kept straight forward passing into an old field and were soon in comparative safety by lying down under the brow of a hill. You must not forget that all this happened in the night, the moon was dimly shining, but she soon withdrew herself from such bloodshed.

The cannonading was kept up briskly till nearly daylight when most of the enemy's guns ceased responding for want of gunners I believe. "Our battery," the Iowa 1st, had in the meantime been reinforce[d] by another Battery. For about an hour before day light there was perfect silence and I got a <u>few</u> minutes sleep.

May 1st. Aurora came and with her returned the deep bayings of the "dogs of war" and mingling with them the shrill shrieks of those "flying demons" all together forming a kind of music that heard once will not soon be forgotten. While this artillery duel was going on our regiment and the 11th Wis.

March 28, 1863–June 23, 1863

were stationed behind the 1st Iowa battery to support it in case of the rebels charging on it. We were lying flat upon the ground with [paper torn—new sheet follows:]

Page 5th
In Camp 22 miles from Port Gibson
Six [miles] from Black River & 26 from Vicksburg
Continuation of yesterday's Letter —
This morning about 3 o'clock we left yesterday's camp and after a quick march of about 12 miles we reached our present stopping place. I would say camp, but the word does not express my meaning. The whole army is arranged in order of battle and we had the good fortune to get a shady fence corner for our place, where I am now writing.

I will now begin where I left off yesterday. I had first mentioned the storming of the enemy's battery and the capture of three guns, flag & prisoners. We, the 22nd, while performing our share of the work had to force our way through a dense cane-brake, and, while stumbling through briars and tangled canes, over logs and into gullies, the bullets of the enemy were whistling around our ears in a manner that persons of nervous sensibilities would not admire. It was here that Adj't D. J. Davis received a wound that was only prevented from being serious by his pistol slightly turning the course of the ball. After we emerged from the thicket and the enemy had been forced to retreat, cheer after cheer from the victorious army rent the air and this was the end of the morning's battle. Then followed scenes of a more serious and less exciting character. Long files of prisoners were marched off to a more secure place. The dead & wounded of both sides had been left lying upon the green sward where they fell and now they were being carried to a church near by which we used as a temporary hospital. After resting a short time, we started out to attack the enemy again, for they had only fallen back about two miles. The battle in the afternoon raged more fiercely and the ground was contested with more stubbornness than in the morning. The hardest and most dangerous work that we had to do during the whole day was supporting a battery in the afternoon. The rebels had their artillery on a hill a short distance in front and as they replied to our battery the shot & shell flew over us — screaming (or screeching) in their own peculiar manner, causing very queer sensations to say the least — and went crashing through the trees behind us or plowing the ground before us or striking the fence rails lying around [and] threw dirt and splinters in our faces rather unceremoniously. One large, unexploded shell came bounding along the ground within a few feet of me, severely wounding Lt. Francisco, Co. "H," and very narrowly missing several others. When a charge of grape shot poured into us, the cries and groans of the wounded could be distinctly heard above the din of battle. At one time during the afternoon the enemy attempted to flank us and charge <u>our</u> battery. The 22nd quickly came to the rescue and poured such deadly vollies into their ranks that they were compelled to abandon their attempt and retreat with a heavy loss. It has since been ascertained from prisoners and by the dead left on the field that we did more execution than any other troops engaged. It is needless to tell how many narrow escapes we had and how the balls flew around us like hail, yet in the midst of this storm of lead and iron we were kept from harm and came out unscathed. A Heavenly Father was kindly watching over us and shielding us from the deadly bullets. This thought comforted and cheered me more than any thing else could have done.

The fire of the enemy slackened towards night and finally ceased all but a battery of two guns which for an hour or so kept up a furious fire when they were dismounted by our cannon. This ended the firing, and as it proved, our part of the battle. We then returned to the place where we first attacked, got our haversack & knapsacks and went back to the last Battle ground where we slept soundly all night for we had fasted all day and our systems were terribly exhausted. Sleep never seemed sweeter to me than it did that night. The next morning, May 2nd, we started out to meet the enemy again as we supposed but none of them could we find. They had precipitately retreated leaving many of their dead on the scene of action. Gen. Osterhaus' (I believe that's the way to spell it) Division had, simultaneously with us, attacked the right wing of the rebel army (we were on the left) and signally defeated them there, completely routing them as we had done. Thus ended the "Battle of Port Gibson."[15] On our side were engaged, our division, Gen. Carr's and Osterhaus' division all the time and Logan's and Hovey's Divisions during the latter part of the fight. Each division will not average more than 5000 men. The number of the enemy has been variously estimated from 15 to 30 thousand. They also received reinforcements during the battle. Our loss in killed and wounded was between 6 and 6700 not more than 175 of whom were killed. The loss of our regiment was 2 killed: Robertson of Co. "B" and Whittinger of Co. "H" on the ground and a man of Co. "E" who died the day after the fight. Our wounded are 3 Lieutenants: Francisco Co. "K", Henderson company "H," and DeCamp (MD)? Co. "G," and 12 privates. In our company 1 man had a toe accidentally shot off by carelessness. The loss of the enemy is said to be 3700 killed & wounded. We buried a great many of their dead. Seven guns were captured from the rebels and a good many disabled that they took with them. We took 500 prisoners, at least, and 1300 stand of arms. These figures may not be correct but they are as near the truth as I can find out.[16]

May 2nd. [W]e marched over part of the Battle ground and on to Port Gibson, about four miles distant. On the scene of action yet lay many of the dead, with their ghastly upturned faces. Dead horses also lay around in many places. All along the road to Port Gibson were scattered rebel guns, blankets, haversacks & articles of clothing which they threw away in their retreat, or rather flight. They retreated across a bayou [Bayou Pierre] a short distance this side of Port Gibson and burned two fine suspension bridges & the G[rand] Gulf and P[ort] Gibson RR bridge to impede our progress. They evacuated Grand Gulf, spiked (with nails) 9 large guns which they were unable to take with them & retreated across Black River. They have opposite us a force said to be 100,000 strong. Against them we can bring 8 divisions besides 30,000 that Gen. Sherman is bringing from G[rand] Gulf. Unless they attack us, we will not have a battle for several days. L Yenter & all the neighbor boys are well. You will find enclosed a secesh envelope that I picked up on the Battle field. The rebs forgot to take their knapsacks with them & the negroes divided the spoil.

Write soon

My love to all, George

Saturday, May 23, 1863 — Headquarters Carr's Division — [near Vicksburg, Mississippi]
Dear Howard,
We received a letter from Pa a few days ago written from Marengo, dated April 28th. That is the last intelligence we have had from home. Having an opportunity to send a letter to the river, I hastily write a few lines to relieve your anxiety on our account. I am in very good health but Lycurgus has not been very well for some time past. There is nothing serious the matter, only another attack of biliousness. We are immediately in the rear of Vicksburg. A terrible fight is going on.[17] This is the fifth day since the attack began. The 22nd was in the battle yesterday & suffered severely. They stormed one of the strongest rebel forts & were terribly cut up. The official report just handed in is 157 killed wounded & missing. Col. Stone was wounded in the arm. Lt. Col. Graham wounded & taken prisoner. Capt. Robinson Co. I killed. Several Lts. killed & severely wounded. Messenger wounded & taken prisoner. Company F is detailed as Carr's provost guard & was not in the battle, though we are not free from danger. We have to guard headquarters, prisoners, etc. We took Black river Bridge, have possession of railroad between here & Jackson. Took 5 or 6 thousand prisoners & about 100 cannon since we have been in the State. Haines Bluff is ours. I have not time to write any more.[18]

Your Brother, G A Remley

P.S. will write soon & give particulars   GAR

Monday, May 25, 1863 — Camp of 22nd in the rear of Vicksburg [Mississippi]
Dear Howard,
This letter though addressed to you is to be considered written for the benefit of all and, as Pa is equally anxious to hear from us, I would like for you to send it to him if he is not at home when you get it. By this means we will save our postage stamps, which are very scarce down this way.

Day before yesterday I wrote a short letter home to let you know how and where we were. In this I will enter more into detail and give you our history since the 8th, the date of the last regular letter I have written.[19] You may think it strange that we do not write more frequently, but you must remember that our communication with the North has been, for a long time, almost entirely cut off and until recently we had no chance to send letters to the river. The last two letters we have received were one written by Howard dated April 12th and one by Pa dated the 28th. I think we have perhaps missed one. This much by way of explanation.

When I wrote last, the 8th, we were near Black river drawn up in line of battle expecting an engagement with the enemy every day. The enemy not showing a desire to meet us there we slowly marched towards Jackson [Mississippi] keeping on the South side of Black river. About this time, the 12th, company "F" was detailed as Gen. Carr's provost guard and after this time we were not with the regiment. Our place in camp is at Gen. Carr's Headquarters and on the march in the rear of the ambulances. Our duties are various such as guarding headquarters, keeping a crowd from collecting around the surgeons while operating and from the hospitals where the wounded lay, taking temporary charge of prisoners and taking up stragglers, while on the march. The movements of our company were necessarily slow, as the road was for miles blocked up by long ammunition and baggage trains and as we toiled along through the dust and under a burning sun we consoled ourselves with the reflection that <u>provost guards</u> did not have to carry knapsacks. If we <u>had</u> to carry them that in addition to other duties would make our position an unenviable one, as it is we like it pretty well. On the 14th we passed through Raymond, 18 miles from Jackson, near which our advance had met the enemy, two days before and repulsed them, taking several hundred prisoners.[20] The dust did not trouble us much this day for the rain came down in perfect torrents and the whole country was flooded. Sometimes we would have to wade through water nearly waist deep and long before night every part of any clothing was completely drenched. Lycurgus not being well rode on our wagon all day and protected by his rubber blanket he kept himself dry and comfortable. That night we camped within five or six miles of Jackson, having marched 16 miles through the mud. I say "camped," that is if, lying on the ground with a blanket over you can be called camping. The next morning, learning that, after a short but sharp fight, our forces had driven the rebels from Jackson and taken possession of the town, we about faced and retraced our steps as far as Raymond, then taking the Vicksburg road we stopped for the night about 2 miles on this side of the town.[21] Lycurgus walked today and did not catch up with us till nearly dark. The road had dried off since the rain so that walking could be done with comparative ease. I saw and drank water from the famous Mississippi Springs. The water is not as strongly impregnated with sulphur as that of the White Sulphur Springs in Va. but still it has a decided sulphury taste. The buildings do not show much taste either in the architecture or arrangement on the grounds. They are of the plainest kind and have been used by the secesh as a hospital. They are now entirely deserted.

March 28, 1863–June 23, 1863

Raymond is or rather was a pretty little town. The courts house, a fine large building now used as a hospital for wounded rebels, and many neat & tasteful residences surrounded by lawns, luxuriant with evergreens and other beautiful shrubbery, show what the town was at one time; while ransacked store houses, deserted and plundered dwellings, large hotels filled with rebel prisoners — some of them perhaps in sight of their once happy homes — and streets crowded with artillery, baggage trains and soldiers tramping backwards & forwards show what it is now and painfully exhibit the ravages of war.

On the morning of Saturday, the 16th, we again started on our way to Vicksburg. When 8 or 9 miles from Raymond, our advance guard met the enemy in force and then followed the hotly contested battle of "Champion Hills."[22] After a desperate hand to hand engagement the rebels were compelled to retreat in disorder from their chosen position and fall back, closely pursued by our troops, as far as the Black River bridge, some 8 or 10 miles from their first position. Our Division was held as a reserve today, hence the 22nd was not engaged. The 24th & 28th were both in the battle and the 24th suffered severely. Cousin John Remley came through safely, but I do not know how he has fared since. Cousin [Elias] Frank [Remley] of Marion was not in the fight.[23]

The rebels were expected to make a stand at the Bridge, one of their strongest places, but a few shells from our siege guns and a charge, made by the 23rd Iowa, sent them towards Vicksburg, running like frightened sheep. This occurred Sunday the 17th.[24] In the mean time we, the provost guards, had on Saturday morning stopped at one of the "General Hospitals" about a mile in the rear of the battleground, when we soon had as many prisoners as we could take charge of, between four & five hundred. Dr. White got Lycurgus to do some writing for him such as making out lists of the names, regiments, etc. of the wounded & also the situation and severity of the wound. Early Sunday morning, Lycurgus left the Hospital with the surgeons for the field of Battle and he remained with White, who accompanied our forces to Vicksburg, until the 21st when he again joined the company. Saturday evening, seeing that our poor fellows, who lay there wounded, were suffering intensely for want of some one to give them water, bathe their wounds, change their positions, etc. I voluntarily remained with them performing those duties, nearly all that night and the next day, Sunday until 12 o'clock when I was relieved by persons regularly detailed. I hope that I may never again be called upon to witness such scenes of suffering and horror as I looked upon that night. Were I to live a thousand years their impression could never be effaced from my memory. To hear a man deprived of an arm or a leg, beg to have those limbs covered up, "that they felt cold" or to see the eager gasp of the dying man after a sip of cold water or to hear him earnestly plead to be allowed to get up that his sufferings might be alleviated, is painful in the extreme, but these things and far more than these greeted my senses as with a candle in one hand and a pail of water and a

"HE DIED IN HOPE OF A BLISSFUL IMMORTALITY"

cup in the other, I picked my way <u>among</u> the wounded and <u>over</u> the <u>amputated limbs</u> that were scattered around the Hospital grounds.

About noon Sunday, with my physical nature almost completely worn out, <u>we,</u> with our prisoners, left the Hospital and moved forward to Saturday's scene of strife & remained there all day Monday, the number of prisoners being in the mean time increased to about 1500. Dead men, mostly rebels, were yet lying unburied on many parts of the Battle ground. The work of burying was going on as fast as possible. They were buried in heaps & some times thrown into a gully and slightly covered with earth. One of our men lay there with his brains shot out and was yet alive & breathing more than 24 hours after the fight. Horses lay around in every direction and almost an unlimited number of knapsacks, blankets, clothing, haversacks, canteens, guns & accouterments were scattered over the battlefield. I counted 23 bullet holes in one tree as I walked past it. The battle was a hard fought one but the victory complete.

The morning of Tuesday, the 19th, we moved onward with our charge and camped a short distance on this side of Black River. We crossed the river, a small, narrow stream, on a pontoon bridge, the rebels having burned the railroad bridge hoping thereby to impede our progress. The next morning the prisoners taken here at the bridge joined our squad increasing the number to about 4000 and that day we marched through to "Chickasaw Bluffs" on the Yazoo river a short distance below Haines Bluff where we "provost guard" severed our connection with the deluded followers of Jeff Davis. They will probably go on up the river. Our gunboats are stationed at the landing and transports bringing provisions, troops & ammunition are continually arriving. The 21st, after a march of 16 miles, we found ourselves once more at Carr's Headquarters, where I met Lycurgus again and where we remained watching the progress of [the] fight until the night of the 23rd when Gen. Carr kindly informed us that, as our regiment was so greatly reduced in numbers, we might join it in a few days, until Vicksburg falls. So now instead of being spectators of the fight we are participants. When the regiment made that charge, it seemed very hard to see them fight so bravely and not be allowed to give them that assistance they so much needed.

The attack on Vicksburg began Tuesday the 19th and is yet going on. It has as yet been an artillery fight for the most part, though there has been some storming and sharp shooters are popping away all the time. For the last 2 or three days the rebels have not replied more than that many times with their cannon. It is impossible for them to work their cannon for our sharpshooters are within 200 yards of their fortifications and when a rebel head ventures to show itself above the breastworks a dozen bullets are sent whistling around causing it to quickly withdraw. And if a cannon dares to show its grim muzzle above the battlements of the forts, shot and shell from our artillery soon dismount it or at least give it a gentle hint to be more prudent in future. The gun & mortar boats are very leasurely shelling the town and fortifications on this side. Even now, while writing, I can hear the dull boom of the mortars on the river and presently see, over the rebel forts, the puff of white smoke and hear the report peculiar to the bursting shell. This scene at night is splendid: first the flash, like that of distant lightening, coming up from the river, then the track of the shell, describing a parabola in the air, distinctly traced by the burning fuse, and last but not least the vivid glare of intense <u>sulphuric</u> flame, quickly followed by the loud report echoing and reechoing among the surrounding hills.

We the 22nd are now on a hill, about 700 yards from the enemy's works stationed here as a support for a battery. We have dug rifle pits from which we occasionally try our skill as sharpshooters on the butternuts that happen to show themselves above their breastworks. Yesterday, Sunday, I spent nearly the whole day in this kind of work. To tell the truth I did not think of i[ts] being Sunday until late in the evening. It is as much as I can do half of the time to tell what day of the week it is.

One half of our company is now out in the rifle pits near the enemy's works practicing sharpshooting while the rest of us are lying here sweltering in the hot sun, with the rebel bullets whistling over us admonishing us not to make ourselves too conspicuous.

A few words about the charge of the 22nd of which you will have doubtless heard before this reaches you. On the 22nd of this month the 22nd Iowa stormed one of the strongest rebel forts, drove the enemy from and took possession of one end of it, and kept our flag — not the regimental flag — on the top of the earthworks for about five hours, when the rebels made a charge, regained possession of the entire fort and made prisoners of some of our men who were in the fort — among whom was Harvey Graham — the others escaping amid a perfect shower of bullets.[25]

If those regiments that were relied upon as supports had done their duty, we would not only have got one end of the fort but all of it and instead of being driven back we could have held it against almost any force. It was a sad day for Johnson and adjoining counties. It is not necessary, and indeed I could not now, give you a list of the killed & wounded. Lewis Yenter, Logan & all our neighbor boys so far as I have been able to learn are well.

May 26th. Yesterday the rebels sent a flag of truce into our lines and there was a few hours cessation of hostilities. The butternuts crowded on top of their earthworks and seemed anxious to make as great a display as possible. During this truce some of our men were sent to the fort that the 22nd stormed to bury the dead that lay just outside of the fort. The rebels talked & joked with the men thus engaged. To get us to bury our dead because they were becoming offensive to the rebels was one object of the flag of truce but I do not know whether it was the only one or not. Today the firing is kept up pretty briskly. Several times have the rebels essayed to drive large droves of horses, mules, cattle, etc. into our lines, but each time they have been driven back by our shells. They don't want to feed them and yet don't want them to die in the town, so says Rumor.

The work is prospering and I think Vicksburg will be ours before many days. The troops are in good spirits and hopeful.

Now a few words in regard to Lycurgus: He has not been perfectly well for just a month to day, but he has been on duty part of that time. He first had the "Billious diarrhea" and that made him very weak. Within the last few days his disease has assumed the form of Billious fever. The worst feature of the case is that he is so intensely blue; the "Blue Devils" have complete possession of him and he does not try to resist their influence or make the least effort to drive them away. Yesterday I got an ambulance and took him to the hospital and such a woe-be-gone expression as he had on his face I never before saw; but after I had fixed him a bed and got the doctor to see him and prescribe for him, he looked fifty per cent better, entirely like a new man. There is nothing serious the matter with him yet, only an attack of biliousness but it is my candid opinion that if he does not resist these "Devils" they will not "flee from him" and if he <u>will</u> not <u>try</u> to banish such feelings and be more cheerful it will be a long time before he gets well. I am going to the Hospital in a few minutes to see him and let him see this and give him a chance to state his own case. I have heard that letters do not go further North than Young[']s [P]oint and will not until Vicksburg is taken. If this is true, it may be some time before you get this. Write frequently, your letters will come to us. I am glad to hear that you & Milton are getting along so well on the farm and that your neighborhood is improving so much. I long for the time when I can see you all again and trust it is not <u>very</u> far distant.

My love to all the family.

Your Aff Brother, Geo A Remley

PS Don't forget to send this to Pa and tell him that we are in the 2nd Brigade of the <u>14th</u> (not 12th) Division, 13th Army Corps Army of the Mississippi.

GA Remley

[Lycurgus continues:] **May 26**
Dear Ma,
I write lying on my couch in the open air suffering with a severe attack of sickness to explain a few things omitted by Geo. First I will say that run almost to death with diarrhea and very weak[,] I still determined to go through with the fight at Port Gibson as far as in me lay. Though exhausted at the close of the day, I still stood it through. May 3rd I was taken more seriously ill, and from that day to this, have been unfit for duty, sometimes unable to stand alone five minutes. Tis true I reported once for duty when I thought myself nearly recovered and that is the time that Dr. White procured my services with the <u>free</u> consent of the Captain who knew I wasn't yet well. I thought those services were to be of real good, but as it turned out it was only for the private accommodation of Drs. White and Peabody.

Upon the whole, however, it was signally providential that I went with White, as I had a mule to ride and I couldn't <u>possibly</u> have stood marching or the fifth part the work of any one of the company.

Well last Friday I was taken worse again and since than have had quite a serious time no appetite whatever — parched tongue frequently and burning skin all the time. I don't know whether it is bilious fever or not. One word about the Blues Geo says so much about. The truth is I had been shamefully neglected — not by Geo. — he was with the company, but the fault of some one. There I lay in a very hot place my tongue parched and nothing to relieve me but warm impure water and the day I went to the Hospital I was nearly all morning entirely alone. Besides I wanted some medicine which I couldn't get. Enough surely to give any one the blues. Well when I came to the Hospital and Geo. had made me a nice comfortable bed (on the ground) and Dr. Lee had kindly and sympathetically prescribed for me and I had been refreshed with cool cistern water, I of course felt better. I feel quite unwell today.

All is for the best. My love to all

Your Affectionate Son, Lycurgus

Thursday, June 4, 1863 — Hospital of 22nd in rear of Vicksburg [Mississippi]
Dear Pa,
Your last letter dated May 23rd came to hand yesterday and that is the latest intelligence we have had from Iowa. A letter from Howard written the 3rd was received on the 27th of May. My last letter home was written on the 25 of May. It was a long one, of eight or nine pages, and was direct[ed] to Howard; but for reasons indicated in it I requested him to send it to you as soon as he had read it. As you are specially interested in and solicitous concerning our health and personal welfare, I will touch upon that subject first.

As for myself I never had better health or felt better than I do now. Lycurgus, as I have intimated in former letters, has not been very well for a long time. About the time we left Perkins Plantation he was attacked with a kind of billious diarrhea, which being very severe at times, greatly reduced him both in flesh and strength; still he managed to keep up [his] spirits, drag himself along and stay out of the Hospital until about the 24th of May [when] his disease changed to the billious fever and I brought him over here, to the Hospital. The fever increased and his case became more and more serious till night before last, the 2nd, when he sweated freely nearly all night and the next morning. The crisis was then passed, so the doctor said. Since then, though he does not feel any stronger and is, in fact, very weak, the fever has been gradually leaving him and his symptoms are now decidedly favorable. I forgot to say that the fever had gradually assumed a typhoid form and that Dr. White began to consider his recovery a little doubtful. When first brought to the Hospital, he lay for several days in the open air under an apple tree, every part of the buildings and yard of a large mansion being full of wounded men at that time, then for a short time in a tent and since that time he has been, along with the rest of the sick belonging to the 22d in the lower part of a large, horse-power cotton gin. It is open at the sides, but I got Lycurgus a good cotton bed (mattress), so he is better off in that respect than most of the others.

Day before yesterday, Dr. White and Capt. Cree both concurring, I was detailed, temporarily, as a nurse in the Hospital, so that I could attend to Lycurgus better. I have thus described his situation so minutely, because I knew that these particulars would interest you. Now for the <u>finale:</u> Dr. White has promised that, as soon as Lycurgus is able to bear the fatigue of the trip he will give him his discharge and send him home. It is very likely Providence permitting that you will see him in Iowa again before six weeks shall have passed away. Capt. Cree does not like to part with him but as it is considered best for Lycurgus he is perfectly willing. One <u>word</u> more and I am through with the subject. Lycurgus, though he had concluded to apply for a discharge, had not yet done so, hence Dr. White offered it of his own accord. White is very kind to <u>us</u> and is doing his best with the 22d. The health of the 22d is very good considering the climate and all the hard ships they have endured. We have now between 34 and 40 here in the Hospital and only three or four of these are considered seriously ill. The regiment is no longer the "big 22d." I do not suppose we could muster more than 350 effective men, at the present time. Yesterday we lost five men, three of them died of sickness and two were killed by sharp-shooters while with the regiment on the hill that I spoke of in a former letter.[26]

To day even while I was writing the above, another poor fellow lying within a few feet of me ended all his earthly sufferings. This is the exception not the general rule. The "seige of Vicksburg" is progressing slowly but surely. The "anaconda," or this part of it, is gradually tightening its folds and the destruction of the doomed city is now merely a question of time. We are daily extending and strengthening our earth-works, working only at night and using all the available "black help" we can procure. Preparations are now being made for a general bombardment of the city and works. Huge seige guns and mortars and immense quantities of ammunition and army stores are being collected here for that purpose. Sharp-shooters still keep up a steady fire, on both sides and hardly a day passes without two or three men being killed in the rifle pits. Our artillery occasionally gives the rebels a foretaste of what they expect one of these days; but they very seldom reply. Yesterday as an ammunition train passed near here they threw four shells and as many solid shot over this way some of which struck pretty close to us, the others passing over. A great many deserters come into our lines from Vicksburg. They all agree in saying that the rebels are very scarce of water. That they have plenty of fresh beef — killed by our shells, but are on quarter rations of meal, little salt, nothing more. They, ungrateful wretches, occasionally give us railroad-iron from their cannon, in return for the fresh meat. <u>You</u> can <u>rely on that.</u>

At night we can very distinctly hear the Vicksburg clock strike and are able to regulate our time by it.

Cattle, dogs & even cats can be heard every night and the pickets at one time are talking and joking with each other and then in a few minutes send their respects from their guns.

The part of Mississippi that I have seen is very different from what I expected to find. It is not mountainous but still is very hilly and much cut up with deep gullies whose banks are some times 20 or 30 feet high and frequently perpendicular. This together with dense timber and innumerable cane brakes greatly impede the operations of an army.

The weather, since we have been in this State, has been as a general thing remarkably fine. It is now almost intolerably hot. I have not slept in a tent since the 27th of April when we left Perkins Plantation. Most of that time all that I ate or drank was cooked in a small fruit can.

While in Missouri we "played soldier" but since then we have been acting it out in earnest.

Gov. Kirkwood is here and brought with him a lot of "sanitary stores," the benefits of which our sick are now enjoying. I have not seen him yet.

I am glad to hear that your part of the country is in such a prosperous condition and that our old neighborhood is filling up and improving so rapidly. I hope that your term at Marengo will pass away pleasantly.

Tell Allie that she must improve her time and opportunities to the greatest extent possible; for the time is fast approaching when other things will occupy her attention. I am truly glad to hear that she is doing so well. I hope you will pardon the sacrilege of connecting the head of Washington with anything, even an envelope, that has treason's foul mark upon it, but it is the best I could do this time. A Hospital is a very unfavorable place for writing. I suppose I have had to get up forty times since I commenced writing.

Write soon for there is nothing that does so much good as letters from home. You can take my money and use as you please. I will want it, if I ever get back, to help advance my education. Give my love to Allie and all at home when you see them.

Your Son, Geo. A Remley

Tuesday, June 9, 1863 — Hospital of 22nd Iowa — [near Vicksburg, Mississippi]
Dear Mother,
Having an opportunity of sending letters directly to Iowa by our orderly-sergeant H. A. Tidd, who is discharged, I could not let it pass without writing you a few lines. The last letter I wrote to any of you was dated the 4th and directed to Pa at Marengo. In that I gave a[n] animate account of the state of our health, etc. I hope you have received it before this time. Day before yesterday we received two letters, both written by Milton, one dated the 11th and directed to Lycurgus containing 9 postage stamps, the other was to me and had no date but was mailed the 28th.

As you may see from the heading I am still in the hospital. I am sitting by Lycurgus keeping the flies off him with one hand and writing with the other, just now, however, Lycurgus offered to do that for himself until I get through writing. Since I wrote last Lycurgus has been gradually improving but as is usual in such cases the improvement has been very slow and tedious. Lycurgus bears it very patiently and as a general thing is in good spirits. I hope he will recover fast and soon be able to leave this unhealthy country and return home where he will receive such attention and be cared for as a sick man cannot be in the army. Lycurgus is, however, very comfortably fixed here. As I said in my last, he has a good bed and our Hospital is the coolest and most comfortable place I have met with in this country. It is admired by all who come here for its neatness, order & refreshing coolness.

I write this note merely to let you know how we are and to relieve your anxiety on our account. Do not be so anxious or think so much about us. Remember that there is One watching over us who is able to protect and keep us from harm and bring us safely through all these dangers and trials that we now encounter. Tell Milton that I will write to him as soon as I can find time. There is every prospect of Vicksburg's speedy fall. It can not hold out against us much longer.

My love to all

Your Affectionate Son, Geo A Remley

Tuesday, June 16, 1863 — Hospital of 22nd in rear of Vicksburg [Mississippi]
Dear Mother,
I have not heard from home since I received Milton's letter of May 28th; I am extremely anxious to hear from you. On the 9th of this month I wrote you a short letter giving an account of Lycurgus' health and prospects of recovery.

This time it becomes my painful duty to let you know that God in his infinite mercy & goodness has seen fit to remove Lycurgus from this world of sin and suffering and sorrow and take him to that far better, brighter & more glorious world above, where there is no more sickness or sorrow and where I trust he is now as the Angels in Heaven. He seemed to be doing very well and gradually overcoming the disease and the Doctors expressed the strongest hopes of his recovery until yesterday morning [when] he seemed much worse and during the day he rapidly failed. About 3 o'clock in the afternoon he quietly and gently passed away, fell asleep in Jesus.

He requested me to tell you that "he died in hope of a blissful immortality." All along through his illness he expressed complete resignation to the will of God knowing full well that whatever He did would be for the best and during the latter part of it he seemed impressed with the idea that he should not get well. As it was impossible to send the body North, he was buried in the soldiers' grave-yard near here.

Do not grieve on account of him Ma, for he is a thousand times better off where he is. God was done with him here in this world and took him home to himself in Heaven, where he is forever free from the pain and suffering and misery of Earth. O, Mother, let not your heart be troubled for God does all things for the best. He does not willingly afflict the children of men, but makes all things work to-gether for the good of those that love him and put their trust in Him.

I will send some of Lycurgus' things home by the first opportunity. In a small sealed package left with you, you will find his will. He desired you to open it.

I can not write any more now, but will write a longer letter soon. Send word to Pa immediately.

Your Affectionate Son, George A Remley

P.S. I send this by Capt. Shrader from the North Ben   G A Remley

Thursday, June 18, 1863 — Camp of 22nd in rear of Vicksburg [Mississippi]
Dear Ma,
Day before yesterday I wrote a letter informing you of Lycurgus' death, which I hope you will have received before this reaches you. I sent it by Captain Shrader (formerly Doctor) of Sheceyville who has gone home on a sick furlough and I think it will reach its destination much quicker than by mail. It is hardly necessary for me to tell you that I do most deeply sympathize with you in this our sad bereavement, for here far away from home in a strange land and surrounded by temptations and danger in every form, I can not but keenly feel the loss of the one to whom I could always look for counsel and sympathy.

Yet, since our loss is his eternal gain, it does not become us to grieve as those who have no hope, but we should earnestly and joyfully look forward to the time when we too shall put away this mortal evil and go to meet him and forever dwell with him and the Blessed Saviour in that far happier clime above. Let us remember that the Lord gave him to us for a time and that when his mission here was fulfilled and his work finished, the Lord took him home to himself, where he is far better off than we who remain.

Day before yesterday, the 16th, after an absence of two weeks, I returned to the company almost completely worn down by my constant watchings. I think I weigh at least 12 pounds less now than I did when I went to the Hospital and felt much more like a sick man going to the Hospital than a well man reporting for duty. Capt. Cree and all the boys are very kind and seem to sympathize with me. The Capt. in particular has been very considerate and attentive for some time past.

I am at present engaged in doing some writing for Gen. [Michael K.] La[w]ler and am of course relieved from all other duty. This is a very easy position, but it is impossible to tell how long it will last. It may be permanent and may continue only a few weeks.

The 22nd is fast decreasing in number. We can muster now only a few over 200 men for duty. No longer the "Big 22nd." One of company was killed last Saturday.[27] Lewis Yenter & all of our neighbor boys are well.

I send home by Walter Saxton, a discharged soldier, (the man who Pa married to Mr. Jamison's daughter one winter at our house), all the valuables, etc. that belonged to Lycurgus. You will find the list below. Mr. Saxton will take them to you.

"HE DIED IN HOPE OF A BLISSFUL IMMORTALITY"

> Watch & Guard
> Pocket book & contents - $4.40
> Paper case & writing materials
> Needle Book & contents
> Pocket knife & looking glass
> Bible & Memorandum Book
> Soldiers Hymn Book
> Suspenders & one Shirt
> Case knife, fork & spoon

None of Lycurgus' clothes (except janshs which I returned to the Captain) were worth sending home as they were almost worn out. His rubber blanket he gave to me. I have also kept a few things which I will keep strict account of.

I hope you will write often for it takes so long for letters to reach me. My love to all the family.

Your Affectionate Son, George A Remley

Hospital 7 o'clock P.M.
Mr. Saxton having already started, I send this by someone else.[28]

Tuesday, June 23, 1863 — Head Quarters 14th Division — [near Vicksburg, Mississippi]
Dear Pa,

Yesterday morning I received two letters: one from you written on the 13th inst and the other from Howard dated the 11th. Both were truly welcome, as all your letters are, for they bring tidings of health, happiness and prosperity at home.

This is the first intelligence I have had from any of you since the 7th of this month at which time I received two letters, both from Milton and the last one bearing the date of May 28th.

Since the 7th I have written several times giving you a truthful account of all that has transpired in the mean time. I have no doubt but that all these letters have reached you long ere this.

My health is tolerably good; but owing to various causes I do not feel as strong as I did a month ago and I know that I will not weigh as much by 12 or 15 pounds as I did then. Indeed, unless you have experience[d] it, you can not <u>even imagine</u> the enervating effect that the hot and sultry weather of this Southern climate, has upon one's system.

The entire system — mental, physical and nervous — is weakened and prostrated to a degree that I never felt, nor even had any idea of before. This is not the case with me alone, but every one here even the strongest and most health[y] feel this way to a greater or lesser extent.

Our regiment is still the busiest of the busy. In fact our Division (Carr's) has had the honor of being in the advance ever since we have been in this State and Gen. McClernand says that we will keep our present position till Vicksburg becomes ours and then we will have a chance to rest a while.

March 28, 1863–June 23, 1863

About three fourths of the time, day and night, our company is on duty of some kind, working on the entrenchments or standing picket guard at night or lying in the rifle pits, close to the enemy's works, all day while the Sun pours down his heat until an egg would almost be cooked without any fire. All this, especially the rifle pit work is attended with considerable danger. The boys are continually telling of hair-breadth escapes and hardly a day passes without some one, in our Brigade, being killed and perhaps several wounded. Since the 16th, the day on which I returned from the Hospital, I have not been on duty in the company but was detailed to do occasional jobs of writing for Brg. Gen'l Lawler, until yesterday; when Gen. Carr desiring Aj't D. J. Davis to send him a clerk. I was released from my Brigade duties and sent over here to act in that capacity. The position is an easy one but, were it not for the great advantage that a knowledge of this kind of business is to a young man I would much prefer being with the company and sharing its toils and dangers. That is what I enlisted for. And besides this, Capt. Cree, I think, would rather have me with the company, though he signified a perfect willingness for me to remain until I had "recruited my strength." Taking all things into consideration, I think, that I will stay here about two weeks and then take my place in the company.

The siege is still progressing favorably and our rifle pits are gradually encroaching on the enemy — being along almost the whole line within 50 yards of the rebel works and some places within a few feet — and in a few days we intend to keep the enemy's pickets inside of their own works, at night. Joe Johns[t]on is still hovering in our rear but he does not give any great concern and perfect security in that quarter by our Officers. There is a rumor in camp to day that there is fight in progress somewhere near Black River; if such is the case, Joe Johns[t]on will be properly cared for. The speedy fall of Vicksburg is confidently looked for and notwithstanding the many hardships and discouragement the troops are in excellent spirits.

The health of our regiment is, I suppose, as good as could be expected under the circumstances, yet there are a great many unfit for duty mostly on account of diarrhea or something similar to it. Discharges and leave-of-absences are becoming quite common. I hope that I shall not have to avail myself of either until the war closes.

It is remarkable how many of our wounded die. Dr. White gave it as his opinion that one of every two of the wounded would not survive and I think that his prediction has been fully verified. It is comforting however to know that they start North immediately where they will enjoy a cooler climate and better attention.

The water we drink here is obtained by digging holes three or four feet deep in the bottoms of ravines that abound in this part of the country. It is better than a great deal we have had since we left Missouri, but cannot compare with that of our well "way up in Iowa." I would give a great deal to have such water as that to drink.

"HE DIED IN HOPE OF A BLISSFUL IMMORTALITY"

Apples, peaches, etc. are beginning to ripen here, but, owing to the number of troops in this vicinity, they cannot become very abundant so far as any particular individual is concerned. Blackberries are ripe and <u>very</u> abundant. We <u>frequently</u> treat ourselves to stewed blackberries and occasionally to stewed apples or peaches.

The rebels are using their artillery more than they did some time ago. It is no uncommon thing for shot and shell to pass, <u>screeching</u> over our heads.

One night not long ago they shelled our camp but fortunately did not hurt any one. One piece passed through those tents and touched no one.

Do not let the fear that your letters will not reach me hinder you from writing long letters and often, for I believe that I receive all you write.

We are in the "Department of the Tennessee" and the Army is "The Army of Tenn." Gen'l McClernand has been relieved of his command here and Gen'l E. O. C. Ord now fills his place. I do not know the cause of the change.[29]

I am truly glad to hear that you are getting along so well with your school and that Allie is improving so fast and learning so well.

I will write a letter to Milton as soon as I have time. I will say to you what Milton says to me "You cannot write too often."

Give my love to Allie & all at home when you see them.

Your Affectionate Son, George A Remley

Sunday, June 28, 1863 — Warrensburg, Missouri
My dear Nephew,
We have been expecting to hear from you for some weeks.[30] Notwithstanding I am in your debt a letter. Since you left Mo. I did not know whether a letter directed as heretofore would reach you, but concluded to try it. And my main object is to hear from you, for we know that you & George have been in these terrible battles, fought near Vicksburg. I will be anxious to hear from you while we know you are in so much danger. In a letter rec'd from your Father a few days since he informed me that you & George had escaped unhurt so far. We have been hoping to hear of the possession of Vicksburg by the Government Troops & will hope on, for it is believed by most persons here that if Vicksburg is taken, quiet will soon be restored in Mo. Something that would be desirable just now. For while I am writing Citizens & Soldiers are gathering in the Street, preparing to go some 8 miles from here in search of Bushwhackers who burnt some Union mens houses last night & committed other depredations. That Class of desperadoes are becoming numerous in our county. I have some fears that this summer is to be a hard season to live through. My own impression is, that very much depends upon getting Vicksburg it will be a terrible back set to the Rebels and when we once get full possession of the Mississippi River, Rebel prospects will be gloomy indeed. Does it not appear strange that the people of the Southern States continue to be misled by dishonest & wiley Politicians whose only care is self aggrandizement. We know that there are as honest & good men in the Southern States as lives any where, and yet when we look on them as the enemies of our country and consequently our enemies, it is hard for us to feel kind toward them. But if we have a desire to pray for

our enemies (an impossibility to the Natural heart I think) we may pray for them of the South who have been our friends and are our relations. As for me I do acknowledge that my heart is hard against the enemies of our Government. The greatest desire of my heart is to see them whipped into their duty. Conquered entirely so that the [coming] generation & generations unborn, may hereafter Fear to Rebel against this Government. And this I think is for their own good. I have never had any objections to the institutions of the South, And sometimes feel sorry to see & hear so much said about the nigger. When the Government of our Fathers recognises the right in Certain States to own & control slaves, so do I. If that same Government for the sake of the perpetuity of itself and for the good of all concerning, concludes that slavery cannot longer exist without continually endangering us as a Nation I am still agreeing with the Government. And if I were convinced that those managing the affairs of our Nation had done wrong or had acted unwisely, yet I am still with that Government, yes for my Government right or wrong, nor have I in any instance found fault. We need not expect that all our Rulers will do exactly right or that every man claiming to be Loyal is truly so, for it will continue to be, as the past has proven, That many men will prove faithless & treacherous. From my youth up I have had a contempt for men whose business is Politicks. I have seen the intreague, Rascality, and deceit, shown forth in Them so much & so long that I think I am right in looking on them with suspicion, & believe that they would lay burdens on mens shoulders grievous to be bourne [that] they would not touch with one of their fingers. I am aware that we have always had Statesmen in our Nation who were honest, but since the signers of the Declaration of Independence & a few others since them, have died I fear, that our best men now are only degenerate sons of Noble Sires; Those men who fought for, and framed our Government I have always looked upon with Reverence; Thinking that God blessed and mightily aided them in the establishment of our Government the equal to which is not [illegible] upon earth. Therefore I thank God for giving us such men, and that I was born in America; And Pray God that there is enough righteous men still in our Country, for whose sake our Heavenly Father may save our country from the threatening evils that surround us. Have you been able since your removal from Mo. to keep up your regular Prayer Meetings in Camp. I hope so. May our Armies be successful in subdueing & putting down Rebellion & you & George spared to enjoy the fruits of Victory is the earnest prayer of your Uncle,

Wm. Zoll.

Monday, June 29, 1863 — Oxford, Iowa
My Dear Husband,
About an hour before we got your letter we heard the report of Lycurgus death which I tried not to believe, it was too distressing to bear. Milton went up to Mr. Jamison's early this morning to know the truth, did not see Mr. Saxton he being at his father's but learned it to be a sad reality. I am so distressed I know not what to do. Can it be possible that I shall never see my first born son again? O how can I bear it, bear it. He died in Mr Saxton's

arms a very calm happy death. George's not writing by Mr. Saxton makes me think he was not present or what is the reason we can't hear from him. I am now so uneasy about George his brother is gone and he is left alone and what will become of him. The destroying angel has entered our family and is taking one by one we will soon all be gone. But I do hope at last we will make an unbroken family in heaven. But if I could only go first to avoid all this distress and suffering which I must endure while in the flesh. I have no doubt but Lycurgus has gone to heaven. I always believed him to be a devoted christian he certainly has reaped a world of misery though it greaves us so to part with him. I hope Allie will try to bear it and give her heart to God. And may we all profit by this sad bereavement.

Your poor afflicted wife, Jane C Remley

[Written on the reverse of Jane Remley's letter:]
Dear Pa,
We have heard the distressing news which I have been dreading for some time. I have feared that Lycurgus would never get well ever since George wrote but Ma would talk of his coming home and seemed to be looking for him and when she heard of his death it almost killed her. How I wished you were at home! The neighbors are all very sympathising & kind. All is for the best.

Your Aff Son, H M Remley

[Monday], June 29, 1863 — Iowa City, Iowa
Dear George,
Your long and interesting letter of May 29th has lain for some time unanswered because of pressure of other duties, etc., etc.

Sabbath evening I was very sorry indeed to learn of the death of your brother L[y]curgus.

When war causes the death of such intelligent and worthy men as he, it becomes an awful scourge upon any country. I know he never would have enlisted except from a sense of duty and the consciousness of having done his duty together with a well founded hope in Christ doubtless made his deathbed pleasant even though far from home. You have my sympathy George. Do not be discouraged by this affliction but take a christian view of it. You are in the path of duty and therefore of peace and safety. Should your earthly house also be dissolved you may hope for a better house on high. I hope God in his providence will spare you to engage for many years in the more peaceful pursuits of life for which I think you are better adapted and more inclined.

My brother was at Haines Bluff when he last wrote. He is 1st Lieut. of Co. A, 27th Reg. Wis. Vols. He is brigaded with the 40th Iowa etc. under Gen. Kimball. I would like to have you make his acquaintance if convenient. Duncan of the Republican is in the 40th you know.

I hope this epistle will find you rejoicing in Vicksburg. Write soon.

Truly Your friend, Chas. E. Borland

Chapter Three

"A Bright and Glorious 'Fourth'"

— VICKSBURG SURRENDERS —

Saturday, July 4, 1863, 10 o'clock AM — Head Quarters 14th Division — [Vicksburg, Mississippi]
Dear Howard,
This is the "Fourth of July." A bright and glorious "Fourth" it is and long will it be remembered as such by this army, for just now — at 10 o'clock AM — Gen'l Pemberton has accepted an unconditional surrender, and I now hear cheer after cheer from our men expressing their joy at this long looked for event.

Yesterday morning Pemberton offered to surrender on certain conditions; Grant replied that he would only accept an unconditional surrender.

Another conference was held in the afternoon which lasted till 10 o'clock at night. The result was that if the rebels concluded to accede to Grant's terms, they were to make it known this morning at 10 o'clock by displaying white flags on their fortifications. This has been done and Vicksburg is ours. Gen. Grant has intimated, not to the rebels however, that he will parole the prisoners and let them go home. Where we will go or what we will do is yet a matter of uncertainty. I hope the 22nd will get to go north to spend the rest of the summer.

Last night for the first time since we have been here there was no firing any where along the line; all was perfect quiet.

The night before I was wakened by the balls whistling over me and the firing caused by an attack by the rebels on our rifle pits and ever since we have been here we have been so accustomed to continuous firing, whistling balls, and exploding shells that to pass a night in quiet was something out of the regular order of events.

Early this morning along the entire line a national salute (blanks) was fired by our artillery in honor of the day. The rebels crowded on the tops of their fortifications but did not join in the celebration.

All is perfectly quiet now very good and, as you may see from the heading, I am still at Gen'l Carr's Head Quarters.

It is quite probable, however, that when we moved from this place, I will return to the company. I have been here ever since the 22nd of last month. I sleep and take my meals (Breakfast & supper) with the company. I do this because I prefer it and because the walk over there — 1/2 mile — does me good. We have had our tents and cooking utensils nearly three weeks and we are now so well fixed for "house keeping" that I [hate] to break up. I would as soon spend the summer here as any where in the South. I have a good bedstead or "bunk" made of canes and have a very comfortable sleeping arrangement, but the heat musketoes & flies usually keep me awake till about mid-night. The musketoes are not very bad but the flies are so numerous that they will eat up a pint of sugar in a half a day if it is left uncovered. This is a fact!

The paymaster has given us a visit lately and paid us two months (March & April) wages. I received $26.00 but for want of an opportunity I have not sent any home.

It is not safe to trust it in a letter nor by the express lines we have down here, so I have concluded to wait for further developments.

You need not send me any more postage stamps for I have now enough to do me for a while. For the special accommodation of the soldiers the paymaster brought with him an immense quantity of stamps and I got some of[f] him. They were sold here at Hd Qrs and there was a tremendous rush for them. $100 were sold in about an hour.

I hope you are enjoying yourselves today and having a good time at your celebration. I will write again as soon as I can. I have not heard from home since the 22nd ult. when I rec'd 2 letters from you dated the 11th & the other from Pa dated the 13th. Write frequently.

Your Affectionate Brother, Geo. A. Remley

Saturday, July 4, 1863 — Oxford, Iowa
My dear Son,

We rec'd the first intelligence of our severe affliction by Mr. Saxton. Since that we have rec'd your letter of the 18th ult., but that of the 16th which you give the particulars of the sad event has not yet come to hand. You can imagine how much your Ma is d[e]stroyed, and indeed all of us are deeply afflicted, but we try to bear it as Christians ought to bear the chastenings of a kind Father who "does not willingly afflict nor grieve the children of men." We console ourselves with the reflection that God does all things right, that he is too wise to err, and too good to do wrong, that he will cause all things to work together for the good of them that love him and are called according to his purpose.

We rec'd your letter of the ninth of June one week before Mr. Sax[t]on arrived, but yours of the 4th did not come to me in Marengo till last Monday the 29th. On Sat. the 27th we first heard of Lycurgus's death. Monday the 29th I came home, Tuesday the 30th your Ma & I went down to see Mr. Sax[t]on & heard from him. We are very thankful that you were permitted to attend him in his last hours & that he rec'd every kindness & attention consistent with inadequate arrangements of a temporary hospital and was attended by kind, christian friends in his last moments. He has indeed received his final discharge & is no doubt gone home to his Heavenly father to those mansions which Jesus has prepared for the reception of his 'returned soldiers.' I feel to day like I too would like to lay my armour by, and dwell with him above. May God in mercy grant that we may all be ready, when ever he calls us to enter into that rest which remains for the people of God! We are now deeply anxious on your account. You say that when you left the hospital, you felt more like a sick man going into the hospital than one about to report for duty. If you are sick & cannot endure the hardness of a soldier's life, I do hope you will receive an honorable discharge & come home. Do not wait till it is too late. May God preserve you, my boy! We are much relieved by the information in your last that you have duties to perform at the head quarters of Gen. Lawler, which during the time, will exempt you from the duties of an ordinary soldier. We do hope and pray that your education, talents & good conduct may so commend you to the powers that be, as to secure for you a place where you can be employed in duties more congenial to tastes & habits & more consistent with your health and safety.

They are having a lively time in Pennsylvania now, but I hope they will make Gen. Lee rue the day he crossed the Rappahannock. We are waiting with the utmost impatience to hear of the fall of Vicksburg & think that when it happens we shall soon see you at home again.

There was a very flattering notice of Lycurgus in the last Republican which you will see in due time.

Your afflicted Father, James Remley

My dear son,
I am sorry I cannot bear my affliction with more fortitude which becomes a christian under such circumstances for I think we have no reason to doubt but that he is in the mansions above and has escaped all the evils of this wicked world. George let me urge upon you to try to get a discharge if you find your health failing.

Your afflicted Mother, Jane C. Remley

Thursday, July 16, 1863 — H'd Qrs 14th Division 13th A.C. — Camp before Jackson, Mississippi

Your letter of the fourth of July was received yesterday morning and I embrace the first opportunity of writing again. I wrote day-before-yesterday and now again to-day because I know that you are anxious to hear from me as often as possible. But I am equally anxious to hear from home and hope that you will let me have the benefit of, at least, <u>one</u> "regular, weekly epistle." If you and the boys are too busy, at any time, to write, tell Allie to write to me. I would be glad to have her do so, and tell me all the news, how she is getting along with her Algebra, Music, etc.

As it regards my health, I am getting along very well. When I left the hospital I did, indeed, feel very much worn down and exhausted by close confinement, loss of sleep, etc. I lost 20 pounds in weight while I was at the Hospital and owing to the hot weather and prostrated state of my physical nature I have not been able to recruit any since. About the time we left

Vicksburg I weighed 120 pounds, but I do not think I would weigh quite so much now. Before I went to the Hospital my health was uniformly good; but since it has been variable and fickle — some days I feel perfectly well, and other days quite unwell — a feeling generally caused by derangement of the stomach, etc. I have felt much better for the last few days and think that I will soon be all right. Much as I would like to be at home and see all of you once again, I would not, were it offered me, take a discharge; much less ask for one. I want to see the boasted strength of the Confederacy completely broken, every hand that is raised against our Government struck down and peace once more restored to the whole country, then and not till then will I be content to leave the army and return home.

Well, here we are settled down before Jackson just as we were before Vicksburg.[1] The same scenes that were enacted before that place are now being repeated here. Even now while I am writing, I here a sharp musketry fight going on — an occasional shot from the cannon supplying the place of bass to the lighter notes.

The rebel fortifications are represented as very strong, but our men have them already encircled and closed in by a parallel line of earthworks, upon which the rebels have made sally after sally in vain, for every time they have come out, they have been driven back rather faster than they came. The railroad from Jackson to New Orleans has been torn up by our cavalry but that leading East from Jackson is in full operation, and the rebels are and have been using it to the best possible advantage. When we destroy this one the 60,000 men now said to be in Jackson will be in a pretty tight place. We have as yet only three Army Corps here and I do not know of any more troops on the way. We are in no hurry to attack the rebels here and it has been done in but one instance — that of Gen'l Lauman and he was removed for it — but we are using every endeavor to provoke them to make sallies upon us. When the rebel army now here is defeated and demoralized as it will doubtless be, before long then, if the news we hear from [George] Mead, [John] Dix & [Nathaniel] Banks proves true, the "Confederacy" may be considered "gone up," and we will have some prospect of returning home.

The position of the 22nd is pretty close to the enemy's works and the music of bullets has become so common that it no longer excites admiration. Yesterday evening while I was there, on a visit, a ball came past making a noise more like a shell than a bullet — this was caused by the ball being put into the gun wrong end fore-most — said to be the work of the new rebel conscripts, who do not care about fighting at all. A few days ago company "F" was sent out as a support for two Co's of skirmishers. They followed the skirmishers closely and, when nearing a fence on the edge of a wood, they were suddenly met by a perfect hail storm of bullets coming from every tree and fence corner in sight (nearly). The rebels commenced throwing down the fence to let some cavalry through for the purpose of capturing the whole squad. The three companies then in a precipitated manner beat a hasty retreat, each one taking care of himself as best he could. And it was

July 4, 1863–September 19, 1863

well for them that they did so for they barely escaped capture that way. Had the rebels instead of trying to capture, poured a steady fire into them they would have been cut to pieces — as it was Co "F" did not have a man touched — the other companies lost several. Some of the boys, Lewis Logan among them, nearly killed themselves running and have not been fit for duty since. I wasn't there and I am glad of it for I would not like to run from the rebels.

I am still here at Division H'd Q'rs and, for anything I know to the contrary, may remain here a long time. In fact I cannot get away, so I suppose I may be considered as a fixture here, doing the [will of] Gen'l W[illiam] P. Benton, who now commands the Division, Gen'l Carr being home on a leave of absence. Capt. Cree & the rest of the company would rather have me with them, especially as I am a sergeant now and I believe myself that it would [be] better for me; I could take more exercise. My mess arrangements have improved somewhat since we left Vicksburg. There are 9 or 10 orderlies here around H'd Q'rs and we formed ourselves into a mess and have a stout negro man to cook for us, pay him $10 per month. He formerly cooked for Gen'l Benton and is an excellent hand at the business. For instance we had for dinner mutton soup, beef steak, biscuit, Tea & sugar; everything was good and got up in good style.

Tell Ma that she need not cease her labors of love in behalf of the soldiers for fear that we never receive any benefit from them. Those who are well indeed very seldom do but the sick have cause many times to bless the "sanitary commissions" for fruits, jellies, and other delicacies also soda crackers, potatoes, lemons and even ice. This I <u>know</u> to be the case, at least to have been the case while I was at the Hospital. They also had shirts & drawers manufactured by sanitary commissions. It may be and no doubt is true that some of what is sent never reaches its destination, but the greater part of it does.

The weather has been cooler and more pleasant for the last few days but the dust is very annoying. I saw, in the "Republican," the notice you spoke of. I had written to the Editor, giving him the facts of the case and requesting him to continue the paper & change the address. Dr. White requests me to give you his respects and say that he "sympathises deeply with you." Dr. White has been very kind and attentive and is yet to me. He is not very well and has a leave absence in his pocket, but says he will not use it till this fight is over. He is doing the best he can for the Regiment now.

I will finish on some rebel paper; some that was got in Vicksburg and sold for $2.50 per quire. Writing would be a pretty dear business if we had that much to pay for such paper. I had a letter from Charlie Borland not long since and he told me about his appointment, prospects, etc. He receives $500.00 per year. He is going east to recruit his health before he enters upon his new duties.

Uncle Wm. Zoll after an <u>unexplained</u> silence of about three months broke loose again. Col. Stone arrived here last evening from Iowa. His health is much improved.

I have a volume of Plutarch's Lives with which I spend my leisure moments that I happen to have.

This is a beautiful country and were it not for war & its ravages, I would like to live here. It looks very desolate & deserted now. The citizens fled as we approached leaving in some cases pieces of furniture half way out of the doors. When we came here near this place, [there were] two large & splendid libraries one belonging to a Doctor & the other to a former <u>Governor.</u> The soldiers pillaged the houses, carrying off almost every thing movable, looking glasses, chairs, carpets, Dishes & every thing, books included. That is where my Plutarch came from.

The water we have here is very scarce and of an inferior quality. I hope we will not have to drink it long.

I am glad to hear that your prospects for a good crop are so flattering and that every thing at home is prospering so well.

Give my love to Ma, Allie, Clara and all the boys & tell them to write frequently.

Your Affectionate Son, George A. Remley

Saturday, August 29, 1863 — Memphis [Tennessee]
Howard,
At Memphis all right.
Start for New Orleans in an hour or two. My love to all.

Your Brother, Geo A Remley[2]

Wednesday, September 2, 1863 — Vicksburg, Mississippi
Dear Ma,
After a slow and tiresome trip down the river I have at last without accident, got back to Vicksburg. We arrived here yesterday about noon and I am now on the steamer Atlantic ready to start for New Orleans. The 22nd is now in the neighborhood of that place and by day after to-morrow I expect to be with them. When I get there I will write a long letter giving you an account of my trip and <u>things in general.</u>

My health has been very good since I left home, and I think I can stand another year's campaign equally as well if not better than I did last year's.

The weather, on my way down here was so cool, the greater part of the time that I almost regretted that I had not brought my over-coat with me. Yesterday was very pleasant and to-day is quite warm and I think by the time we get to New Orleans the weather will be warm enough to suit any one.

Capt. Cree who left Iowa City the day before we did is with us now. We over-took him at Cairo.

Yesterday I saw the wreck of the City of Madison, a boat that you will remember was blown up here two or three weeks ago. The explosion was caused by a percussion shell being carelessly let fall into the hold where they were loading ammunition.[3]

We will soon have 120 tons of the same material stored away in this boat, so I suppose we will have to live for a while over a small magazine.

The Atlantic is just up from New Orleans and while on the way the guerrillas made about a thousand bullet holes through her. I wish we had our rifles with us so that we could return the compliment if they undertake such a thing on our way down.

I hope you will let me hear from home <u>at least</u> once a week, bearing in mind that letters are liable to be lost in going so far. I will write often, but if from any cause you should not hear from [me] as frequently think you ought to, I hope you will not give your self any uneasiness or anxiety on my account.

My love to all, Mr. & Mrs. White included

Your Affectionate Son, George A Remley

P.S. Direct to Memphis & be sure to put 13th Army Corps in the direction and I will get the letters.

Friday, September 4, 1863 — Carrollton [Louisiana]
Dear Howard,
I have only time to write a few lines this time. We arrived at this place a few hours ago, just in time to find that the regiment had embarked on transports with ten days rations, for some point in the southern part of Texas. They landed at a place called Algiers opposite New Orleans, intend taking a railroad west for about 100 miles and then march across the country towards Galveston, Texas.

It is a kind of a <u>raid</u> and the sick, camp equipage, baggage, etc. were left at this place, where they had been camped about two weeks.

This place — Carrollton — is three miles north of New Orleans and is in fact nothing more than a continuation of that place. Now in regard to myself. In the first place, I am well. It is now about eleven o'clock at night and tomorrow morning we furloughed men & Cap't. Cree intend taking the six o'clock train for New Orleans and try to catch up with the Regiment. We take nothing with us except our guns & blankets and I don't know when I will have another opportunity of writing.

We are now in the 2nd Brigade, 1st Division 13th Army Corps. I want you to write often and direct your letters to Vicksburg. Lewis Yenter is well & gone with the regiment.

My love to all.

Your Aff Brother, Geo. A Remley

Tuesday, September 8, 1863 — Bayou Beauf, Louisiana
Dear Howard,
After many vexatious delays I had last night the satisfaction of overtaking the regiment in this out of the way part of the world. I have a great many things that I would like to tell you about what I have seen since I left home, but time, place and opportunity will not permit me to so as fully as I would if I could see you "face to face." I will try to give you some idea in regard to

our present location. Bayou Beauf — pronounced Beff — is a stream of water 3 or 4 hundred yards wide and about 12 feet deep at this point, connecting Red River, I believe, with the Gulf. The country is low and almost perfectly level and the current is so slow as to be almost imperceptible. We are seven miles from Brazar [Brashear] City and I don't know how far from the Gulf, but we are near enough to be within reach of tide water. The tide rises about inches here. Musketoes, gallinippers, crab fish, gars and alligators are some of the luxuries of this country.[4] Well, about 70 miles west of New Orleans where the rail road crosses bayou Beouf, I found the regiment camped — if lying on the ground without any tents can be called camping — the boys mostly looking much better than they did when I left Vicksburg and enjoying to the fullest extent of their capacities, the above mentioned luxuries.

As a temporary protection from the burning rays of the sun and the heavy dews, we have a shelter made of small poles and covered with sugar cane stalks and the broad leaves of the plant that the common palm leaf fans are made of. These leaves are sometimes four or five feet across. The weather is intensely hot in the day time and cool at night. The intensity of the heat is, however, greatly lessened by a refreshing breeze that comes the greater part of the time from the Gulf of Mexico. The principal objection to a campaign in the swamps of Louisiana is the scarcity and impurity of water. I hope it will be better in Texas.

I will now give you a few items concerning my trip down the river that may possibly interest you a little. I left Iowa City on the 6 o'clock train Tuesday the 25th, passed through Davenport, where I saw Charlie Johnson, about 9 in the evening and arrived at LaSalle by 2 o'clock in the morning of the 26th. Slept till late that morning on the platform of the Depot building, soldier fashion. At 2 o'clock that day we started for Cairo and running all night reached that place about 8 the next morning. A few minutes before I got on the cars at Iowa City, I was introduced to Mr. Humphrey, of Old Man's Creek, who immediately gave me an introduction to Mrs. Humphrey, who was on her way to Bloomington, Ills., at the same time consigning her to my care until she should reach her destination. Of course I accepted the charge and I had no reason to regret it for I found her a very intelligent, agreeable and sociable companion. At the end of her journey she seemed very grateful for my services and kindly invited me to visit her when I return again from the army. If it was possible, I would transfer the invitation to you & let Miss Elizabeth have the benefit of it.

After being delayed at Cairo, procuring transportation, etc. till after dark — the 27th — we started down the river on the "City Belle." The weather was very cool and we had a strong head wind, from the south, accompanied by considerable rain. This with the crowded state of the boat made that part of the trip very unpleasant. About daylight on the morning of the 29th we arrived at Memphis. Spent the day in looking at the town after having got our transportation down to Vicksburg, ready to start on the first boat. Memphis is a wealthy City and has a great many fine buildings.

I have often heard of music being made by steam but I never had the pleasure of hearing it before. The steamboat "Lady Jackson" has an organ on board in which steam takes the place of wind and when we left port this evening playing several well known tunes as she steamed down the river, the scene was one of the most beautiful & pleasing I ever witnessed. At a distance it would call to mind the dying swan and her fabled songs. Just as the sun rose on the 30th we left Memphis. Passed Helena just 10 hours after starting and spent all forenoon of the next day on a sand bar. The river is very low and this is a common occurrence in steam boating. We were at last pulled off by another boat and went on our way rejoicing. Passing Millikens Bend — an old camping ground of ours — Young's Point and Yazoo River we reached Vicksburg about noon on the 1st of Sept.[5] By night we had our business arranged and all of our things on board of the Atlantic — a splendid steamer — but the boat did not leave until the morning of the 3rd. We stopped about 2 hours at Natchez that evening and I had an opportunity of seeing the town. Part of the town is on the river bank and the other part on the top of a high perpendicular bluff. We passed Port Hudson during the night, which I regretted very much. We expected to be fired into by the guerillas, for they salute nearly every boat that passes in that manner, but were agreeably disappointed.[6] Late in the day on the 4th we arrived at Carrollton, where we learned that the regiment had just started on this expedition. We went to the camp of the regiment and on account of the unavoidable delay in drawing rations, and procuring transportation we did not start again until the morning of the 7th. We took the cars for New Orleans passed through that place and crossed over to Algiers on the opposite side of the river. After waiting till late in the afternoon we started for this place riding on top of freight cars loaded with mules. It seemed almost like returning home to get back to the regiment once more.

On my way down I wrote home from three different points: Memphis, Vicksburg and Carrollton. I got along very well with my box until I reached Carrollton when finding that I would have to leave it, I opened it and had the benefit of the contents as long as I remained, but when I left I gave the things to the sick & convalescent of our company. I might have sold the butter for .40 cents a pound. I left the butter, etc. belong[ing] to Hopwood & Gans with Gans who is at Carrollton.

Day after tomorrow morning we take up our line of march westward but where we are bound I don't know. We are now in the 2nd Brigade, 1st Division, 13th Army Corps, Department of the Gulf and you can direct your letters accordingly by way of New Orleans instead of Memphis.

Write as often as you can.

Give my love to Ma and all the rest of the family.

Your Affectionate Brother, George A Remley

Saturday, September 19, 1863 — Brashear City, Louisiana
Dear Howard,
Nearly a month has passed away since I left home for the land of Dixie and I have not yet had the slightest intelligence from any of you. It seems very strange that such should be the case; but I know that the distance is very great and the facilities for sending mail are extremely uncertain, hence, I suppose, I must not attach any blame to you for the non-arrival of letters, until your negligence is proved by their date.

The long time it takes a letter from home to reach one here is what I dislike more than any thing else in being so far away. I hope that you too will bear this in mind, remembering also that some of your letters may never reach their destination, and write frequently, the oftener the better. I have written four times since I left home — the last time was on the 8th — and would have written again sooner, but I have been waiting, daily, expecting to hear from you; but in this respect have been sadly disappointed. Since I returned to the army my health has been remarkably good. My furlough was not spent in vain and had the expense been four times as great, I would not regret that I availed myself of it. The health of the 22nd is better now than it has been at any time since its organization. This I think rather remarkable considering where we are and the kind of water we have to drink. After duly considering both sides of the question I have done what I intimated before I left home that I should probably do: that is join the company instead of returning to Division Head Quarters. The labor and hardships to be endured may be greater with the company but I had two good and sufficient reasons for re-joining it. 1st, Captain Cree wished me to do so. 2nd, I think it is decidedly better for my health and interests generally to be with the company. Company "F" has 36 men here with us now, all but three of whom are fit for duty. The sick and convalescent have been left at Carrollton or sent up the river.

We have not yet gone as far into the country from the river, as I supposed, when I wrote last, we would before this time. On the 10th we left our camp on bayou Beauf and marched about 12 miles — only seven by railroad — to this place — Brashear City — where we have been ever since. We are still camped on the same bayou that we were on when I wrote last, but here the tide rises higher and the water is more salty than where we were then. Porpoises are frequently seen plunging about in the bayou. They seem to be huge monsters ten or twelve feet long and five or six feet wide and are perfectly harmless.

Drills, inspections and reviews are the order of the day, "hard tack," pickled pork & the government bill of fare and a rubber blanket my only bed.

This will give you some idea of the kind of life we lead. Our bill of fare is generally lengthened considerably on private responsibility. Although guard and picket lines are numerous, private foraging parties can be seen, almost every evening, coming into camp heavily loaded with sweet potatoes, oranges, honey, chickens, etc. The potatoes are the largest of the kind I ever saw, some of them being about 18 inches long and four or five in diameter. They are very abundant in this country and form an important item in our living. Oranges are very plenty; the trees some places lining both sides of the roads and forming beautiful groves around the dwellings. They are nearly ripe, are pleasant to the taste and the doctors say are very wholesome. I wish I could send you a barrel or two of them. I know it would be quite a treat.

The weather for the past two weeks, has been quite warm and thunder showers very frequent until night before last we had a cool drizzly rain and since then the air has been cool and Autumn-like. Pure water is very scarce in this country — the best that can be got being cistern water, but unfortunately the cisterns are nearly all dry. The rebels it is said bored holes into them and let the water out when they evacuated this place. Well-water is not considered fit to drink here, but we have to use it from temporary camp wells, about 12 feet deep. Even cisterns cannot be made under ground, but are huge tubs, like that in the Oxford house, sitting on blocks at the corners of the houses.

There is a strong probability that we will start westward tomorrow or next day but exactly where or how far we will go, it is hard to tell — Galveston is said to be our destination. The 19th Army Corps started yesterday. When the regiment left New Orleans they started with 10 days rations and expected to be at Galveston by this time, but only why the programme was changed and we were allowed to remain so long at this place, I cannot tell, unless it was that the rebels made some demonstration, near here that demanded attention. The 28th Iowa is here and I was at their camp on a visit yesterday. I did not see Cousin John Remley, for he was left at Carrollton sick.

Lewis Yenter is well and looks better than he has done for a long time. I don't believe he has written a letter since I started home on furlough. No more furloughs, except to sick men are being granted now.

Do not forget to write often.

Give my love to Ma and all the family.

Your Affectionate Brother, George A Remley

Chapter Four

"Our Grand Expedition...into Texas"

— WINTER QUARTERS ON THE GULF COAST —

6 — Saturday, September 26, 1863 — Berwick City, Louisiana
Dear Ma,
Day before yesterday evening I was rejoiced by the appearance of a letter from home; it was written by Howard and dated Sept. 3rd. Thus you see, it takes about twenty days for a letter to reach me from Iowa! This is the sixth time I have written home since I left there and in order that you may know whether you receive all of my letters or not I will number them, placing the number at the top of the first page of each one. If you would do the same thing, I think it would be an improvement.

    My health continues good. I feel better and stronger than I did when I left home. Lewis Yenter and Logan and all the rest of the boys from our neighborhood are well and in good spirits. Since I wrote last we have moved our camp across the bayou — about two miles from the former camp — preparatory to our starting out on our grand expedition across the country into Texas. Plantations, with their large collection of buildings, negro quarters, sugar houses, barns, sheds, etc., frequently look like a small town and are named accordingly. The one on which we are camped at present is called Berwick City and is owned by a man who claims to be a British subject and enjoys British protection, but even that can not save the fences from the "soldier's ruthless hand." We are camped on a beautiful, grassy piece of ground and like the entire country it is perfectly level. The water that we have for drinking and cooking purposes is obtained from a stagnant pond that your cattle in Iowa would scarcely touch. The water is thick with mud, alive with frogs and creeping things and when boiled a green scum rises to the top. To make coffee we boil it and let it stand overnight to settle. I have not drank any of the water yet. I will give you a little insight into our domestic arrangements. Four of us — three sergeants and one corporal — live together and keep house on our own responsibility. Our present dwelling house is a <u>board</u> roof, supported by four stakes, with boards leaning up against it on three sides; thus forming a shelter about 8 feet square. Four rubber and two woolen blankets is the amount of bedding material we have with us. Bread, honey, sweet potatoes and coffee constitute breakfast. For dinner and supper the fare is the same, frequently substituting beef soup for the potatoes. This soup is made of corned beef (sometimes pork), rice, crackers and some of the above mentioned water, and is in reality very good. Oranges form the dessert, for each meal.

September 26, 1863–November 11, 1863

We are now having fine weather; the days warm and pleasant and the nights cool and very favorable for sleeping soundly. I hope this kind of weather will last until we get through the long march that is now before us. When the rainy season "sets in" traveling through such a low flat country will be very unpleasant. We sent to New Orleans a few days ago for our knapsacks and they have just been brought into camp. If mine has not been pillaged, I will have larger and more plenty of paper to write on next time.

This country is intersected in almost every direction by bayous. These bayous in this particular vicinity are called by the natives "the Bay"; but whether the bay has any <u>given</u> name or not I don't know. An evening scene on the bayou is very lively and interesting. Boats of almost every kind, from the small log canoe to the large ocean steam ship may be seen passing backward and forward over the water and the above is lined with "boys" plunging about in the buoyant water like so many porpoises. Spring boards, projecting far out over the water, are fixed on the bank and from these a continuous stream of "boys" pour headlong into the water.

Stationed along the bank may be seen numerous individuals with pole and line in hand patiently watching and waiting. These are the crab fishers and their "name is legion." The sea crab looks something like a craw-fish only more so. The flesh is tender and very delicately flavored. They require no preparation for the kettle, but are thrown into the boiling water while alive and kicking.

Brashear City is a very small place and deserves the name City about as much as Williamsburg does. The principal buildings are the Depot and a few houses inhabited mostly by negroes.

There are several regiments of Negro troops in this vicinity. I wish there were ten times as many. Some of the officers are black. They can beat the white shoulder straps in "putting on style."

Write to me as often as you can find time to do so, for you can think of many things to tell me that the boys forget to mention. Tell Pa to write; I like to get letters from him & wish he would write oftener. I suppose his school is nearly out.

My love to all of the family.

Your Affectionate Son, George A Remley

7 — Thursday, October 8, 1863 — Camp of the 22nd near New Iberia, Louisiana
Dear Pa,
A few days after I wrote my last letter we received marching orders and the fourth day from that found us at our present location, fifty miles from Brashear City. We arrived here on the 6th and expect to remain here only a few days. Since we started on the march I have had no opportunity of sending a letter back to Brashear City and am writing this now only to have it ready whenever a mail does happen to go out. I say <u>happen</u> because there is no regular way of conveying the mail to the terminus of the rail-road and it goes only when there is no necessity of sending there on business.

"OUR GRAND EXPEDITION...INTO TEXAS"

I have received but one letter since I left home and am of course very anxious to hear from you again. I hope you will write often and make all due allowances for mis-carriage and delays. Your school at Marengo is doubtless out before this time and you will now have more time to write than you formerly had.

My health is still very good. This rough kind of life agrees with me better than ever before. I never felt better and stronger than I do now and have fattened up so that you would hardly know me. The health of the regiment was never better than now. We are almost daily receiving accesssions to our number from the convalescent camp at Carrollton and by the return of the furloughed soldiers, fresh and vigorous, from the North.

We are just entering a rich and productive country, one that has never before been run over by a union army and as a consequence abounds in horses, cattles and all kinds of stock. It may truly be said of us that we live on the fat of the land. We do not draw full rations from the Government while on such a march as this, but whenever we think it necessary "special requisitions" are "sent in" and "heavy draws" made upon some neighboring plantation. The Government rations — hard crackers, bacon and coffee — increased by the fresh beef, mutton and pork, chickens, geese, sweet-potatoes, honey and molasses that are obtained as the proceeds of the said "special requisitions" when cooked as a soldier only knows how will make a dinner good enough for any one.

The rebels have but recently vacated this part of the country and only do so as our army advances. The 19th Army Corps and two Divisions of the 13th under the command of Major General Franklin from the Army of the Potomac form this expeditionary army. The 19th Army Corps has led the van[guard] thus far and has been gradually driving the enemy before them, having had several skirmishes already. The rebels were concentrating a force at New Iberia and were expected to make a stand there, but did not. We will follow on after them and are liable to have a brush with them at any time. Nearly all of the able-bodied negroes have been run off into Texas, but sugar and other kinds of property not so easily transported were necessarily left behind to the tender mercies of the Yankee soldiers. On our way here we camped one night on a large plantation belonging to a Frenchman who had at least 2000 hogsheads of sugar stored away in his sugar houses.[1] The negroes say that the rebels never expected us to come into this part of the country and thought everything was safe but they will find out that they were sadly mistaken. Millions of dollars worth of sugar is yet in the country and I have heard that measures are being taken to have it transported to New Orleans as fast as possible.

To any one who never saw anything of the kind there is something interesting to be seen in walking through a sugar making establishment. In one of these I saw 1025 hogsheads of sugar just as it was taken out of the evaporators and left to drain. The hogsheads were on a floor of loose boards and under the floor a large vat made to catch the molasses. In this one the molasses was about three feet deep.

September 26, 1863–November 11, 1863

Our route thus far has been up Bayou Teche, which though very narrow is navigable for steam boats. One came up with us loaded with provisions, ammunition, etc. It presented a rather strange appearance as, at times, it would suddenly emerge from the woods and seem to be walking on the land like a thing of life.

One night on our way here we were surprised by the appearance of the paymaster, about 2 o'clock A.M. when we were asleep. I received four months wages, 68.00 dollars, but have not yet sent any of it home. Adams express company has an agent here and some of the boys sent money home through the company, but as they will not hold themselves responsible for it considering the distance and risks to run, I thought it unsafe and concluded to wait until next week when the commissioner appointed to take the vote of the regiment will be here, and send it by him. I have heard, and hope to report is true, that Mr. Turner is the man. I hope all of the commissioners will be on hand promptly for I think we can do more towards putting down the rebellion that way than in a whole years campaign. We are ready to give a good account of ourselves.[2]

The weather is very good, cool and pleasant. I am very thankful for this as we are on the march without any tents or any kind of shelter besides the rude sheds that we construct of the flat rails that the fences are made of and boards torn off barns, etc. Before we left Berwick City we had a rain which lasted two or three days and almost completely drowned us out, but I managed to live through it without any serious damage. The nights are quite cool but there has been no frost yet. Most kinds of trees are as green as they were in mid-summer. I have seen some persimons and walnuts but they are not very plenty. Pecan nuts are abundant. They are very good when perfectly ripe and taste much like hickory nuts but when green they taste bitter like the white-hickory nuts you have in the yard. I believe I have mentioned the only kinds of wild fruits I have yet seen. Pea-nuts are cultivated and grow in the ground like potatoes.

When a camping ground is reached, no sooner are the arms stacked and ranks broken than the men rush for the nearest fences, barns, etc. yelling like so many savages. Whoever is quickest and gets the most boards before guards are put out is the best off. Fences, barns, negro quarters, etc. are torn down and carried to camp on short notice. It is with difficulty that guards can stop the work of demolition and if they happen to belong to eastern regiments it is almost impossible.

The 19th Army Corps is composed mostly of eastern troops and the 13th Army Corps of western boys and between them there is not a great deal of good feeling.

It is getting dark and I can not write much longer. I have just heard that Mr. Turner has arrived and stopped writing long enough to speak to him. He looks very well. A few minutes ago I was notified that a mail would leave for Brashear City tomorrow morning by a boat that came up this afternoon.

Lewis Yenter is well but does not write home often. Write soon and tell me all the <u>news:</u> how you are getting along, whether Milton and Allie have started to school or not and about your prospects generally.

Give my love to Ma, Clara, Sidney & Fred and the rest of the family.

Your Affectionate Son, George A Remley

P.S. Oct 9th 4 o'clock

Start on again this morning at 6 o'clock G A Remley

8 — Monday, October 12, 1863 — Camp near Vermillionville, Louisiana
Dear Pa,
I wrote you a letter on the 8th of this month and sent it by mail but this one I would send by Mr. Turner who will start for Iowa tomorrow of next day. Until today I had received but one letter from home since I left there, but to make up for past delinquencies, today I received two letters one from home written by Howard, Clara, Ma and yourself, dated Sept 20th and the other from Milton in Iowa City and also two papers, the "Republican" & "Christian Times."[3]

8 — Tuesday, October 13, 1863 — Camp near Vermillionville, Louisiana
Dear Pa,
This is election day and I fully intended to write you a long letter and send it by Mr. Turner, who starts early tomorrow morning but alas for human expectations! I was appointed clerk of the election and consequently have only time to write a short note. On the 8th, the day Mr. Turner arrived I wrote a letter and sent it by mail. I do not know when I will have another chance. The voting is nearly done and we have stopped for dinner and all afternoon and perhaps night I will be busy helping to count the votes. 294 votes have been cast, there will probably be 300 in all. Last year there were about 600.

My health is very good as Mr. Turner can tell you.

I send by him $65.00 which you get and put to some good use. If you want to obtain all the pay, bounty, etc. that was due Lycurgus you had better apply to W. C. Luce of Iowa City who will give you all necessary information. Nothing can be done about it here. The papers are all at Washington ready for you to obtain the money.

6 o'clock PM. Stopped work for supper and I write a few more lines. Stone has 221 majority, Tuttle getting only 36 votes. The others of the same stripe in proportion.[4] Charley Johnson arrived here day before yesterday. He looks very well & is in good spirits.

After a long dearth of letters I received quite a benefit day before yesterday in the shape of two letters one written by Howard, Clara, Ma, and yourself and the other by Milton in Iowa City and also two papers the "Republican" and "Christian Times."

The 22nd is stationed here, about a mile from the camp, of the Division, for the purpose of running a small steam mill and grinding corn, to save the transportation of hard crackers. I don't know when we will leave.

Write soon.

Your Affectionate Son, Geo A Remley

Wednesday, October 14, 1863 — Oxford, Iowa
Dear Bro Geo,
It has been sometime since any of us, at home, have written to you, and we have rec'd several from you, so I think you deserve one. We are glad to hear that your health has improved so much and that you enjoyed your furlough so much and so pleasantly.

First and foremost, you need not expect much of a letter this time for I am writing in the Sitting room & Pa is trying to rub up his "whistling faculties" and Ma & Clara are sewing and talking, etc. and I am not a soldier yet and can not write under every disadvantage.

We are well and very busy and will be so until the weather shuts down upon us. Mit's being away makes me have a great deal more to do than I had before and now since the frost has killed the prairie grass, we have had to keep the colts up.

Thursday morning, 5 Oclock, Oct 15/63

I could not stand it any longer last night, so I got at it early this morning. I went to the election the other day, the first that I was ever at in Oxford, but did not have the privilege of voting. Nearly every voter was there and more votes were cast against the <u>democracy</u> than ever before. Silas Emory, the disgusting pup, is a copperhead and attends every copperhead meeting any where near, calls himself a copperhead, is allways telling about the nigger coming here etc. and abusing the union men as abolitionist etc. The other day while threshing at the McCandelesses he said that Jeff Davis was as good a man as Lincoln. I asked him how, if he meant as good a union man. He said <u>any way</u>. Then I walked up to him and told him he was a lying scoundrel and if he said Davis or Lincoln before me again I would knock him over. That cooled him off considerably. The union leagues are flourishing and are a <u>little</u> more than people suppose.

Your Aff Bro, H M Remley

[Included with Howard's letter:]
My Dear Son,
I cannot get rid of the impression that we must get at least one letter a week from you. It is more important that we should hear from you than you should hear from us. You know we are not surrounded by danger as you are but have peace and plenty and getting along as well as we can under the circumstances.

It seems strange L. Yenter don't write home. I hope you will not neglect writing home weekly unless you are placed in circumstances you cannot. If prayers will avail any thing you will be preserved through this war.

Your Mother, J C Remley

9 — Monday, October 19, 1863 — Camp near Vermillionville, Louisiana
Dear Howard,
It has been nearly a week since I wrote my last letter home — which I sent by Mr. Turner — and though I do not know when there will be an opportunity of sending this, I will write now in order to be ready, for we never know when a mail is about to leave until a few minutes of the time it starts. This is the ninth time I have written home since I left there and have received in return only three letters — one from Howard written Sept 3rd, another from Howard, Clara, Ma & Pa dated Sept 20th, and one from Milton written the 26th — these are the only times I have heard a word from you. Was there no letters written between the 3rd and 20th of Sept? If not, you are sadly behind in your "weekly epistle" and I hope you will do better in [the] future for you must remember that I am equally as anxious to hear from you, as you are to hear from me. The distance and the uncertainty of the mails should be no excuse for <u>not</u> writing but should rather cause you to write more frequently.

In your next I would like for you to tell me whether you have received all that I have written up to the date of this. By Mr. Turner I have sent, a letter to Pa, which I requested him to put in the Post Office and also $65.00 in greenbacks, which I requested him to keep until Pa sends for it. I hope he will get home all right. The rebels burn so many boats on the river now that traveling is very dangerous.

The hot season is now past and we are enjoying clear, cool and pleasant weather, the most delightful I ever saw. This country certainly cannot be called unhealthy at this season of the year. I don't know how it will be when the rainy season comes on and the land is mostly cover[ed] with water.

My health still continues good; and the number of sick in the regiment is smaller than ever before. There are only two now in the Hospital; one of them, however, is John Klenk. He is not very sick, only a slight derangement of the liver.

The pale, sickly look that we all had while in the rear of Vicksburg has given way to a healthy, robust appearance. A stronger, and better looking set of men than the "Iowa boys" is no where to be found and the eastern troops always suffer by the comparison. General Banks and the eastern troops generally are most cordially hated by a majority of the 13th Army Corps. The causes of this state of feeling are various. When Banks review[ed] the 13th Army Corps at New Orleans, he at first was inclined to reject them on account of their ragged and war-worn appearance. This was a deep insult to the veterans of Vicksburg and hence the beginning of their dislike. Since we have been in this State rebel property has been uniformly guarded, stringent orders against "private foraging" have been issued and it was even carried so far as to authorize the (rebel) citizens of Vermillionville to "form into companies and arm themselves against all foraging and marauding parties white or black." This order gives men, who are inoffensive citizens while we are here but, according to the testimony of the negroes, rebel soldiers — uniform and all — as soon as we are gone, the privilege of shooting down a union soldier whenever found away from camp or in other words it establishes a band of bush-whackers and is diametrically opposite to our preconceived notions of the manner in which rebels and their property should be treated. Banks may be a good General and popular among his own men, but the 13th Army Corps heartily wish themselves back under Grant.

The 22nd is still detached from the Brigade and is occupying the same camp that we were when I wrote last. The mill that we were running then has been stopped and there is some talk of our moving tomorrow. Our next destination is supposed to be Opelousa a town 25 or 30 miles north of here. There was heavy cannonading heard in that direction the other day caused by our troops shelling the rebels out of a swamp.

Notwithstanding Gen'l Banks "stringent orders" and the numerous guards, patrols, pickets, etc. that result from said "orders" we are still living on the "fat of the land" and this will continue to be the case as long as there is anything to be had in the country, for the guards being soldiers and sympathetic creatures cannot always see things in the same light that Gen'l Banks does. In addition to what is obtained on private responsibility, foraging parties are sent out into the country every day or two with wagons to bring into camp corn, beef, potatoes, etc. which are issue[d] to the men in the same manner as the regular rations. Thus you see we have plenty to eat and nothing to do but guard our own camp and of course have as good times as it is possible for soldiers to enjoy.

There are more men in this vicinity, remaining as citizens, than in any part of Dixie I have yet been. They are mostly foreigners and claim foreign protection and pretend to be Union men, but the negroes say that they are mostly soldiers and assume [foreign] citizens[hip] only when only our troops are present. The inhabitants are mostly descendents of the old French and Spanish settlers and even yet the French language is spoken in many places almost exclusively by both black & white. There are, however, very few genuine black negroes here, but they are of all shaded between black & white and go by the name of Creoles. I have not time to write any more now for it is getting dark and I can't see the letters as I make them.

Oct 26th — Near Opelousa, Louisiana 8 o'clock PM
I have not yet had an opportunity of sending this letter back to New Orleans. I will therefore add a few lines.

Long before day-light on the morning of the 23rd I was awakened by the unwelcome intelligence that we had orders to march at 6 o'clock. A cold, drizzly rain that was falling at the time was the only thing that made the news unwelcome. This day's march was one of the most disagreeable I have yet experienced. All day the cold rain was driven into our faces by a strong wind from the North. The ground was slippery and muddy and in many places covered with water about six inches deep. This was Charley Johnson's first experience as a soldier.

At night when we stopped to camp everything looked blue I can tell you. We were all wet and cold with no fire, no tents nor any kind of shelter. Boards were soon found and fires started and shelters made and long before bed time I had my clothes dry and made myself comfortable and as much at home as possible under the circumstances.

Charley & I parched some pop corn, "pulled taffy" made from some nice sugar and then went to bed and slept as well as we ever did at home, at least I did. Thus it is with the soldier and by repeated experience he learns our thing to perfection — that is under whatever circumstances he may be placed — to adapt himself to them as much as possible and "let come what will" to make the best of it.

Early the morning of the 24th we were again on our way. The wind still blew cold from the North and as we had to march directly against it, though it had cleared off and the sun shone bright, we had by no means a pleasant time of it. About the middle of the afternoon we reached our present camp, three fourths of a mile from Opelousa. We had hardly got things fixed in camp before I was detailed to take a squad of men and guard a "foraging train" — going out into the country after corn — and did not get back to camp until nearly midnight. As there was danger of the train being attacked we had orders not to ride and you can guess we were moderately tired. There have been six or seven of our regiment taken by the rebels while they suffered in the same way.

Today I was out again with a forage train. We had fifteen wagons and got corn, sweet potatoes and dried corn-blades (fodder). No private "foraging" was allowed but that made no difference with me, for our mess has [an] abundance of everything on hand and did not want any more. We have orders to be ready to march to-morrow morning at seven o'clock. The general supposition is that we will go back to New Iberia; if so, I will have a chance to send this. The whole Division is going back and it is very probable that we will not come back to this part of the country again.

I forgot to state that our brigade escorted a train of 400 loaded wagons from Vermillionville to this place.

The 19th Army Corps passed through this place five days ago and is by this time some distance in the advance. They had a small fight near here and drove the rebel army, said to be fifteen thousand strong, before them. It may be possible that our Division is destined to go to Mobile instead of going to Texas. There is certainly no necessity of sending a large Division — containing four brigades — to New Iberia to guard a train back here, for the Rebels have no force in our rear except small guerilla parties.

September 26, 1863–November 11, 1863

Here I was interrupted by the announcement that some "sugar molasses" we had on the fire boiling was ready to "pull." At [it] we went, greased our plates to receive the molasses and after waiting a few minutes for the molasses to cool we were pulling away like fine fellows. As soon as we had pulled the "taffy" enough for it to become perfectly cold, it became un-pullable; hard as rock candy and brittle as glass, but it is decidedly the best thing of the kind I ever tasted. Four of the five us who were at it blistered our hands in the operation.

The "boys" nearly all are hearty and in fine spirits. John Klenk, Lewis Yenter, etc. are all well. I don't think Lewis Yenter has written a letter since about the 9th of August. If Mr. Yenter inquires about him, you can tell him that he is well and that the reason he does not hear from him probably is because he (Lewis) does not write.

New Iberia — Nov 1st — We are here again at New Iberia but how long we will remain or which way it is intended for us to go it is impossible to tell with any certainty, but circumstances seem to indicate that we will return to the Mississippi river and perhaps go to Chattanooga [Tennessee].

It does not make any material difference to me where we are, whether we go to Texas, Chattanooga or stay here. If we go to Texas, I may get to see some of my relations.[5] At any rate I would like to see the country and the only objection I have to going there is the difficulty of hearing from home. Though several mails have come to the regiment I have not received a letter since Mr. Turner was here, but I hope to get one before long as mail is expected to arrive nearly every day while we stay here.

There is a mail going out this afternoon at three o'clock. This will be the first chance I have had of sending a letter for more than 2 weeks. This place is on Bayou Teche and has a telegraph line established to New Orleans and is within twenty four hours communication with that place by steamboat to Brashe[a]r City and thence to New Orleans by railroad.

The bayou is very narrow, looks hardly wide enough for steamboats, but it is deep enough to make up for what it lacks in width. Water lilies and other aquatic plants in many places cover the entire surface of the water for miles and make it look like a long, narrow meadow. Although we are about 76 miles from the Gulf yet the country is so nearly level that the effect of the tide is very discernible, the backwater rising at least one foot.

The weather is not so uniformly good as it was a few weeks ago. Coming from Opelousa here we had to march two days in the rain. It is successively cold, warm and rainy, taking about a week to get once around.

I saw Cousin John Remley yesterday. He looks well and is at present detailed as a teamster.

A few days ago I had an opportunity of being permanently detailed as clerk for the Surgeon in Chief of the Division. The Surgeon in Chief Dr. Brashear was very anxious to have me, but I told him I would not go without Capt. Cree's consent and as he would not give it the matter dropped there. If I had been a private, there would have no trouble about it.

This is Sunday, but there is no quiet Sabbath rest for me. We have no Chaplain, no preaching nor any thing of the kind. The noise and confusion of camp is as great as ever and there is no outward circumstance to show that it is Sunday. Card playing, profanity and blasphemy seems to be on the increase in the regiment. Gambling has been carried on very extensively since we were paid off last time. I shall be glad when this cruel war is over and I will no longer be compelled to be familiar with such things.

Give my love to Ma, Pa, Clara, Sidney & Fred and remember me to all inquiring friends.

Your Affectionate Brother, George A. Remley

10 — Tuesday, November 10, 1863 — Berwick City, Louisiana
Dear Howard,
The date of my last letter home was Nov 1st and since then we have been marching so much that I did not have time to write and even if I could have written there has been no opportunity of sending letters away from camp. After an absence of more than a month we have got back to Berwick City again on the opposite side of the Bay from Brashe[a]r City.

We arrived here today and as there is a probability of leaving for Texas or some where else at any time, I write a few lines this evening and if we stay here a few days I will write again and tell you everything more in detail.

I am still enjoying excellent health and all of the neighbor boys are well except Lewis Logan who is complaining a little. We are having cool weather here just now, but have only had one slight frost.

I have not time to write any more by this mail but will try and give you a benefit tomorrow.

Give my love to Pa, Ma and all the rest of the family.

Your Affectionate Bro, Geo A Remley

11 — Wednesday, November 11, 1863 — Berwick City, Louisiana
Dear Pa and Ma,
After a long dearth of news from the North in general and home in particular, on the 5th of this month I was much rejoiced by the receipt of a grateful abundance of letters and papers and among them was one from home, dated Oct 14th, written by Howard and Ma. Enclosed within it was a "small memento" from you which was gratefully received. I hope that this will not be the last one but that every time a letter is written you will favor me with a similar memento and occasionally venture to send a large one on your own responsibility.[6] It had been nearly a month since I had heard a word from home and I assure you that I was glad to get such a good long letter. Ma says in her "contribution" that that was the third time a letter was written to me from home since I left there, that being the case I have received all that had been written up to that date, but none since. More than two months and a half passed away since I left home and I have heard from you only three times! I hope the obsolete custom of writing a "weekly epistle"

will be revived again, for you must remember that though you may have cause to suffer more anxiety on my account than I do for you, yet the soldier needs encouragement, needs to be cheered in the performance of his arduous duties and needs something to help him bear up under the trials and resist the temptations incident to a soldiers life. Nothing can do this more than kind, sympathetic, loving words from home, written by those we love most and best. If you wish to "give aid and comfort" to the soldiers in no way can you do it better, so far as my case is concerned, than by writing frequently, the oftener the better.

I will write at least once a week whenever we are situated so that letters can be sent North. Yesterday I wrote a short letter to Howard and my last before that was dated Nov 1st. I would have written sooner but for the reason that we have been marching nearly ever since and have had no chance to send out letters.

A little more than a month ago we left this place on what was supposed to be a grand expedition into Texas but it has proven to be nothing more than a feint, made for the purpose of drawing the rebel forces this way while a landing was being effected somewhere on the Gulf coast. This has been done and the 1st Division has returned to this place and is said to be under marching orders for Brownsville said to be on the Matagorda Bay or at the mouth of the Rio Grande where General Banks is said to have made a landing. Before this reaches you I may be treading the old battle ground of Palo Alto or some other "historic place." The nineteenth Army Corps, during this expedition, preceded us a few miles and though on its way back has not yet arrived here. The rebels did not make a stand but continually retreated as we advanced keeping up pretty sharp skirmishing in front most of the time. When we began to fall back the rebels followed us up, annoying us considerably. About twenty miles beyond Vermillionville — part of the 4th Division, 13th A. C. being in the rear, the rebel cavalry about 5,000 strong and the regiments of infantry made a dash on our rear killing 18, wounding 85 and taking 538 prisoners and one piece of artillery. The rebels suffered severely both in killed and prisoners, but I have not heard the numbers.

The rebels in this part of the country are nearly all mounted and are well acquainted with the country — know all of the roads, bayous, crossings, etc. — and under these circumstances it is almost impossible for infantry to cope successfully with them. During the entire expedition my health was excellent and spirits good and I enjoyed myself as well as I have done at any time since I entered the service. Our table was supplied with the best the country afforded and the meals got up after the most approved, modern style. Genuine Confederate money can be had for from 5 to 10 cents on a dollar from the negroes and when the orders against "foraging" were too strict we always made use of this expedient for obtaining whatever we considered necessary for home consumption. Confederate money though it does not pass as readily as "greenbacks" is nevertheless current among a certain class of the citizens. There are many citizens who remain at home and enjoy the protection of our army and yet cherish the most intense hatred towards the "Yankee soldiers" and everything that comes from the North; and are not at all backward about expressing it. Ex Governor Mouton, whose residence near Vermillionville our Regiment had the honor of furnishing guards for said, it was his misfortune to be born in the North. This shows something of the spirit that animates them.

If you will take the trouble to refer to a map, you can easily tell what route we took and how far we went into the country towards Texas. We passed through Franklin, New Iberia and St. Martinsville. This far road lay directly up Bayou Teche which has been cleared of all obstructions — wrecks of transports and rebel gunboats that the rebels were compelled to destroy about a year ago to prevent them from falling into our hands — as far as St. Martinsville. Then we left that Bayou and went in a south west direction as far as Vermillionville. Here we changed our course and went North to Opelousa, the entire distance from this place being about 120 miles. You must not think that we were "more than a month" marching this far and back for we did not in reality march half of the time. We had our knapsacks to carry, but as the blankets were hauled for us, they were not very heavy.

The weather during our expedition was variable; sometimes it was clear warm and pleasant and the roads dry and at other times cold and windy or wet, muddy and disagreeable. Sometimes we would lie down at night with a clear starry sky over us and before morning would be wakened by the rain coming down in torrents and find ourselves in pretty much the same condition as "drowned rats" are generally supposed to be. Frequently we have had to march all day through a cold, drowning rain, over a muddy, slippery road and stop at night tired, wet and hungry with no shelter, no fire, no place to sleep but the cold wet ground. Imagine yourself in such a condition and you can readily sympathize with us. If you had to go out on the prairie some cold rainy night and make yourself comfortable till morning with nothing more than two or three blankets, you would have some idea of what we very frequently have to endure.

We are now having some fine autumn like weather. The days are pleasant as could be desired — not too warm nor to cold — and the nights are cool — quite cool — with out frost however. We have had but one _very_ slight frost here yet and this is nearly the middle of November.

Most kinds of trees are yet green and grass, weeds, etc. yet look as if summer had not departed. A few days ago I saw apple and peach trees in bloom for the second time this season. Gardens are being made in many places. I have seen all kinds of garden vegetables — beans, peas, cabbage, etc. — growing finely and in all stages of growth. Okra becomes 10 or 12 feet high! Persons living here say that they have better tomatoes about Christmas than at any other time of the year.

Sometimes, however, it gets cold enough here to form icicles on the trees eighteen inches long. So the negroes say.

September 26, 1863–November 11, 1863

Directly opposite Brashe[a]r City on the shore of the Bay is a large mound — about 150 feet square and 20 feet high — on the top of which is a solitary tomb with no inscription whatever. This is said to be the resting place of a notorious pirate by the name of Berwick, who flourished a long time ago, from whom this place derived its name.

Gulf steamers come up the Atchafalaya Bay to Brashear City. There is one there now waiting to take the first Brigade on board.

The 22nd is considerably larger than it was a month ago. Furloughed men are returning and nearly all who were left at the convalescent camp at Carrollton have come back to the regiment.

The report about a battle having taken place near here that you speak of is without the slightest foundation.

I know you must feel lonesome sometimes, situated as you are with no one about the house but Ma, Howard and the little children and I wish I could be with you to do what I could towards cheering your lonely hours. I hope that time will soon come. Do not give yourself an undue anxiety on my account for the same God who watches over all of us is able to take care of me here as well as if I were nearer and I trust that he will do it.

We have no chaplain now and never had one that amounted to much. A good, working Chaplain would be of immense service to this regiment and I do not see why some one does not apply for the place.

Charley Johnson is well and seems to like soldiering very well. Lewis Yenter is well but I don't believe he ever writes home any more. He is a queer genius to say the least.

L. Logan is not very well but nothing serious is the matter.

It is reported that a landing has been made at Brownsville, the Rio Grande, and also at the Matagorda Bay, but which place we go to I don't know.

Give my love to Howard, Clara Sid & Fred & tell them to write me sometimes.

Your Affectionate Son, George A Remley

Chapter Five

"Into Texas Proper"

— MATAGORDA ISLAND —

Tuesday, December 8, 1863 — Port Vadalla [Cavallo], Texas[1]

As there has, as yet, been no opportunity of sending letters away I will add a few lines more to let you know where I am now.[2]

Well, we have at last got into Texas proper. Those barrier sand islands have been left behind and I have no particular desire ever to visit them again. We are now on the extremity of the peninsula that separates the main part of the Matagorda Bay from the Gulf [of Mexico] and though the character of the country is in many respects, much like that of the islands yet it is a decided improvement on them. The entrance of the Bay, which is between this point and Matagorda Island, is about a mile and a half wide and we were over two days trying to cross before we succeeded in doing it. On the evening of the 5th we left the camp that we occupied when I wrote the first part of this letter and moved to a place about two miles distant where the schooners that are constantly plying between the two shores usually land. The vessels were large enough to accommodate only one company at a time. Company "C" attempted to cross that evening but unfavorable winds and tide compelled them to return. The next day about noon company "F" and also Lt. Col. Graham, Major White and Adj't Davis embarked on one of the schooners and tried to effect a crossing but as none of us knew anything about managing such a craft we most signally failed. We poled and rowed and worked the sails and rudder against both wind & tide until night and were then forced to put back again to our old starting place. It was dark, by the time we reached it and raining and then I had to get my supper and find a place to sleep after that.

It was Sunday and that was the way I spent the evening. The next morning, the 7th, was perfectly calm and the sea smooth and we concluded to try it again. This time we succeeded but had to row all the way across with a pair of common oars.

You must not think that this was the only way of getting troops over that there was. The rest of the troops crossed in steamboats, but we being only a small detachment were left to work our way across as best we could. When we landed we joined the part of the regiment that was left at Berwick City. In the evening we had our tents issued to us and in a short time we had them up and <u>furnished.</u>

December 8, 1863–March 8, 1864

I gathered some grass to sleep on and had a very comfortable bed. That was the first time I have slept in a tent for a long time and it reminded me of old times, seemed almost like getting home again.

I think it quite probable that we will stay here several weeks, before starting on an expedition into the interior of the country, for the purpose of fully equipping and re-organizing the army.

General Fitz. Henry Warren, an Iowa man, is here and rumor says is to take command of our Division. I hope he will. Gen C. C. Washburne, who at present commands the corps, is the proprietor of Washburne's lumber yard in Iowa City.

I have not said anything about my health but not because it was not good. I never had better health. Charles Johnson is well and sends his respects to you. Lewis Logan was left at New Orleans sick so I can not tell how he is now. He was pretty sick when we left. L. Yenter & all the rest of the boys are well. Tell Howard that Lewis has received the letter he wrote on the 27th of Oct. Both "Republican" and "Christian Times" come to me regularly. Since I have been here I received both for Nov 4th. I supposed you are having some regular winter weather up in Iowa by this time. Here it is warm & pleasant; today it was quite warm. The Bay water is not too cool to bathe in. I hope you will write frequently as possible. Give my love to Ma, Howard, Clara, Sidney and Fred and believe me to be

Your Affectionate Son, George A Remley

15 — Monday, December 21, 1863 — Port Cavallo, Texas
Dear Pa,
After waiting and watching for a letter from home for a long time, in vain, I was at last, day before yesterday gratified by the arrival of one from you and Ma bearing the date of the date of Nov. 14th, which though more than a month old was nevertheless welcome for it brought news more than two weeks later than any I had yet received from home. I am very sorry that I am so situated that it takes so long to hear from you, but that cannot be helped so I suppose I must make the best of it. Yet I hope you will not allow two weeks to elapse between your letters any oftener than can be helped, at least not more than twice a month. The mail has left here but twice since we arrived in Texas and each time I sent a letter home, a long one, "No. 13," which started from here on the 7th of this month and the other was "No. 14," written on the 15th to Ma.[3]

Charley Johnson received a letter from home mailed the 25th of Nov. and the "Christian Times" of the 19th was brought to me by the last mail, this is the latest intelligence I have had from the North.

Nothing gives me so much pleasure as to hear that you — notwithstanding the war, hard times and scarcity of hands — have prospered in so great a degree and are now in a fair way of getting rid of all encumbrances and once more becoming a free man, in a pecuniary point of view. And if the "mite" that I have been or may be able to contribute shall do anything towards hastening that desired end I shall be very glad. I am glad that Alice and Milton are getting along so well in their studies. Alice must have improved her time well while she was at Marengo last Summer to be able to take a place in the Junior Class with Milton. I received a letter from Charles Borland a short time ago and he speaks very highly of Allie and says she is a "very good student."4

Now a few words in regard to myself. My health is as good as I could desire it to be. I feel thankful for this, for a man in ill health has not much of a chance in the Army. It will soon be a year and a half since I enlisted. The longer I am in the service the better I like it. I do not mean that I am perfectly satisfied with this kind of a life, but being placed in almost every variety of circumstances, I have learned to adapt myself to them and be cheerful and contented where ever I may be. I enjoy myself as much as it is possible for any one, similarly situated, to do. The knowledge of the fact that everything at home is in such a flourishing way contributes no little to my happiness.

Well, we are still camped here on the "end of the peninsula." There was a small town here once but it is said that the rebels destroyed it about a year ago. There are now only two houses to be seen. The place was called & is marked on the map as Port Cavallo, not Vadalla as I stated in a former letter. It is now called DeCrow's Point from the name of the man who owns and lives in one of the above-mentioned houses.5 I tell you this so that when you see either of these names you may know that they refer to the same place. We have been here since the 7th of this month and are likely to remain some time longer, but how long it is hard to tell. The rebels yet have possession of the upper end of Matagorda Bay. We are now at the entrance of the Bay and I believe that this point will be made the base of our future operations in to the interior of the State at least until Galveston is taken. Troops from New Orleans arrive here every few days. Quartermaster and Commissary stores, wagons, mules and all kinds of Army supplies are being unloaded in abundance.

This is a fortunate thing for us who are already here, for the past two weeks strong winds from the North and the rough sea have really interfered with the landing of supplies and rations were beginning to run rather short, but still we had plenty to eat. It has been uniformly the case that where the Government furnished us least we have lived the best.

Before we leave here the army will be reorganized and fitted out completely. Clothing, of which some of the men are very much in need of, is now in the harbor ready to be unloaded. Fortunately my wearing apparel is yet in good condition. My coat that I brought from home comes in play and is doing excellent service.

The monotony of camp life is relieved by occasional reviews, inspections etc. while the daily company and Battalion drills give us good appetites and keep our blood in circulation.

The weather here is far different from what you are having up in Iowa. We have had nothing colder than a hard frost down here yet while you, no

December 8, 1863–March 8, 1864

doubt have had some pretty severe weather by this time. They have here every now and then what the "natives" call "Northerners." It will be warm and pleasant — the wind probably blowing from the South, when all at once it will wheel around to the North and blow a perfect gale for a day and some times two, then it will gradually moderate, stay warm for a few days — perhaps a week or two and then the same thing will be enacted over.[6]

During the prevalence of these North winds, though it is not cold enough to freeze anything, both man & beast suffer intensely with cold: more than they would in a colder climate.

Sometimes rain accompanies a "Northerner" and then the suffering must be great. We have had none of the latter kind yet this winter. Today it is cloudy and raining a little but it is not cold. We have our tents now and could stand a pretty severe "northerner" with comparative comfort.

Wood is very scarce and all of our fuel for cooking has to be collected off of the beach. I have marched over sixty miles on Texas soil and sailed in sight of the coast nearly all the way from here to the mouth of the Rio Grande and have not yet seen a tree or even a shrub in the State. Some places along the shore there is considerable driftwood.

Extensive fortifications are being made at the upper end of Mustang Island, where we landed (opposite) and the place is garrisoned by the 20th Iowa & a negro regiment. Ft. Esparanzo, opposite here, is garrisoned by the 23rd Iowa. Fortifications will soon be commenced on this side of the channel.

I am glad the money I sent by Mr. Turner ($65.00) got home all right. If I had as good an opportunity, I would send you a little more. On the 14th we were paid off again. I received two months wages ($34.00) and would be glad if the greater part of it were at home, where it would do some good. I was looking over some accounts the other day and found out that on my trip home, from the time I left the regiment until I joined it again, I spent all together $40.65. The fare cost $19.70. My subsistence only $3.30. Clothing (Hat, shirt, boats & shoes), subscription for the Republican and incidental expenses amounted to $17.65, making in all the above named sum. Besides the expense of

The mail leaves immediately & I must break off

My love to all

Your Affectionate Son, George A Remley

16 — Wednesday, December 23, 1863 — Port Cavallo, Texas

Dear Ma,

Last Saturday I received the letter of Nov 14th written by you and Pa and yesterday evening one from Howard dated Nov 23rd came to hand. I suppose it is not necessary for me to say that I was glad to receive these letters for that word is not expressive enough to indicate my feelings. It had been a long time since I had heard a word from home and I was beginning to think it very strange, especially as letters for others came through in a short time that is without any unusual delay.

"INTO TEXAS PROPER"

Day before yesterday (the 21st) I wrote a letter to Pa which I was compelled to break off rather unceremoniously on account of the sudden departure of the mail, but this time I don't expect any such interruption, for the mail may not leave again for two weeks. Howard wrote me a good letter the last time giving many items of interest both in regard to home and neighborhood affairs. I like such letters and shall not complain no matter how often they come. Howard says that you and Pa were in Iowa City, partly to consult a Doctor about your finger. I am very sorry to hear that your finger is still stiff and sore, no better than it was when I was at home. I had intended to inquire about it a great many times; but every time I wrote I forgot it. I hoped, however, to hear that it was that it was getting better instead of remaining "about as it was."

Time flies! Thanksgiving day is past and Christmas is almost here. Day after tomorrow is Christmas Day. I can almost imagine that I can see you busy at work among the mince pies, doughnuts, cakes, suet pudding, chickens, turkey, and other "fixins" getting ready for a "big" Christmas Dinner. I have become so simple in my tastes and abstemious in my habits that these inventions of luxury never give me any troubles or concern and I hardly ever think of them, except when something like the present occasion calls them to mind.

I suppose the hard farm work is all done by this time: the corn all stored away, hogs disposed of, beef killed, sausage made and everything stowed snugly away in winter quarters. The long winter evenings are at hand when sleigh rides, spelling schools and social parties become the order of the day. Tell Howard he must improve the time and "shoot folly as she flies." When the "buck wheat cakes" are all eaten, supper is over, the dishes washed and you all gathered around the cheerful lamp in your room: reading, sewing, talking or <u>thinking:</u> let no thoughts of me, then, disturb your peace or interrupt your enjoyment, but, if you think of me at all remember that I am well, comfortably situated and not exposed to the inclemence of such a climate as that of Iowa and though far away and engaged in an uncertain warfare, yet there is One whose eye never sleeps and in whose power to protect distance can make no difference. Do not then give <u>yourself</u> any uneasiness on my account, for He will take care of me. I am willing to risk and abide the consequences.

As it may interest you I will try to give you an insight into <u>our</u> culinary department and domestic arrangements generally. By <u>our</u> I mean the mess of eight of us who occupy the same tent. Our tent, a Bell tent, is large enough to accommodate eight men very comfortably. Charley Johnson and I sleep to-gether. We have a good bed made of dry grass and, though it is on the "cold, damp" ground, I sleep as soundly as I ever did on a feather bed.

A cracker box set up on one edge makes a very good little table. A newspaper is the table cover. On the table are several books and papers also a choice collection of beautiful sea-shells. These look well and would be an ornament to any drawing room. I wish I had a chance to send some of them to you.

December 8, 1863–March 8, 1864

If you could take a peep at our "family circle" some evening after the candle is lit, you would see an interesting picture. One perhaps pouring over an old arithmetic, one completely absorbed in Byron, another reading an old letter over and over again and others interested in a paper or magazine or perhaps amusing themselves playing "checkers." We are decidedly a literary set. We have Byron's (complete) works and a book that treats of Ancient Mythology. Harpers and other magazines we borrow from Mrs. Harrison, the wife of the pilot of this harbor, now in the employ of the Government.

The Iowa City Republican and the Christian Times come to me pretty regularly, hardly ever missing a number, but they are usually about a month old when they get here and sometimes two numbers come at once. Nevertheless I prize them highly and would not willingly part with them. You may wonder whether there is any card playing in our tent. To show matters in their true light I am compeled to admit that there is. I am sorry that such is the case, but five of our number do so frequently play for amusement. They never gamble any. The remaining there never touch the cards and, I can speak for myself alone, I never feel any inclination to know anything about them.

Now for the culinary department: In the first place, the wood we burn is of a very poor quality and cooks, you know, can never succeed well without good wood. And all that we get is drift wood, generally pretty well soaked, gathered up on the beach. Our cooking utensils consist of, one camp kettle, a "dutch oven," and two frying pans, besides two small tin buckets, and in these we cook all of our "Grub." Two of us cook at a time, taking <u>day about</u>, so that each man's turn comes only once in four days. Charley & I have to be cooks tomorrow. I never cooked any until since I was at home. We always hired a cook before that, but now we find it more convenient and agreeable to do our own cooking. We do it up in style too. On our bill of fare is beef soup, bean soup and mutton soup thickened with rice or crackers, fried meat, roasted meat or boiled meat, crackers dry, stewed or fried, beans baked or boiled, sugar and coffee, also pepper, salt and vinegar.

Of meat we usually draw half pork (in brine) and half fresh meat. We draw plenty of soap and candles. Common soap will not do any good in salt water, but rather makes matters worse. We have a kind of soap made on purpose to use in salt water, called "salt water soap" issued to us since we have been on the Gulf. The coffee we get now is put up in small sacks containing eight pounds each and marked "Pure roasted and ground coffee." This substance is supposed to contain some of the coffee <u>element</u> and may for all I know to the contrary, but whether it does or not is a question that will admit of considerable discussion. If we want dried fruit, sugar or any thing <u>over and above</u> the regular rations it can be got, on an order from the captain, at the Commissary Department for very reasonable prices. About a week ago we were slightly curtailed in our provisions and we bought some coffee, sugar, crackers and candles. Coffee sells at 33, sugar 12, crackers 5 and candles, I believe, 25 cents per pound. There has not been a day, since I have been in the army that I did not have plenty to eat. Pa says that he thinks I must have been very hungry to eat crabs cooked in the way I "described." Tell him that that is the only way it is possible to cook them and that we did not eat them because we were hungry but for the novelty of the thing and because they were good, for the same reason that persons eat oysters.

I will now make a few miscellaneous remarks. In the first place I want to ask Howard why his letter was not mailed until 2nd of December when it was written Nov 23 and 24th? As it is both impossible and not desirable to keep up a separate correspondence with direct members of the family I want Howard to consider this letter as answering his. I write more frequently than you do and sometimes direct to one and sometimes to another, but all are written "pro bono publico." Howard says, that you had "received the two letters" I "sent by Mr. Turner." I sent only one which I requested him to mail. The money I wrapped in a piece of old paper and told him to keep until it was called for.

Rainy days have proved a great advantage to me, in one respect at least, for most of my letters from home "may be attributed" to them. I hope the long winter evening and stormy days will benefit me in the same way this winter.

I am glad to hear that the Freeman farm has been sold to some <u>one</u> who intends to make a permanent <u>settlement</u> and hope you will find the new comers, as Pa says a "nice family" and agreeable neighbors.

Have Davis got his new house finished or did he move into it as it was when I was there.

Judging from some of your former letters I had supposed that Miss Sarah McElfish was a little girl and in a letter to Howard, Nov 18th, I made some remarks & inquiries that were entirely superfluous had I the slightest idea that she was "Aunt Sally." I ask her pardon for making the mistake and acknowledge myself sold.

Howard say[s] that Creed will "go up" before long.[7] I wonder if he will take the Post <u>Mistress</u> along with him. I would like to know how they feel on the war question by this time. Does <u>she</u> talk as much treason as formerly; if so, ask Howard where his Union League is. Howard ask whether we have any "Union Leagues" in this army or not. Tell him that I belong to a "Union League." Its members number several hundred thousand and we do not allow as much treason to be expressed in our presence as you tolerate up there in Oxford.[8]

I hope that there will be no more volunteering done in Oxford. The time for that is past, long ago. I want the draft to come off and bring out some of the <u>rampant copperheads.</u> You seem to be "down on" soldiers marrying before the war is over.

What do you think of Lewis Gohen's marriage? <u>He</u> went home scarcely able to walk or talk and was married in a short time, I am glad to hear that he is getting better and hope he will soon be able to rejoin his company. Howard says that he has sent on for his discharge papers. That will not do

December 8, 1863–March 8, 1864

him any good; for he tried his best to get them before he left and did not succeed and it is not very probable that he will do any better now. It is generally considered that a man who is able to get married is well enough to be a soldier. Gohen will get himself into trouble if he is not careful. Lewis Logan is yet at New Orleans, sick in the Hospital. I heard from him the other day. He is getting better and if he can't get as much as he <u>wants</u> to eat, he will soon get well again. A few weeks ago there was some talk of him being discharged, but Capt. Cree would not sign the papers and so that was the end of it.

Lewis Yenter is well and looks about as well as he has at any time since he has been in the service. Tell Howard that he answered his letter punctually. He does not write very often. It seems such hard work, and he can't think of any thing to say, that I don't blame <u>him</u> so much.

All the rest of the boys from our neighborhood are well. The health of the regiment is very good and the "boys" generally look well. One man from company "A" died a few days ago.[9] This is the only death that has occurred in the regiment for a good while.

Christmas Day 1863
I wish you all a merry Christmas. I hope you will have a pleasant and happy time to day and enjoy yourselves as much as possible.

I can almost imagine that I can see Sidney and Freddy running about in their "copper-toed boots" with their eyes sparkling with <u>fun and frolic</u> and their tongues running, anxious to tell what "Santa Claus" put in their stockings last night and who owes them "Christmas Gifts" this morning. Tell them I think of them often and intend to write them a letter some of these days. Well, this is Christmas morning. And a bright and beautiful morning it is too. It is warm and pleasant, the air soft and balmy and the sky clear. A gentle breeze is blowing and even the low murmur of the ocean sounds soft and subdued this morning. All nature seems in harmony with the day.

The nights are glorious! It is impossible for me to describe them and do justice to the subject. Last night would have been a splendid time for a sleigh-ride if we had the snow. I have been talking about sending up North for some but I am afraid it would not last long. I wouldn't live in a country where it didn't snow. It does not seem natural to have warm weather in the Winter and no snow at all.

As my prospect for a Christmas Dinner is not very bright, I will feast with you today <u>in imagination</u> and see if that will answer as well as the reality. The power of imagination is said to be great. I instead put it to the test. Last Christmas we were in Salem, Mo. and I remember that many a wonder was expressed where we would be in a year from that time. Now we are away down here in Texas and the question very naturally arises, [w]here will we be next Christmas? The past year has been an eventful one in my life and I have passed through many scenes that I never wish to see repeated. What the coming year will bring forth none can tell, but I hope that before it shall have rolled around "this cruel war" will be "over" and peace reign instead of war and bloodshed. One thing we know, however, that whatever does happen all will be for the best. And I can cheerfully await the issue confident that all will come out right in the end.

I did not save a lock of Lycurgus' hair; I did not think about it but wish now that I had done it.

You requested me to send you a lock of my hair. I cheerfully do it. You will find it enclosed in this letter. Also a picture, which is the only "Christmas gift" I am able to send you. It is only a tolerable "picture": but I guess it docs pretty well considering the subject and the place it was taken in. I hope it will reach home without being defaced or smashed all to pieces.[10]

Yesterday I spent the whole day doing some writing for Capt. Cree. Was making out the "Pay and Muster Rolls" for these two months (Nov & Dec). Capt. Cree frequently gets me to do such work for him.

My duties as sergeant are not very laborious. I am not on duty much oftener than once a month and even then the duty is not severe. I could almost any time, on application, get a position as clerk at headquarters, but with the company I can content myself better and have better health. It is rather too confining at headquarters. Moreover there is some chance for promotion in the company but out of it none.

Our Sutler has just arrived from New Orleans with a large stock of goods. Every thing bought at a sutler's establishment has to be paid for at an extravagant rate. Butter that is old enough to be self-supporting sells at 50 cents per pound. Cheese almost able [to] walk at the same price. Small green apples three or four for a <u>quarter.</u> "Sour kraut" twenty cents per pound. Soda 50 cts @ pound. Ink 15 cts for a very small bottle. Writing paper 50 cts per quire and scarce at that, and other things in proportion.

It is said that the next time we move the sutlers will be placed in the advance of the entire army. The reason assigned is that no one is able to stand their <u>"charge."</u> I saw a quotation from Virgil the other day and I want Howard to let me know whether the translation is correct or not. It is this, "illi Lao-Coonta petunt," and may be found in the Aeneid Book 2nd 212 verse. The translation is <u>"they all went a coon hunting."</u>

I do not know how long we will stay here: but I <u>think</u> we will move soon. The 1st Brigade has gone to Indianola, across the Bay, 15 or 20 miles north west of here.

Dec 26th 9 o'clock PM Have been busy all day with the Pay & Muster Rolls and finished them. The long expected clothing has come at last and we will have a better looking group on dress parade after this.

There has been quite a change in the weather since yesterday morning. Today was warm and cloudy and raining a little. About dark the wind whirled round to the North and now a regular "Northerner" is literally "making things howl." It is growing colder fast.

I think it likely that there will be a chance to send this letter to New Orleans tomorrow.

Give my love to all. Good Night.

Your Affectionate Son, George A Remley

17 — Sunday, January 10, 1864 — Indianola, Texas
Dear Pa,
It is now a little more than two weeks since I wrote my last letter home and before this reaches you, I suppose you will be expecting one and wondering why I don't write. I expect to send this letter to New Orleans by Lieut. Smiley of Company "G" who starts home on the next boat that leaves here. When that will be depends somewhat upon the weather. On the 30th of Dec. I received Howard's letter started Dec. 2nd and finished the 5th and on the 7th of this month your letter dated Dec 12th came to hand.

Our communication here in Texas, with the outer world is imperfect and it is impossible for letters to come and go with any degree of certainty or regularity and if the weekly letter does not punctually, make it[s] appearance you must not blame me, but attribute the delinquency to the force of circumstances. We never hear any news here until it is about two months old and then by the time it reaches us it so exaggerated and twisted that we don't know what to believe. I almost feel as if we were in another world so seldom do we hear of any thing that transpires outside of our immediate vicinity. I hope this state of things will not last long, but I suppose there is no help for it as long as storms are so frequent. I used to think that the "sunny South" where cold winds never blow would be a grand country to live in, but a short sojourn in that land has wrought a great change in my feelings in this respect. Give me a country, like Iowa, where there is cold enough to make it pay a person to get used to it. Here one day it will be so warm that the "boys" go about with their coats off and perhaps the next day will be cold enough to "freeze the horns off a muley cow," so they say I have never witnessed that phenomenon, yet, but don't know how soon I may for it is pretty cold. Since I wrote last we have had five or six regular "northerners" following each other in quick succession and one, who has never had any experience in the matter, can form no adequate idea of the keenness with which the cold is felt. There is a pond, a short distance from here, which though the water is much more salty than that of the bay, has been frozen over several times. In cisterns the ice formed three or four inches thick. There has been no snow and very little rain. Today is cool cloudy and drizzly with a North wind. Howard says that the Saturday after Thanksgiving the mercury was down to -8° That was a cold day here. We were down at the end of St. Joseph's Island and had orders to march early that morning. When morning came the wind was blowing, the sand flying and Oh! but it was cold! We ran to the sand hills to get out of the wind as much as possible and cook our breakfast. Did not start as soon as we expected, on account of the storm, and we were just preparing to eat dinner when the bugle sounded to fall in and we had to leave the dinner uneaten and plod our way through the sand, against the cold North wind, the sand filling our eyes and blinding us worse than snow. It was pretty rough but we had to "grin and bear it." So much for the state of the weather.

I will now tell you where we are and how we came here. We are at Indianola on Matagorda Bay near the mouth of Lavaca River, twelve miles from Lavaca and fifteen from Port Cavallo where we were. Indianola was before the war a town of about eighteen hundred inhabitants a good proportion of whom were German. The town is composed of two parts about three miles apart called Old & New Indianola. The 11th Wis. is at Old Town which is as far as our pickets extend. Last Sunday, just a week ago to day, we left our camp at Port Cavallo and arrived here about dark that day. It was one of the cold rainy days and the bay being rough we could not make much head way against the wind. We left our tents behind and the prospect for comfortable quarters that night was not very bright. Vacant houses, however, supplied the deficiency and we have, since then, got along very well in that respect. Since we have been here we have drawn no rations except fresh beef, from the Quartermaster's Department. Fresh beef and corn bread has been our diet for the past week and it will be worse than that before another week unless a boat loaded with rations comes soon. Corn is very scarce and the only way of grinding, rather cracking, it is by means of hand mills and three or four small wind mills set up on posts about 12 feet high. Flour or wheat bread is not to be thought of. Our corn-bread we obtain from the citizens by paying twenty five cents for a cake six inches by ten and three fourths of an inch thick. It is made up with the bran in it somewhat after the manner of chicken feed, a little salt being added to give it a taste.

This luxurious living <u>might</u> tend to bring on the dyspepsia but our daily drills correct any such tendency. Though several times I have not known at one meal where the next one was to come from, I have never yet gone hungry.

We, <u>the right wing of the regiment,</u> are quartered in the City Hospital in the out skirts of town and are acting as a reserve picket force. We have a good comfortable room about ten by fifteen feet. Eleven of us occupy it, sleep on the floor and take up our beds in the day time. We have borrowed a small parlor stove and stick the pipe out the window and when the wind changes we change windows.

From our windows looking towards the country thousands of cattle can be seen roaming over the plain, but we are not allowed to go out and kill them on private responsibility.

Squads of rebel cavalry can be occasionally seen in the distance but they never venture very close, at least not often.

Yesterday evening, however, the 11th Wis. had some skirmishing, rebels were driven back. We were on dress parade at the time.

We are liable to have a fight any time. Gen'l Marmaduke with a force variously estimated from 1,500 to 15,000 is said to be some where in our vicinity.

December 8, 1863–March 8, 1864

There are several regiments in this Division enlisting in the Veteran Volunteers. Most of the 11th Wis., 33rd Ill., 8th & 18th Ind. have already re-enlisted. Those who re-enlist will obtain furloughs and go home. This will weaken the force here.

The entire force at this place is in command of Gen'l Fitz[-]Henry Warren.

The chaplaincy of the 22nd has been temporarily filled from the ranks. The present incumbent is a private from Co. "B," a whole-souled, zealous kind of a man, devoted to the good cause but he has the misfortune to be crazy about half the time. I wish we had a good working man for a Chaplain. He might do much good, but unless he <u>worked</u> more than Mr. Allender, the former Chaplain, he might as well be in Boston as here.

I am truly glad to know that you think of me at the throne of grace and remember me in your prayers. I feel grateful for your advice and have been trying ever since I have been in the service and, by the grace of God, do still intend to try to follow it. I have not yet done anything that I would be ashamed for the world to know. Christ in his prayer for his Disciples says "I pray not that thou shouldest take them out of the world; but that thou shouldest keep them from the evil" (John 17:15). Will not God yet protect those that put their trust in him?

My love to Ma & all the family.

Your Affectionate Son, George A Remley

18 — [c. January 10, 1864 – February 1, 1864] — Head Quarters 1st Division 13th A C, Office Provost Marshal — Indianola, Texas
Dear Pa,
On the 10th of this month I wrote you a letter and sent it to New Orleans by Lieut. Smiley of Co. "G" who was on his way home. With him I sent you $25.00 which he promised to leave with Mr. James Smith at Iowa City. I have not received any letters from home since the 7th, when yours mailed the 14th of Dec. came to hand. Yesterday a mail arrived here, but there was nothing at all for me. I have no doubt that the intervals between my letters are as long and perhaps longer, but you must remember that mail communication between the North and this part of the world are not perfectly established and that during the prevalence of the North winds, which are frequent this season of the year, it is almost impossible for vessels to land on any part of the Texas coast. I may have an opportunity of sending this away in a day or two or it may be a week before a boat leaves here.

You will infer from the heading of my letter that I am not with the company and after all I have said on the subject, will probably be surprised at it. Well, it is not my fault and I had no choice or anything to say in the matter. I will tell you how it happened. Last Saturday evening an orderly rode down to our quarters and asked me for my name, company and rank in full and the next day (Sunday) an order was sent down from Division Head Quarters requiring me to report there for duty, immediately. I had just returned from meeting at the Church so off I posted to H'd Q'rs and commenced my duties immediately. I do not know how Capt. Cree will like it as I have had no opportunity to talk with him on the subject; for when we left Decrow's Point, Capt. Cree being a member of Court Martial that was convened there remained behind and did not arrive here until yesterday.

Though at Division H'd Qrs I am not in exactly the place I had before. There I was in the Adjutant Gen'ls office, now in the Provost Marshal's. Captain J. R. Jackson, the Division Provost Marshal, is a pleasant and agreeable sort of a man and I think we will get along very well together. We have been very busy for a few days straightening up things and bringing system and order out of confusion for the former incumbent conducted the business in a loose way. I have been very busy all day and it is now about 11 o'clock PM and I am writing in a hurry and hope you will excuse the disconnection of the letter.

I like the place and business very well, better than in the Adj't Gen'ls office for there is more life and variety about it and after we get settled the confinement will not be so great.

When I have more time I will give you some of my experiences in the Provost Marshal's office. We have all kinds of persons, citizens and soldiers to deal with and sometimes the office is crowded with men, women & children after orders to draw or buy provisions from the Commissary Department. A large number of the citizens of this place are in destitute circumstances and are obliged to have rations furnished them by the Government or starve. With regard to my boarding, etc., I am much more pleasantly situated than I was before. I eat at Gen'l Benton's table and sleep here in the office. Gen'l Benton has command of the Division and has his Head Quarters in the Casimer House the largest and best Building in town.

Our office is a nice, cosy room with a cheerful fire burning in the grate; well furnished with chairs, tables, marble-top-bureau with looking glass, etc. When the rebel troops left this place a great many of the inhabitants went with them leaving every thing. Their houses and furniture are made use of by our troops. There being no timber in this vicinity fences, tables and even dwelling houses receive rough usage at the hand of the ruthless invaders. As long as troops are quartered here wood for cooking purposes will be a necessity — <u>military necessity</u> — even though the town should suffer somewhat by it.

My health still continues good and indeed there is very little sickness of any kind among the troops. Company "F" never was in a more healthy condition than now. Charley Johnson looks well and seems to enjoy himself hugely. I don't know how he will get along without me to "Bunk" with him; but suppose he has found some one else by this time. Lewis Yenter has got himself a new pair of shoes and a new suit of clothes and looks much better than he did. Lewis Logan has not rejoined us yet. I have not heard from him for a good while.

December 8, 1863–March 8, 1864

The 2nd Brigade — 22nd included — has moved to Old Town, in sight about three miles from here. A little over a week ago three or four hundred rebel cavalry advanced upon the town and we came very near having a fight. We were all out in line of battle ready to receive them. A battery of 4 pieces was brought to bear on them and they scattered like frightened sheep. About forty shells were thrown at them wounding several men & horses. They did us no damage. Rebels are in sight every day but they make no demonstration against us & run whenever we send out after them. Magruder not <u>Marmaduke</u> is in command & is said to have a pretty strong force. There is some probability that we will remain here a month or two. I will write again when the press of business is over. Write often as you can & believe me to be as ever your affectionate son, George A Remley

Jan 20th 1864
I find by the postmark of your letter that they are frequently detained several days, sometimes nearly a week at Oxford P.O. I wish you would inquire into the cause. My love to all.

Tuesday, February 2, 1864 — Hd Qrs 1st Div 13th A.C., Office Provost Marshal — Indianola, Texas
Dear Howard,
It is a little more than a week since I wrote to you last and I have been trying ever since to get a chance to write you a long letter but have not yet succeeded. I will not promise you a long one this time for it is now about 9 o'clock PM and getting later very fast. A large mail came in to day but there were no letters for me. The last I have had from home was one written by you on the 26th of Dec. Today the Republican of the 30th of Dec. & the 6th of January arrived and that is the latest intelligence of any kind I have had from Iowa.

In your last you say that you "don't know where I am"; "whether" I am "in Texas at all or not" and ask to be enlightened on the subject.

If you have not been satisfied on that point before this time, I will state for your special enlightenment that I <u>am</u> in Texas, in the town of Indianola, on the Matagorda Bay, in the southern part of Texas near the Gulf of Mexico. If you will take the trouble to consult any good map, you can tell very near where I am.

Well, in regard to myself I am at Division H'd Q'rs, have plenty to do, am in good health and spirits and am more pleasantly situated in all respects, except in regard to the mail, than I have ever been since I entered the service. How long this will continue is impossible to tell, but the prospect for continuance is good. While I think of it I want to mention one thing, in my last letter I told you to direct your letters to me at Div H'd Q'rs, but upon more mature deliberation I think that it would be better to direct as you have always done, for my stay here may be a month or it may be six months, yet while I remain here I am always sure of my letters by going to the Regiment after them and, as I have a horse to ride, that is not much trouble, but when I return to the company I will not be so fortunate and there would some difficulty in getting my letters until the direction could be changed again. So to avoid all risk of miscarriage you will please address me as with the company.

I think it very probable that we will remain here two or three months yet before any permanent advancement is made towards the interior. My reasons for thus thinking are: 1st The forces we have there is not sufficient to hold all important points and keep our line of communication open, should an advance be made. 2nd The soldiers are rapidly enlisting in the "Veteran Volunteer Service" and are allowed to go home on furlough, taking arms & equipment with them, which certainly does not indicate a speedy forward movement. The 33rd Ills. has already gone, the 8th and the 18th Ind. are nearly ready to go and will start soon, and the work of re-enlistment is rapidly progressing in several other regiments. The 11th Wis. the only regiment in our Brigade that has been in the service long enough has re-enlisted.

3rd The state of public feeling in Texas is such that the people need only to be encouraged and enlightened in regard to the true policy of the Government and then the work of the conquering the rebels in this State is three fourths done. It is therefore the avowed plan of the General commanding the forces here to use every possible means to awaken the minds of the people in the interior and set things before them in their true light. To accomplish this, orders, explanatory and conciliatory have been issued and copies of the President's proclamation printed and are designed to be distributed among the rebels in every way it can be done. I send you a sample of the orders.[11]

Deserters from the rebels frequently come inside of our lines and seem glad to get into a land where they can have plenty to eat. They take the oath of allegiance freely & report that many of their comrades would like to come if they could get away. When our troops first came to this place there were two companies of rebels here who had to be driven away by their own men at the point of the bayonet to keep them from coming over to us.

A woman & a little boy came 68 miles on horseback, alone, to procure something to eat for her children at home. She told a pretty hard story. Her Husband was conscripted and was obliged to leave his oxen hitched to the wagon in the road. A neighbor, father of the little boy, was shot down in his own door because he wouldn't go.

The population of Indianola (New & Old) is now 602 about two thirds of whom are in destitute circumstances and are furnished provisions by the Government. They are mostly families of rebel soldiers who are now with Magruder at the head of the peninsula above Matagorda.

The ladies personally entertain <u>Union</u> sentiments but occasionally we meet one who is very bitter against the Yankees. A certain young lady was asked to attend a party by one of our Officers. She was highly indignant. Her father's family had always been considered respectable people and she hoped that she would never disgrace them by going to a ball with a Yankee.

December 8, 1863–March 8, 1864

Before I enlisted I used to read about soldiers marrying for three years or during the war, but I never saw a practical illustration of it until I came here. There have been several cases of the kind among the soldiers here, the ceremony being performed by the Chaplain of the regiment or some commissioned officer, it does not make any difference to them, which.

Parties and balls are frequent and the usual amount of flirtation is carried on, but such things have no attractions for me, down here and at this time. Solomon says there is a time for every thing, this is a time for war. There will probably be time for other things hereafter.[12]

The weather is splendid, delightful. For two or three weeks in the last of December and first of January the weather was very disagreeable and not at all to my taste as you have doubtless discovered by a former letter, but excepting that "spell of weather" we have had nothing that comes up to my ideas of a winter in the South. I expected rain, sleet, mud, etc.

Six of our men while out scouting towards Lavaca a few days ago were captured by the rebs. and the rest sent into camp on the double quick. I was at Old Town yesterday and today too. Charley Johnson, Lewis Yenter, etc. are well. Lewis Logan is improving rapidly. Remember me kindly to Mr. Mars & all inquiring friends.[13]

My love to all.

Your Affectionate Brother, George A Remley

Sunday, February 14, 1864 — Hd Qrs 1st Division 13th A.C., Office Provost Marshal — Indianola, Texas
Dear Pa,
My last intelligence from home was your letter of January 16th which I received yesterday, a week ago. By the same mail I received one from Milton dated Jan. 9th. Several mails have come since then but there was nothing for me except The Christian Times and the Republican containing the Governor's Message and the proceedings of the "Board of Supervisors," nothing else of consequence.

Your letters are full of interest and are a source of great pleasure to me, coming, as they do, full of news from home and expressions of affection. Letters themselves are love-tokens from friends at home and you have no idea of the eagerness with which they are looked for when the mail arrives and the disappointment when the words "none for you" are heard. My health still continues good, never has been better at any time since I joined the army than it is at present. I weigh about thirty pounds more than I did when I was at home. The climate of Texas agrees with me so far, but I don't want to stay in this part of it till next August, then I am told there is sometimes a good deal of sickness and occasionally the yellow fever at the principal ports on the Gulf Coast, this one included. There is very little sickness among the troops. I never saw the men feel better and look better than they do now. It is just one month ago today since I came to Division H'd Q'rs. It seems to me but a short time, not much more than a week. Time flies. Oh, how rapidly! Just seventeen months ago tonight I sat in the cars, about to start forth upon a new and untried life, trying to look into the future and wondering how many of those then leaving friends and home would ever return again to see them. How many hearts that then beat high with hope and expectation have been stilled in death! How many more will be before "this cruel war is over" none can tell, time alone will reveal it.

Since I have been here it has seemed to me less like soldiering than ever before. It reminds me, frequently, of teaching school. I have a house to live in, sit on chairs, write on a table and eat meals that would not disgrace any table off of dishes, the genuine article not in plates and cups. No part of my living is soldier-like except the sleeping arrangements. I sleep on the floor with nothing between me and the soft side of a pine board but a rubber blanket. It would almost kill you to sleep that way a week wouldn't it? I wouldn't exchange it or this kind of weather for a feather bed. I know you will think "sour grapes any how" if you don't say it; but you must remember that I have become accustomed to it and like it.

My duties in the Provost Marshal's Office are not so onerous as they were for the first two weeks. I have become more accustomed to the business and can do all of the writing much easier and faster than at first. Attending to the wants of citizens give us more work than any thing else. At first we issued rations for only a few days at a time, but the last time we issued 'till the first day of next month and of course we are greatly relieved by it.

Capt. Jackson the former Provost Marshal has been superceded by Capt. Botsford, of the 16th Ohio, and now almost the whole care of the business devolves upon me. I give and sign passes, give orders for provisions to citizens, make details, take charge of prisoners and attend to the business generally occasionally referring the matter to the Provost Marshal.

Sutlers, trying to smuggle in whiskey along with their goods, give us considerable trouble; for Gen. [Napoleon] Dana's orders against it are very strict, and we have to watch them very closely or they will get some landed in spite of us.

About a week ago Gen'l Benton was ordered to report at St. Louis as a member of a Court Martial about to be convened there, and he will probably be gone two or three months.

General Fitz[-]Henry Warren now commands the Division. He is decidedly a military man in every respect, but one that is he has always managed to gain his celebrity somewhere else besides on the battle field. He is a strict disciplinarian and rules with firmness and decision. As to his personal appearance, he has a tall, commanding figure, a stately step — walks with military precision — and has a stern and rather forbidding, looking countenance. Generally goes about Head Quarters with a tooth pick in his mouth. (I expect if he could see what I am writing he would give me Fitz). He comes out on review in full Regulation uniform. Puts on all of the "style" the law will allow. The contrast between his dress and that of other Generals on such occasions is anything but to his advantage. Their's is modest, neat, tasteful and becoming while his, perhaps I'd better stop. Warren was Col. Stone's opponent for the nomination. By the way I saw Stone's Inaugural address the other day, thought it pretty good. You perhaps remember a Dr. Stone, who was about Iowa City some four or five years ago. Well he is here on Warren's staff with the rank of Captain — now acting as chief of staff — and is a pretty good match for him in height, being about 6 ft 8.[14]

Capt. Morseman is also on staff duty as Act. Ass't Inspector General of the Division. Nick Messenger, 2nd Lieut. is in com'd of the company (I).

It has been about a week since I was at "Old Town" to see the company. I saw them all to day, however, when the Regiment came down to escort the 11th Wis. to the boat, on its way home.

I believe arrangements are being made to get the whole army corps into the "Veteran Service" and the question is beginning to be agitated in the 22nd and I believe that within two weeks nine tenths of the Regiment would re-enlist if an opportunity were offered.

I think this willingness of the old soldiers to re-enlist must be very disheartening to the rebels. They will find that they can't tire us out.

I see in the paper that General McClernand is coming back again to his old Army Corps, the Veteran 13th. He will be greeted by three rousing cheers when he comes here; for the boys all like him and prefer him to any one we have yet been under, not withstanding his motto is "Onward," "Charge." They like him for that.[15]

The winter here is over and Spring is hastening on. The weather is dry, very dry and is as warm and pleasant as May in Iowa. Even this late hour of the night — about 11 o'clock — I am sitting here with my window open and flies and mosquitoes are humming and singing around my head, giving me a slight foreshadowing of what I may expect about June. It is very dry, cisterns are all empty and grass is unable to make a good start on this sandy soil without rain. I forgot to tell you that oysters are plenty here, so abundant that with very little trouble we can have as many as we can eat all the time. Well, I am coming to the end of my paper and with it to the end of my letter. I have only room to say. Give my love to Ma. Tell her I think of her often. My love to all the rest of the family your self included. Respects to Mr. Mars Good night

Your Affectionate Son, George A Remley

Tuesday, February 16, 1864 — H'd Q'rs 1st Division 13th AC,
Office Provost Marshal — Indianola, Texas
Dear Brother Howard,
The business of the day being over, about an hour before sun set I took a walk down to the Boat Landing, partly for the exercise and partly for some oysters. I give the men orders for the boats and permission to go for oysters and get in return as many as I can eat any time I want them, get them opened for me in the bargain. Well, when I got there one of the men got out

his oyster knife and just as he opened them I took them in charge and soon disposed of about two dozen of the largest oysters I ever saw. Happening to think of supper about that time I concluded I would stop because I did not want to spoil my appetite for that meal. Thanking the man who waited on me very kindly I returned, to H'd Q'rs and waiting about a half an hour supper was ready. That being dispatched I started for this office about two Blocks distant. On arriving at the door, the guard handing me something said "Clerk here is a letter somebody handed to me for you." Wasn't I glad? I was almost sure it was from home, for I had been expecting one for some time. I came up into the office, lit a candle, then some dry shingles into the grate and started a cheerful fire and then sat down by the table to read your letter of the 29th ult.

I believe this letter came through quicker than your letters usually do, being mailed the 30th January and arriving here the evening of the 16th of Feby. The contents of your letter were soon devoured and within less than a minute there after — concluding to answer it immediately while the spirit moved me — I was down at the table scratching away at this epistle, but with what success I can't tell yet; but think if the spirit moves in the right direction and doesn't fail me altogether I will get through all right. So much by way of Preface. Now for the letter. In the first place I want to ask you if there were only two letters written to me from home during the month of January? If so I suppose you are excusable on the ground that you did not have <u>time,</u> perhaps sleighing was good and <u>certain</u> individuals, not more than a thousand miles off, demanded your time and personal attention. Be that as it may, one thing is certain, I received only two letters from home written in January — one from Pa dated the 16th and this one of yours dated the 29th. I am very thankful, however, that I have been favored with even this many. You know that it is a failing of human nature to become so accustomed to receiving favors that they no longer excite emotions of gratitude, but are taken as a matter of course and demanded as a right if withheld.

Now I am greatly indebted to you for the interest you take in my welfare in this respect, and the great caution you use to prevent me from falling into a habit so deadening to one of the best feelings of the human breast — due appreciation of benefits. Were it not for such watchful care I would, doubtless, soon begin to look upon letters from home as due me as a right and murmur if they were not forthcoming at the proper time; but thanks to you; volens out nolens I am free from that.

I am glad the "likeness" arrived at home without any serious accident. I have as you say fattened up remarkably since I left home, but about being sunburnt, it is the varnish on the picture that makes it look dark. I am not sunburnt at all indeed, have no chance to under existing arrangements; neither was I when I had the picture taken I knew it was not a good one and considered a good while whether to send it or throw it away I concluded, however, to send it and let you throw it away if you didn't like it. I would

December 8, 1863–March 8, 1864

have had a photograph, in preference to an ambrotype, to send in a letter if it could have been obtained here.

It makes me shiver even to think of the snow and cold weather in Iowa. I know I could not stand it well if I was there now. When the war is over I will have to undergo a re-acclimation.

I "don't mind the weather" <u>here</u> "when the wind don't blow." The Iowa winds are bad enough but they "can't" compare with the wind here that comes sweeping down from the North as if it were trying to blow everything into the Gulf of Mexico. Take to night, for instance, we are having a "norther" now. The wind blows <u>very</u> hard. It moans, it whistles, shrieks, howls and wars around the house as if it were terribly out of humor about something and wanted to gain admittance into the Provost Marshal's Office and make known its complaint. I can hear enough of it where it is and prefer not attending to any such cases out of business hours. You think that facing the wind with the snow blowing in your eyes is pretty hard. Well it is but just imagine yourself marching all day against a wind so strong that you could hardly make any headway at all, with the drifting sand stinging your face filling your eyes so that you can hardly see <u>anything.</u> We have had to do this several times since we have been in Texas. How would you like that? Sand will not melt like snow. How would you like to lie down at night and awake in the morning to find yourself almost buried in sand?

While we were on Matagorda Island and at Decrow's Point, I did not eat a meal that I dared to shut my teeth tight together, on account of the sand.

Most of the dwelling houses here would not be fit to live in in Iowa, they are so open very few being plastered and none <u>underpinned.</u> This is one of the best houses in town, being well finish, plastered, painted, etc. It belongs to Some rebel General. I have forgotten his name. There is nothing of particular interest transpiring in Texas. The rebels are said to be concentrating a force to drive us out of the State, but I don't think there is any probability of their success.

We are fortifying this point and will hold it at all hazards. I think it probable that our Division will remain here as a garrison. Mobile is the center of Attraction just now & is the probable destination of most of the troops in the Dept. Today the 4th Div. is said to have been ordered away from Decrow's Point.

Your debating club must have <u>grand times</u> in the School House. Do you discuss political or war questions. I would like to be there <u>once</u> when the "right of peaceable secession" is called in question. It would be almost as good as a monkey show.

Lewis Gohen and several others for our company arrived here last Sunday, day before yesterday. There were 297 for the Division. I have not seen Gohen yet but am told that he looks well. He is not reported on Muster Rolls as a deserter. Suppose the man arrested him to get the Thirty Dollars.

I wrote a long letter to Pa Day before yesterday. My love to all.

Your Affectionate Brother, George A Remley

Fourth letter this month

Monday, February 22, 1864 — Hd Qrs 1st Div. 13th A.C.,
Office Provost Marshal — Indianola, Texas
Dear Pa,
Last Tuesday — nearly a week ago — Howard's letter mailed Jan 30th was received and answered immediately. Since then I have neither received any letters from home nor written any. A large mail came in this afternoon, but I have not had time to go to Old Town to see if there was anything for me.

It lacks just three days of being six months since I left home to re-join the regiment. It doesn't seem that long to me, the time has passed very rapidly. This is the twenty fourth letter I have written home during that time, averaging four per month. This, I think, is performing my part faithfully, considering that about one fourth of the time our communication with the North was almost entirely cut off and we were so situated that we could not have written if the "communication" had been open.

When I wrote last a "Norther" was just beginning to make itself "felt and feared." Well, that lasted three or four days and succeeded in making every body more or less disagreeable. It gave me a sever[e] cold as a "remembrance" and blackened the tips of the leaves on the trees. That is all the damage I have been able to discover. The last two days have been mild, clear & pleasant as any one could wish for.

Today while some of our scouts — mounted infantry — were out after cattle three or four miles from camp about thirty rebel cavalry made a dash on them and captured fourteen out of twenty, without much resistance. Two of our men were severely if not mortally wounded. Pursuit was immediately made, but the rebels having good horses were well on their way to Lavaca before our men reached the scene of <u>action.</u> The scouts were commanded by a man who has a commission as Captain of a company of Negro Cavalry — having only temporary charge of the scouts — but whose Co. is yet to be organized from negroes scattered, perhaps all over Texas. It is said that our brave Captain — having said commission in his pocket & fearing capture and the death sure to follow — fired one volley at the advance "rebs" and then beat a hasty retreat. This is the second time this has happened since we have been here & should be the last. Three wounded rebel horses and three guns were found by the pursuers.

Being by my self more, now than when I was with the Company, always surrounded by a crowd, I think a great deal more about you all at home, and often wonder what you are doing just at that time. And when Sunday comes I often wonder where the Sunday School lesson is & whether you think of one there. There is a Sabbath School here pretty well attended by the little folks of this place, but they are laboring under many difficulties and more than all are sadly in need of books of all kinds.

Yesterday, I went up to Old Town to see the boys and staid all day. Capt. Cree & all the boys were very friendly and seemed glad to have me visit them. I received while there a letter from Charles Borland, also the Republican & Christian Times. In the Republican I saw a notice of the marriage of Adj't O. B. Lee 22nd Iowa. The same mail that brought this brought the Commission as Adjutant for Samuel D. Pryce, Sergeant Major. That is quite a joke on "Adj't O. B. Lee" and I have no doubt he fully appreciates it. His rank is fifth sergeant, Company "A." The companies in the Reg. have recently been arranged according the rank of their captains. This places Co. "F" on the extreme left of the Regiment & hereafter we are to be the company of skirmishers. Nearly ever since I left, the Co. has been drilling in the "Skirmish Drill." I am sorry I was not with them but I guess when I do go back I can by hard study overtake them again. By the way Capt. Cree told me yesterday that he thought he would send for me in a few days, so I am expecting every day to be "relieved" of my "command" here. I am not very anxious about it either way. It doesn't make much difference where I am.

Fishing is the order of the day now. Co. "F" bought a s[e]ine and keep themselves well supplied with fish. This part of the Bay abounds with fish & oysters. Almost every day a crowd of men can be seen collected at some particular spot on the shore and looking out into the Bay three or four hundred yards the "Alterior" parts of about a dozen men can be seen, they evidently pulling away with might & main at something under the water. They are in two squads about 50 yds. apart and as they approach the shore the labor seems more difficult. Presently one, two, three & then a half dozen men leave the crowd on the Bank & go out to the assistance of those pulling in the net. As the water grows shallow the fishes become alarmed and leap out of the water sometimes traveling six feet or more in the air. Many of them thus escape. The shore is reached at last and from one peck to two or three bushels of fishes may be seen floundering about on the sand. (Fishes are measured by the bushel here). This is repeated several times & the s[e]ine is then transferred to some one else wanting Fish. Give my kind regards to Mr. Mars & all inquiring Friends. My love to Pa, Howard & all the little folks. Do not fail to write frequently.

Your Affectionate Son, George A Remley

Excuse mistakes as this was written in a hurry.

Feb 23rd I understand that a commissioned officer & four men are to be sent home from each regiment to take charge of drafted men. Capt. Botsford, Provo Marshal, is going from the 16th this week, so I will have a new man in his place. I don't know who it is to go from the 22nd.   GA Remley

Tuesday, March 8, 1864 — H'd Qrs 22nd Iowa Infty — Indianola, Texas
Dear Pa,
I have been so very busy for some time past that I have allowed a little more than a week to slip by since I wrote home last. I write a great deal oftener than I receive letters from home. In the month of January there were only two written to me and between the 29th of Jan and the 14th of Feby — the date of your last — I suppose there were none, at least I rec'd none.

Hence I have come to the conclusion that you write only once in two weeks. Yours of the 14th ult. came to hand day before yesterday evening. It was a long and interesting one and gave me much satisfaction, especially as it had been nearly three weeks since I had heard a word from home, Howard's letter of the 29th of Jan being the last. I am glad to hear that my money got home all right. There is a strong probability of our Reg't. being paid again in a few days. We will then get four months wages and I will have some more to send you.

You seem to be decidedly in favor of Texas, but I think if you were obliged to live in this part of it two or three years you would be glad to get back to Iowa again. If you supposed that the coast was wooded, you were very much mistaken. I have seen a great part of the coast between there and the mouth of the Rio Grande and have not yet seen the first native tree of any kind. You ask "if there are no trees what is the ground in its natural state covered with?" It is not covered at all except some places by a kind of wild grass and a low thorny bush that spreads and sometimes forms large thickets. This bush is called "Chapperrell."

So far as I have been able to learn the country for two or three miles along the coast is low, sandy and barren, beyond that is prairie, perfectly level, tolerably productive and frequently cultivated. Beyond the level prairie is the best part of Texas. It is a beautiful, rolling, country, with plenty of timber and fertile prairies, well watered and said to be very healthy. This is the part of Texas I would like to live in. I hope we will not be called away from here without making an expedition into the interior. Perhaps I will get to see a certain Uncle of mine who lives down here somewhere.[16] Do you know what part of the State he lives in, his county and Post Office address. I have forgotten it. It seems from what I can learn, that it is not the intention to invade Texas, from this point at least and that the occupation of this place was rather premature and done without the order of Gen'l Banks. Banks has ordered this town to be evacuated; but as we have very extensive earthwork fortifications here Gen'l Dana asked permission to hold the place. I have not yet heard what answer Gen'l Banks gave, but think it probable that under the circumstances he will let us remain here. I hope he will for this is a much more pleasant place than either DeCrow's Point or Matagorda Island. Another consideration is that we came here offering protection to Union men and pardon to repentant Rebels. All of the male citizens and some of the ladies — more than a hundred altogether — have taken the Oath of Allegiance and if we leave, all of these with their families will have to go with us; for the Rebels would hang every one of them and burn the town. I don't think it would be right to leave them to the tender mercies of the "rebs" after all that has been done. In war, however, "might is right." As it regards the Union sentiment in Texas as long as the Rebels have military possession of the country, it has no chance to develop itself. Deserters frequently come inside of our lines and they all report great dissatisfaction among the Rebel troops. Magruder is very watchful, lest his men will come over to us by companies and Regiments. He has to guard some of them as if they were prisoners. There is a company of rebel cavalry hovering about our lines all of the time and besides these there are no rebel troops of any consequence within forty miles of here. This company is well mounted and armed and they have several times captured some of our men. One man from our company was taken the last time. They are commanded by a man by the name of Capt. Levis, formerly from Cedar Co. Iowa. By the way Gen'l Magruder has a brother now living in Pleasant Valley, Johnson Co. Today a flag of truce was sent in by the enemy. I don't know what the object of it was. Two ladies were brought into the lines. I believe they wish to be sent North. Flags of truce have passed backward & forward several times.

Gen'l McClernand has taken command of the 13 A. C. again, to the great satisfaction of his entire command. About two hours ago we heard a salute fired at fort Esperanza supposed to be in honor of his arrival at that place as he was expected here daily. Just now while I am writing, the cannon are firing down at New Indianola. The natural conclusion is, therefore, that he has just arrived here. Tomorrow or next day we may expect another "Grand review and Inspection." I am glad that I am exempt from that this time.

You were right in supposing that I had changed my residence by the time your letter reached me.

I have changed my base of operations to something more substantial and permanent than I had. I have returned to the Regiment and expect to remain with it. Do not belong to company "F" any more. Have been appointed Sergeant Major, 22nd Iowa [and] Samuel D. Pryce promoted to Adjutant. I have been acting in that capacity ever since the first of this month. A Serg't Major is an assistant Adjutant and you can guess pretty well what the duties are — is the 1st Serg't in the Regiment & first on the non-commissioned Staff — receives twenty one dollars per month. Does not have a gun or knapsack to carry and has as good a time generally as any one could expect in the Army.

Day after tomorrow is the time fixed for the famous draft that has been hanging over the heads of Iowans for so long a time to come off. I suppose "copperheads" up there are beginning to get a little uneasy by this time. I hope there will be no failure this time. I want to see such men as some I could mention not a thousand miles from Iowa City, made to do something towards putting down the Rebellion. The Draft is a powerful thing both morally & physically. The one influence it exerts before the other at the time it takes place. Am glad to see its effect on Silas Ewing. Would like to be there on the 10th inst. & see how it makes that vile reptile — the copperhead — squirm.[17] I am glad to hear that Milton & Allie are doing so well at the University and that they have the privilege of remaining until the end of the term. Allie will soon be able to take charge of a school if she feels so inclined. I received a letter from Milton a few days ago. According to his account he is doing remarkably well. Charlie Borland speaks well of both Milton & Allie & says they are good students. I suppose you are beginning to prepare for the Spring's work on the farm; sharpening the plows & getting harness, hoes etc. in working order.

Have you any of the old snow-drifts left that you spoke about in a former letter.

Charlie Johnson, Lewis Logan, Yenter, etc. are all well.

I will write again in a few days. A few postage stamps would be thankfully received for it is impossible to get them here.

Your Affectionate Son, Geo A Remley

Chapter Six

"To Bid His <u>Dulcina</u> Farewell"

— LEAVING TEXAS —

Thursday, March 24, 1864 — Hd Qrs 22nd Iowa — Matagorda Island, Texas
Dear Pa,
Day-before-yesterday a large mail arrived in camp direct from New Orleans and I had the satisfaction of receiving two letters from home: one was a fragmentary epistle, but none the worse on that account, dated Feby 28th and written by Ma, Howard and Clara and the other was a good long one from you written on the 7th of this month. I was very glad to receive such a large stock of news from home at one time. It was all the more welcome and better appreciated on account of the long time since I had heard from you before. I am glad to learn that Milton and Allie are doing so well at the University and that everything goes along so smoothly and harmoniously at home and throughout the neighborhood.

Nothing gives me more pleasure than to know that notwithstanding the cruel war that is raging and the ruin and desolation that has visited so many households, in our once peaceful land, you are happy and prosperous at home and enjoy comparative freedom from the evils and horrors of war. You at the North ought to be truly thankful that the scene of strife has never been transferred to your part of the country. Though as a people you have made and are still making great sacrifices for Freedom's holy cause, yet you felt the effects of such a war as this in a very slight degree and know comparatively little of the misery and suffering, caused by the presence of an invading army, both upon friends and foes. When we first went to Indianola many of the citizens who were truly loyal were glad to see us come and welcomed us there as friends. They are mostly foreigners and believing that we would permanently occupy the place were anxious to take the oath of Allegiance and would frequently come to us speaking in their broken language, and say "we want to swear" "we want to come back into the old Union." We promised them protection and they were glad; we fed the destitute, both friends and foes, and they thought the Government gracious and forgiving; we took their horses, killed their cattle, burned their fences & buildings, appropriated their property whenever it was wanted, but at this they began to complain a little; we quieted their fears, pleading "military necessity" and assuring them that they would be fully remunerated for every loss and they were satisfied; but, when we announced our intention of evacuating the town, they felt that they had been duped, imposed upon, <u>outraged</u>

"TO BID HIS DULCINA FAREWELL"

and some expressed themselves in no very measured terms on the subject. And when we left there on the thirteenth of this month I have no doubt some of them at least — Union men — were glad to see us go and cursed the day the Yankees came. Some of those who had taken the "oath" having the fear of the rebels before their eyes, preferred to come with us rather than trust themselves again to the tender mercies of the rebels. I will relate some of the incidents connected with our departure. First as I intimated in a former letter a majority of the inhabitants are females — many of them girls and young ladies of an interesting? age — and as a matter of consequence many of the boys formed <u>temporary</u> attachments and some of them were even married. We received orders to start on the morning of the 9th but, as a "norther" which was raging at the time had blown two of the transports, that were being loaded at the wharf, so hard aground that they could not be got off until the wind fell, the order was countermanded. We had already started and proceeded about a mile and a half before the countermanding order reached us. The wind was very high and sand & shell dust were flying through the air like snow, almost blinding us so we were not sorry to turn back. It was amusing as we started to see here & there a soldier slipping into a house along the road to bid his <u>dulcina</u> farewell. Some were standing in their doors crying as if they had lost their last friend. The citizens who intended leaving with us had their household goods & their families packed on wagons and were following. Those who left their families behind were marching along like soldiers carrying their bundles. It was an odd-looking procession, such a one as is not very often seen.

    Between here and Indianola there are two Bayous or rather arms of the Bay, very deep and four or five hundred yards wide. These are the only water to be crossed coming here. Everything being ready on the morning of the thirteenth (early) we again took up our line of march and the same parting scenes were again enacted. We marched down the beach and arrived without accident at the first Bayou. The crossing was effected by means of a ferry boat drawn backwards and forwards between two ropes stretched across. The crossing was necessarily slow & thinking our turn to cross would not come that night, the regiment had gone into camp and the little shelter tents — the other tents and baggage, mine included had been ferried over early in the day — were soon pitched, supper got and everything made ready for a nights sleep. We had hardly gone to sleep when the order came to fall in and within five minutes there after everything was packed up and the regiment again on the move. About a mile & a half from the first is the second Bayou and here we had to wait again. We all stretched ourselves upon the sand, some with and some without blankets. Presently a cold rain began to fall accompanied by a chilling wind and there we lay obliged to take it the best way we could. Very few of the shelter tents had been put up this time and after it began to rain very few of the boys thought it worth while to trouble themselves about it then. This state of affairs continued till daylight, when the rain still falling, we crossed the second Bayou to Matagorda Island. At this place, while part of the 69th Indiana were crossing, the boat being loaded too heavy, sunk and about twenty five — I do not know the number precisely — of that Regiment were drowned. They had their knapsacks & cartridge boxes on and of course went straight to the bottom.

Our present camp is about four miles from Fort Esperanza or the extreme upper end of the Island. The Island here is ten miles wide and the troops are camped in line of Battle across it. A line of Forts and rifle pits were laid out entirely across the Island and for the past week the regiment has been working on them and our part is nearly done. One regiment is stationed about ten miles down the Island doing picket duty and it is said that that regiment is to return in a few days and the 22nd will go down to take its place for ten days or two weeks.

There are plenty of cattle, sheep & deer there, I believe I would as soon stay there two weeks as not.

The weather at present is <u>splendid</u> warm, clear & pleasant, but I do not expect it to last very long. There is something peculiar about the weather here. It will be clear warm and pleasant for a few days and then the wind will suddenly change from the South to the North, bringing clouds frequently a cold chilly rain and what we call a "Norther." In a day or two it will moderate again and then the same thing is repeated. The peculiarity is the sudden change of the wind & the difference in the temperature. I have known the wind to be blowing strong from the South and in less then fifteen minutes it would be blowing a perfect hurricane from the North. An instance of this occurred the other night and our tent came very near taking to itself wings and leaving us in a drenching rain, but by strong exertions on our part this was prevented. As it was we were forced to get up two or three hours before daylight. My sheet is full but if I have time before the mail goes out I will write more. My love to all.

Your Affectionate Son, George A Remley

I see by the papers that certain kinds of articles of clothing may be sent by mail to the soldiers by paying eight cents for every four ounces or two cents an ounce. Tell Ma that I would be glad if she could make it convenient to send me a silk handkerchief, <u>if not contrary to law,</u> or two linen handkerchiefs if she can not send the other one, and two pairs of good, substantial socks. The last, especially would be very acceptable for the socks we get from the Government are hardly worth putting on and it is impossible to get them from any other source. Those I brought from home are about used up. Moreover anything of the kind coming from home will be doubly prized not only on account of real worth but because it is from <u>home.</u> There is some probability of the paymaster visiting us before long. A great many of us will feel relieved when he comes for not one man out of ten has a cent. The pay of the officers has been stopped for nearly ten months and they managed to get along only by borrowing from the men; but as it has been over four months since any of us were paid and we are all in rather straightened circumstances. But it does not make so much difference with the men as with the officers for they (officers) have to buy provisions while the Gov. feeds the men. The sutler gets a great deal of money from the Regt. Prices are exorbitant.   Geo A Remley

March 25th 1864
Dear Pa,
As the mail has not yet gone out I will make a slight extension to my letter of yesterday. This may not be very connected, but will contain a few miscellaneous items that may possibly be of interest to you. I will in the first place give you a little insight into my domestic arrangements. The Adjutant and I have a tent to gether which serves both as an office and a sleeping apartment. It is what is called a wall tent — a tent about ten feet square, shaped like a house, being about four feet from the ground to the square or what corresponds to the eve of a house. We have a good board floor in our tent a certain corner of Which answers the purpose of a bedstead. The furniture consists of a small table, a stool, etc. a large box or chest containing Regimental Books, Blanks, etc. This is also used as a bench to sit on. It is my seat at the present time. The only remaining piece of furniture is a regular army "field desk," having a double lid arranged so that when open it formed a nice table to write on. There is also a set of "pigeon holes," containing files of orders, various kinds of papers, etc., etc. which fits in the "desk" when packed for a march, but is kept on top at all other times. The whole desk sits on a stool to make it high enough. This I believe completes the furniture, except a small looking-glass which hangs against one of the tents poles. Suspended from the ridge pole of the tent we have another pole upon which to hang articles of clothing, towels, canteens, etc. At nine or ten o'clock at night we spread our bed, consisting of three Blankets, two rubbers and three half shelter tents, on the afore-mentioned part of the floor and on this we sleep as soundly as if on a feather bed until wakened by the sound of the bugle, a little after daylight next morning.

Then we get up and wash by pouring water on each other's hands from a canteen. We have a wash basin. The floor is then swept with a broom made of coarse grass, which I forgot to mention, the bed rolled up and by that time breakfast is ready.

Our mess comprises four — Capt. Humphrey, two Lieuts. & another man besides the Adjut. & myself. A small mess box forms the table and a stick of wood & sometimes nothing more than the ground are the only chairs.

This much concerning domestic affairs.

Yesterday and today there was considerable excitement in camp on the subject of furloughs. Several of the Captains of our Regt. thought they would try to get some of their men furloughed — so they made out a lot of furloughs, three or four from each company — and sent them up to Brigade Hd Qrs to get them approved and forwarded. Genl Warren approved some of the first that went up and sent them on, but finding that "still they came" he wrote on them "returned & disapproved" and sent them back. I suppose that will end the matter. Some of the boys had their expectations raised and were of course disappointed. The furlough if at all would be for sixty days.

You have frequently heard of the tarantula I suppose. They are plenty down here and ugly looking customers. I saw one the other day and I assure you that I don't desire a very intimate acquaintance with any thing of the kind. They look like a huge, fat spider from one to three or four inches across, covered with short, brownish hairs. They have teeth, shaped very much like a gopher's claws, and with these they bite savagely. Their bite is said to be very poisonous.

Snakes, lizards and many such creeping things are numerous. There is one the boys call a horned toad, but it does not resemble a toad in the least. It does not hop but runs along the ground. It is five or six inches long, the body three or four inches across has a tail and legs resembling those of the lizzard. Its peculiarity is several sharp horns, like thorns, on the top of the head and the rough jagged appearance generally. It is tame & perfectly harmless.

You spoke in a former letter of the negroes in this part of Texas. There are no negroes here and were none at Indianola except those following the army. The health of the troops here is very good. I believe there are only four from our Regt. in the Hospital. Lewis Yenter, Logan, Gohen, Charley Johnson and all those from your vicinity are well. Lewis Yenter stands a soldier's life very well and seems to be doing well. Charley Johnson looks very well is lively & cheerful and makes an excellent soldier. Company F has received several recruits lately and has more on the way. I do hope the draft will take place in Johnson County and some of the conscripts sent to fill up the Regiment. Lt. Col. Graham and four sergeants have gone to Iowa to "conduct recruits to the Regt" but if they do not draft I don't think many recruits can be got for <u>this</u> Regt. If the draft takes place I know Col. Stone will have the 22nd filled up. Maj. White has also gone home on a leave of Absence and the Regt is now commanded by Maj. [Leonard] Houston of the 23rd Iowa.

We are now in the 1st Brigade 1st Div 13th Army Corps — please don't forget to direct accordingly. Not long since there was a great mania for commission in the "Corps d'Afrique" in the 22nd. Two from Company "F" are now in New Orleans to undergo an examination. One them is Wm. D. Hopwood whose brother recently arrived as a recruit for Co. "F."

It is now past "taps" and I must wind up pretty soon.

Tell Clara that I was very glad to get a note from her and that she must try to write me a letter before long. Sidney & Freddie can help her if she thinks it is too much to undertake alone.

I am glad you are going to have some new neighbors. Let them come the more the better.

Give my respects to Mr. & Mrs. Davis. Remember me kindly to Mr. Mars, Mr. & Mrs. Price and all inquiring friends. Tell Howard he must not forget to write to me occasionally at least.

"TO BID HIS DULCINA FAREWELL"

Tell Sidney & Freddie that I think they have been getting along finely at school & will soon be able to write me a letter.

Give my love to Ma Howard & the little folks reserving a pretty good share for yourself.

Your Affectionate Son, George A Remley

Tuesday, April 5, 1864 — Head Qrs 22nd Iowa — Matagorda Island, Texas
Dear Bro. Howard,
I have been very busy for the last ten days and consequently have not had time to write as soon as I would like to have done. The end of the month and quarter coming together this time there were a great many more "reports" and "returns" etc. to be made out than usual, but, as the rush of business is over for some time, I will now have an opportunity to make up for lost time and average at least one letter per week.

My last was written on the 24th of last month and was addressed to Pa. On the 22nd I received two letters from home dated respectively Feby 28th and March 7th and since then we have had but one very small mail, which did not bring anything for me, consequently we are all anxiously expecting the arrival of a boat from New Orleans every day. We are also very anxious to hear the war news, whether anything is being done, whether the Army of the Potomac has "advanced one inch and fallen back two," whether the world still moves or any thing interesting or exciting is going on outside of Matagorda Island. I am becoming almost heartily tired of this particular part of Texas. It is the meanest and most lonesome place it was ever the lot of a soldier to be confined in. Any change would be preferable to lying here all Summer in the hot Sun and sand without anything to do. Ship Island can not be worse than this. When the wind blows — that is about three fourths of the time — the sand drifts like snow and like snow has the power of penetrating almost every where. Not mentioning the inconveniences and annoyance of having sand in the food, in ones eyes or stowed away in considerable quantities about the person during the day, it is impossible to shut it out or get rid of it any time. At night it blows in on ones face and on waking in the morning does not cause the most agreeable sensations. When writing it covers the paper so that I am frequently reminded of the ancient manner of writing on tables covered with wax, only instead of wax I have sand.

Nothing of particular interest has occurred here since I wrote last. The work on our part of the fortifications has been suspended. The works are nearly completed, the main thing yet to be done is to sod them which will require some time and care. When completed they will be quite formidable. There may be and no doubt are good reasons for making such extensive fortifications at this place, but I must confess my inability to see them.

The paymaster visited these "inhospitable shores" about a week ago. He did not have very plenty of funds and our Brigade was paid only to the first of January. Commissioned officers received checks on the national bank in

March 24, 1864–June 12, 1864

New York instead of "greenbacks." Lieut. Wm. J. Schell Co "F" has resigned and gone home and by him I sent thirty five dollars ($35.00) to be left, upon his arrival at Iowa City, with James M. Smith — the same with whom Lt. Smiley left the last I sent home. Lt. Schell intends going round by way of New York and will not get home until about the fifteenth of May. I settled my clothing account with the Government this time — the first time that has been made since enlisted. From the date of my enlistment to the first of Jan. all of the clothing I drew from the Gov't amounted to a little over forty seven dollars, the value of clothing allowed was fifty-eight dollars & forty cents, consequently I received about eleven dollars on that account in addition to the two months pay. The Gov't clothing is mostly of good quality and lasts well. It is much better than can be bought at the north for the same price. Our great relative, Uncle Samuel, is very provident and takes as good care of his large family as it is possible to do under the circumstances. The troops here are well fed, well clothed and are in good fighting condition. The 22nd is gradually filling up with recruits and I hope that Col. Graham will bring enough with him to entitle the regiment to a full set of field officers and each company to a second Lieut. During the month of March twenty four recruits arrived for the entire regiment. Company "F" received four of them. Co. "G" ten. Some of them are very young and small, entirely too much so for a soldier. That is one of the beauties of the plan of delaying the draft and offering large bounties. The army will be filled up with children and others equally unable to stand the hardships of a soldiers life. You may think it strange, yet it is true, I do hope there will be a draft in Johnson County, Oxford township included. It would do me good to see certain persons I could name be compelled to <u>fight for</u> the Government they are now doing all they can to embarrass and overthrow.

I can neither see the wisdom nor policy in regarding the draft as the worst thing that could befall the state and using every means to avoid it. I think that in many respects it would be a blessing. I am glad to learn that Gen'l Grant does not intend to leave the field. It is reported here that he intends recalling all of the troops from western Texas and employ them in more active operations in Mississippi & Alabama. Such a movement would be hailed with joy on the part of the troops. There would be very few tears shed on leaving this place for <u>anywhere</u> else.

The weather is now quite warm and is as a general thing very good. There is always a breeze — generally pretty strong — blowing towards or from the Gulf. It is only about a mile and a half from here to the Gulf. Just the right distance for a walk and I frequently go there to bathe. There is generally rough water near the shore whether the wind blows or not and it is fun to bathe in the surf and allow the breakers to roll over you. I would not like to venture out too far, for a shark might be prowling around.

The health of the Regiment is good, there being only three in the Hospital. Our Surgeon, Dr. [Alfred B.] Lee, started home on a leave of Absence a few days ago.[1] Dr. Dinwiddie has sole charge of the Regiment. Lewis Yenter,

"TO BID HIS <u>DULCINA</u> FAREWELL"

Logan, Charlie Johnson & all from your neighborhood are well. Lewis Gohen is stout and hearty and can talk as well as he ever could.

I suppose this Spring will be a busy time with you. The greater part of the burden of this year's crop will fall on you. Will Staley will be of great help to you. I suppose you will put Milton through when he comes back, won't you? My love to Pa, Ma & all the family.

Your Brother, Geo A Remley

P.S. A very large mail arrived this afternoon and I had the satisfaction of receiving a letter from you dated March 16th. The Republican of that date also arrived, but it did not have any news in it. Does the small pox excitement still continue in Iowa City? Do not fail to write frequently.

Give my respects to Mr. Mars. Tell him I think of him <u>occasionally</u> & would like to have a chat with him.

Give my love to Clara, Sidney & Freddie & tell them they must manage to write me a letter.

G.A. Remley
Serg't Major
22nd Iowa

Wednesday, April 13, 1864 — Matagorda Island, Texas
Dear Pa,
Tomorrow morning twenty two men from this Regiment start home on furlough and through the kindness of one of them (Serg't Virgil S. Hartsock) I send home a little packet containing some letters from <u>home</u> and a few others that I did not care about carrying with me any longer, also a few shells, collected on Matagorda Peninsula when we first arrived there, and some papers taken from a deserter from the Rebels while we were at Indianola.[2]

When we were camped on Matagorda Peninsula I had a fine lot of beautiful shells, that I would like to have sent home but have had no chance & had to throw them away when we left for Indianola. I have frequently had an opportunity to obtain some rare curiosities but not having any way of carrying them with me could not keep them until I had a chance to send them home.

Last night we had a terrible rain storm, the first hard rain I have seen in Texas, and to day has been a cool windy day. The wind coming directly from your part of the country. Judging from all appearances I think we are elected to stay here for some time.

My health continues good. My weight is now one hundred and forty nine pounds with an upward tendency.

My love to Ma and all the family

Your Affectionate Son, Geo A Remley

Friday, April 15, 1864 — Matagorda Island, Texas
Dear Pa,
This is a beautiful, clear night and though it is now near the hour of eleven I do not feel at all like retiring; I will therefore write a short letter to send to

March 24, 1864–June 12, 1864

you by tomorrow's mail. Everything is perfectly quiet, roll-call is over, the bugle has blown for lights to be put out, the vocal music that has been issuing from a neighboring tent for the past half hour has just quit floating through the air, and the entire camp has settled down to rest. The moon is shining brightly and the stars look serenely down upon the sleeping earth — keeping their nightly vigils as faithfully now, when contention and bloodshed are the order of the day in our land as when all was peace and prosperity. It is some comfort and satisfaction to me to look at the North star and think that the same star is at this moment shedding its light upon you though many miles away. Light emanating from the same source thus forms a kind of connecting link between us. But Oh! How much more satisfaction there is in <u>knowing</u> that the same God, whose Eye never sleeps and whose promise cannot fail, is at this time looking down upon each of us and extending to us his kind, protecting care.

This afternoon I received your letter written on the 27th of last month. I suppose it is unnecessary for me to tell you that I was much gratified at its reception, for you very well know that all your letters are gratefully welcomed. I suppose Howard's farm duties keep him so very busy now that he has not time to write much, but I am glad that you have taken the matter in hand and partially supply the deficiency. Tell Howard that I do not want him to stop writing entirely, but give me a "benefit" at least semi-occasionally. Tell Milton I feel thankful for his "edition" to your last letter. Ask him whether it was a second edition; I think, however, it must have been a "revised edition." I advise him not to attempt to eat hickory nuts and write at the same time, for in that case neither will be done well. Tell him I have written to him several times lately and if he has not received them perhaps it would be well to inquire occasionally at the Iowa City Post Office, for I noticed one advertised for him in the last Republican. My last letter home was written on the tenth of this month. Whenever circumstances will admit I try to write <u>at least</u> once a week.

Some of our men started home on furlough this morning. Twenty two furloughs — five per cent of the number of men present with the Regiment — were granted; for thirty days only. The largest companies were entitled to send only three men home at a time.

I sent a package of letters, that I did not like to destroy, by one of the furloughed men and directed it to be left with Mr. Welton. If you will call for it some time when you are in town you will oblige me very much. It will probably reach there before this does.

I become more thoroughly convinced every day that it will be our fate to remain here all Summer. We are making fortifications here that, in my opinion, are not intended for the rebels alone. I believe we are preparing to attend to France and straighten our affairs in Mexico when the Rebellion is put down. If France is not very careful she will get herself into trouble on this side of the water.[3]

A few days ago I took a ride of about ten miles down the Island and back. I went four miles beyond the pickets and enjoyed the ride very much. My horse was a fine spirited fellow and I assure you I did not "go slow"; he also had a rough kind of gait and I feel the effects of the ride very sensibly yet. I picked a single wild flower which I brought back with me on purpose to send to you, not because there is anything remarkable in the flower itself, but I thought that because it came from this part of the world it might possess a little interest to you.

There is nothing new nor interesting occurring here and I fear that camp life here will become exceedingly dull before we leave.

I must bid you "Good night" and close this hasty letter. My love to all.

Your Affectionate son, Geo A Remley

31 — Wednesday, April 20, 1864 — Matagorda Island, Texas
Dear Brother Howard,

It has been just five days since I wrote my last letter home and during that time, though we have had a mail, I have not received any intelligence from <u>any</u> of you, but as I do not expect to have another opportunity of writing for several days, I will write you a short letter to night.

We are on the eve of making an expedition somewhere, but of its object and destination I can not speak <u>certainly;</u> though it is generally supposed that we are going to make a raid into the country as far as Lavaca for the purpose of obtaining lumber to be used in the completion of the fortifications here. At all events we received an order this afternoon requiring the Major commanding the Regiment to report at Division H'd Qrs, at 6 1/2 o'clock to-morrow morning with three hundred men each having forty rounds of ammunition; and five days rations in his haversack. Also to bring with us all picks and axes that can be spared from camp. This looks like there might be some work to be done. I have heard from unofficial sources that we will go on a transport preceeded by a gunboat, up the Bay as far as Lavaca, land there and get a lot of rebel lumber which is piled up ready for us and then return. After we get back I will give you an account of the trip. I am, ex officio, not obliged to go but it being left entirely to my own inclination, I will of course go. I am glad that something has turned up to relieve the monotony of camp life. I hope to find some letters here waiting for me by the time I get back.

I don't think I have told you in any of my letters yet that our Regiment is now commanded by Major Houston of the 23rd Iowa; there being none of our own field officers present with the Regiment. Lt Col Graham went home some time ago for the purpose of conducting recruits to the Reg't. From letters received from him I learn that he has succeeded in catching the small pox for himself and collecting seven recruits at Davenport for the Regiment. Don't you think he has done remarkably well? He states that when he arrived at Iowa City it was the current report there that the 22nd was full and did not want any more men. This was probably started by recruiting officers from other Regiments. Volunteering is now pretty nearly "played out" and I think that the 22nd stands a pretty good chance of never being filled up again. Perhaps it will be consolidated with some other Regiment. So much for not having the regular recruiting parties at home, all the time that we are entitled to have by existing orders. The 24th and other Iowa Reg'ts took advantage of this long ago, and are now nearly full. So much for the foresight of <u>our</u> officers.

As you well know the 22nd has no Colonel but we all thought that Graham would come back with the eagle on his shoulder instead of the leaf; this would necessarily make the Lieut. Colonelcy vacant. Soon after Col. Graham's departure domestic troubles and the state of his personal affairs rendered it <u>suddenly</u> necessary for Major White to go home. I expect there will be some pretty hard pulling at the wires done before they both get back again. The Regiment was thus left without a field officer, which is contrary to all military rules, and one had to be detailed from another Regiment until one of our own returns. Since we have been here in Texas four of our line officers have resigned and gone home. They are Lieuts. Smiley Co. "G", Morrison Co. "K", Schell Co. "F" & Henderson Co. "H." Lieut. Henderson started home this morning. He is from the North Bend and you may probably be acquainted with him. There are not many of the officers who started out with the Regiment now with us. The race will soon become extinct and a new one take its place. A little more than a month ago a new banner presented to the Regiment by the ladies of Johnson county, I believe, reached its destination. We had no flag at all for some time before that.

We are proud of our new banner, but I am sorry to say that it will not last long. The painting is a great deal too heavy for the silk and has cracked in several places, cutting slits in the silk six or eight inches long.

Col. Graham intends to bring us a new flag, the stars & stripes, when he comes back.

The health of the regiment is still good, though in company "G" there are about a dozen cases of sore eyes. The men thus afflicted are sent immediately to the General Hospital at New Orleans because they would never get well in this sandy country. All of our boys are well. Lewis Yenter is at present suffering with a felon on his thumb; but in other respects all right.[4] So much for the Regiment in general; now for a few words concerning one of them in particular.

I still enjoy very good health. My weight is now 151 pounds with a fair prospect of increasing. I do not care about becoming any heavier for my clothes are already becoming too small for convenience.

My official duties require considerable attention, but are not very onerous. Besides the regular duties connected with the Regiment I have to mount Guard at Brigade Head Quarters every third morning and there, though Genl Warren is commanding the Division, every thing is under his personal supervision, and has to be done up in style. My new position necessitates new expenditures one of which was the purchase of a sword; which is the only warlike implement I have. Capt Cree presented me with a nice belt.

"TO BID HIS <u>DULCINA</u> FAREWELL"

I must bring this running rambling letter to a close. Do not fail to write as often as you can. Give my love to Pa, Ma & the little folks. My kindest regards to Mr Mars

Your Affectionate Brother, George A Remley

32 — Thursday, April 28, 1864 — On Board Steamer "Clinton"
— New Orleans, Louisiana
Dear Pa,

Our steamer has just arrived at the Dock at this place and hoping to have an opportunity to send you a few lines before we leave I will attempt to write them under very unfavorable circumstances. You will doubtless be very much surprised to learn that I am here so soon after I informed you that I expected we would spend the summer on Matagorda Island. When I wrote last, on the 20th we intended to start the next morning on an expedition to Lavaca, expecting to be gone five days. We did go to Lavaca and returned late in the evening of the 24th bringing with us two boatloads of lumber obtained by tearing down buildings. Some rebel soldiers, who were home on furlough at the time we arrived there, delivered themselves up to us professing to be very tired of the war and especially of being obliged to serve in the Rebel army. Unfortunately for the reputation of the 22nd the town was fired while we were there — supposed to have been done by some of the disaffected citizens — and two blocks in the best part of the town were entirely destroyed. On the evening of the 25th we received orders to leave for this place and accordingly the next day the 26th we embarked on the Clinton and have just arrived here. I do not think we will land here or even change boats. This boat will probably take us as far as the mouth of Red River but whether we will go up that river to reinforce Banks or go further up the Mississippi or not I am unable to say. The 23rd Iowa and the right wing of our Regiment came over on this boat. I came with the Right wing this time. The left wing will follow us on the next boat that comes. There are now only two regiments of white troops — besides the half of the 22nd — left on Matagorda Island and they expect to leave soon. The works will be garrisoned entirely by negro troops. The Clinton is a splendid sidewheel Gulf Steamer. The hull is made entirely of iron and the engine is the best I ever saw.

We had a <u>very</u> pleasant trip across the Gulf this time. The water was as smooth and level as the Miss. River. I had not the slightest chance to get sea-sick. We might cross the Gulf a hundred times and not see it as smooth as it was this time. This morning when we crossed the bar at the mouth of the river there was no perceptible change in the running of the boat. The fore-going was written last night in a State room on the boat where it was so dark that I could see the lines at all. I sat on a valise with a pillow on my knees for a table on which my single sheet of paper was spread.

March 24, 1864–June 12, 1864

Friday, April 29, 1864 — Rooms of USC Commission — New Orleans, Louisiana

Dear Pa,

Last evening we arrived at New Orleans and fearing that I would not have a better chance to write home I commenced writing a letter on the boat, but had to leave off very suddenly on being informed that the troops were disembarking. After we got off the boat we marched about a mile to a large building formerly used as a warehouse to store away cotton in known as "Cotton Press No. 1," where we spent the night. It is now about 9 o'clock AM. Two companies engaged in unloading our baggage from the boat. This morning soon after we got up Kenedy, Duncan & I went to the market and got a good breakfast. We then took a stroll around the town until it became too warm for comfort and finally "brought up" at the rooms of the U. S. Christian Commission where we are at this moment improving the time by writing home. No. "69 Carondolet St" is the Place, about two miles from quarters and we availed ourselves of the street cars to get here. These "rooms" are very comfortable, cool & nice, and are well supplied with books, papers, periodicals, writing materials, etc., etc. They are perfectly free to all who wish to avail themselves of their benefits. There is also a daily prayer meeting connected with the establishment. The "Christian" & "Sanitary Commissions" do much more good in the army than many persons at the north suppose. At every town of importance in the South within our lines there are "Soldiers homes" where food & lodging can be had free of charge and "reading rooms" similar to these under their special control.

We will probably remain here two or three days until the left wing of the Regiment joins us and then it is the general impression that we will go to reinforce Banks up the Red River. It is an acknowledged fact that Banks was badly whipped in the late fight. The part of the 13th Army Corps engaged is said to have suffered severely. Letters from the 24th & 28th Iowa state their loss to be very heavy.

Gen'l Banks is held in very low estimation by the Western troops and the sooner some able man, McClernand for instance, takes his place the better it will be for our cause in this Department. We will probably have some stormy times down here before long. Just one year ago we commenced active operations in Mississippi. Just one year from this day the bombardment of Grand Gulf was going on and then the battles of Port Gibson, Champion Hill etc. followed in quick succession. I don't think we will get into the real hard work quite so soon this year but judging from present appearances there will be some as hard fighting this Summer as there was last. I am very glad we have got away from Matagorda Island.

The contrast between the barrier sand banks of the Coast of Texas and the beautiful, fertile, Mississippi Valley is great. The country between here & the mouth of the River is very beautiful.

"TO BID HIS <u>DULCINA</u> FAREWELL"

Your letter of the 7th was received the night before we left Texas. I am very much obliged to you for the stamps they came in the nick of time. I know you would excuse the manner in which this is written were you acquainted with the circumstances. My love to Ma & all the family

Your son, George A Remley

33 — Tuesday, May 3, 1864 — HeadQuarters 22nd Iowa — New Orleans, Louisiana

Dear Howard,

As it is not probable that we will remain in New Orleans more than another day or two at farthest I will write to you <u>to night</u> because a Mail Boat will start up the river tomorrow and I may not have another opportunity as favorable for writing as this. I doubt very much, however, whether <u>you</u> would consider <u>this a very favorable</u> opportunity if you knew the circumstances. We are quartered in a large barn-like building and this room — one end of which is occupied by "these HdQrs" and the rest of it filled with soldiers — is about 300 feet long and 100 ft wide. Even in the most propitious times there would be more or less noise in such a crowd, but on this occasion it is doubly <u>interesting</u> to me from the fact that within a few feet of me there are about twenty five "boys" going through a peculiar kind of Gymnastic Exercises commonly known in army "parlance" as "the stag dance." The screeching noise of the violin, the loud tones of the "caller," the shuffling of heavy feet on the floor and the jarring of my desk, all have a tendency to distract my attention from any one thing and render thinking or writing almost impossible, but nevertheless hoping that you will bear this in mind when you read, I <u>will</u> write a letter but cannot vouch for the quality.

My last was written to Pa on the 29th ult. Yesterday I received a letter from you dated, I believe, the 17th of the last month, also received one from Allie of about the same date. Tell Allie I was <u>very</u> glad to get her letter and will certainly answer it the first chance. This is the time of the month that I have a great deal of business to attend to and when the present rush is over, if not on the move, I will have more time to devote to writing letters. The left wing joined us yesterday morning and since then we have been very busy making our "Muster and Pay" Rolls. This must be done at the end of every two months whether we are payed that often or not. There is some prospect of our being payed tomorrow, probably four months' wages as that much is now due.

It is impossible to even guess with any degree of certainty what will be our destination when we leave here. We will go up Red River to rescue our gun boats if they do not get down before we arrive there. It is rumored in "official circles" that Memphis will be our final destination, after the Red River difficulty is settled. Time will fully decide the matter. I hope we will not remain here for long for such a place as this is not a good place to keep a body of troops in. The temptations are great and the demoralizing influences many; so for the good of the regiment I shall be glad when we get away. We had been away off there in Texas almost outside of civilization for a long time and since we have been here a great many have been giving loose reins to themselves and are doing many things that they will repent and be ashamed of when the more sober second thoughts come as they surely will. Even now I can hear the noise and foolish talk of more than one drunken fellow.

New Orleans is in many respects a pleasant and beautiful city, but yet it has some <u>very</u> dark phases in its character. This is the case, however, with all large cities. I have visited nearly every part of the town. Horse cars run through the principal streets thus the passage from one part of town to another is greatly facilitated. There are many large and splendid specimens of architecture. The new Custom House, not entirely finished, covering four whole blocks, the St. Charles Hotel and a great many others "too numerous to mention." I visited the "Greenwood Cemetery" and others about three miles from the city on the continuation of Canal Street. There are many fine monuments and tombs of rich material and workmanship. I was well repaid in the interesting things I saw for all the trouble and expense of going.

Last Saturday evening as a friend and I were walking along Camp Street we met a crowd of children and grown persons going to church. Being a little curious to know what was going on I learned upon inquiry that there was to be a Sunday School Concert. As a matter of course we went in and I assure you that I have not been so pleased, delighted, beyond all expression, for a long <u>long</u> time. It was so sudden and unexpected to me. The school numbers nearly 250 and judging from appearances they were all there. There were a great many beautiful, sweet, innocent looking little girls and when they sung songs, I will leave you to imagine the effect if you <u>can;</u> but I doubt it.

There were other exercises besides singing, speeches and recitations by the pupils and speeches by the pastor of the church and others. It passed off very pleasantly and was a decided success. I learned that last January the school numbered 70 and eight months ago seven scholars were all they could muster. The next morning I attended Sabbath school and in the evening preaching at the same place by Rev. Mr. Horton. This was the first time I had had that privilege for a good while. Altogether it was quite a treat and if we stay here until next Sunday I will "try it over again."

At some more convenient time I will probably say something about the "Southern Beauties." Their "name is Legion." I have heard considerable discussion about the claims of Northern & Southern ladies to beauty nearest to perfection, but now I will have a chance to form an opinion of my own. I am wandering writing something that will not interest you perhaps.

I am very glad to hear that everything is running so smoothly at home. I am glad that the Sunday School is again in operation. I send my best wishes & kindest regards to the Sunday School collectively and individually. You needn't boast to me how you remember me in particular and soldiers in general, show your patriotism and serve your country by attending all the parties, suppers, fairs, etc. gotten up for the "benefit of the soldiers," I see through all that and understand it perfectly. "Pitch in" Howard & do your best now while the soldiers are away for when they get back you will have to stand aside, be content to remain in the background for a while. (This last sentence is for your own private ear.) Some things in your letter I will answer some other time. Write often. Do not be afraid of writing the same things several times. You don't do it often and it makes no difference if you did for I would rather hear the same things over & over than not receive any letters at all. The "boys" are all well, except the fclon on L. Yenter's thumb. It is pretty severe. My love to Ma, Pa & the littler folks. Remember me to Mr. Mars.

Your Brother, Geo A Remley

35 — Thursday, May 19, 1864 — Simmsport, Louisiana
Dear Pa,
I have an unexpected chance of sending a letter away this morning and though I have nothing to write with except a pencil and no place to write except by sitting on the ground and holding a small book with the paper on it on my knee nevertheless I will write you a few lines.

The right wing is yet at New Orleans and it is hard to tell whether they will join us here or we will return to them. We have not received any mail since we left New Orleans and have had very few chances to send letters away. I wrote a letter home on the 11th just after we had returned from a trip up Red River. Since then we have not traveled very far but have been in daily expectation of going somewhere. We are now at a place on the Atchafalaya river called Simmsport about eighteen (18) miles by water from the mouth of Red River. Banks army, what is left of it has returned to this place and commenced crossing the river yesterday. Banks is famous on the retreat. The gunboats were all saved by taking off the iron plating and some of the guns, part of which was thrown into the river, of those that drew the most water and by building a dam across the river below the falls, thus backing up the water so as to float them over the rapids. The rebels followed the army, which marched overland, to this place and annoyed it all of the way down. They are even here fighting with the rear guard all the time. All day yesterday there was heavy cannonading about four miles from here at a Bayou the Rebels were trying to drive our rear guard fronm. There was also heavy skirmishing with musketry kept up all day.

There are thirty transports here to take one army corps up the River as soon as they can embark. The other army corps — the 19th — and parts of the thirteenth and seventeenth will probably be stationed at different points on the Mississippi to keep communication open. This is the impression prevalent here.

The 24th & 28th Iowa are here but I have not seen any of them yet; neither have I heard anything definite from them. They are said to have suffered severely in the Pleasant Hill fight. John Hoffer, a young man who

March 24, 1864–June 12, 1864

used to work for Mr. Bond is said to have been killed. I have not heard from cousin John Remley yet. I think I will go to their camp about four miles distant if I can today.

The weather is very hot here now in the day times; but the nights are quite cool and dews are very heavy. We have no tents with us except the little shelter tents which do not amount to much. They are much better than none, however, to keep off the Sun and dews. Company "F" is here and the boys are all well with one or two exceptions. Lewis Yenter could not come with us on account of his thumb which was quite painful when we left New Orleans. Lt. Col. Graham has returned from Iowa and is now with the right wing in New Orleans. He brought very few recruits for the Regiment, but I think that was only a secondary object. He came back with a commission for himself as Col., one for Maj. White as Lt. Col. and one for Capt. Gearku Co. "B" as Major.

Now we have a full set of field officers and a bright trio they are.

I am very anxious to hear the news from the North and especially to hear from home.

I see from the Chicago Tribune that the Iowa State University has raised a company of "one hundred days" men. I am glad to see them thus show their patriotism. I shall not be at all surprised to hear that Milton is one of them.

I have not time to write any more now. I hope to be able to make up for all deficiencies when the Reg't gets together again and I have plenty of writing materials.

I hope you will not fail to write as often as you can & if you could send papers occasionally they would be acceptable. Give my love to Ma & all the family.

Your Affectionate Son, George A Remley

36 — Tuesday, May 24, 1864 — Morganzia Bend, Louisiana
Dear Howard,
A mail will leave here in a very few minutes and I have only time to write you a few lines this time. We are here without tents and my writing materials are with the right wing at New Orleans, consequently the facilities for writing letters are very few and besides this there have been very few chances to send mail up the river for the past two weeks. On the 19th while we were at Simmsport I wrote a short letter to Pa but I doubt very much whether it has gone up the River yet. A mail was sent to us from New Orleans day before yesterday that being the first we have had since we left there. By it I received a letter from Pa dated May 4th and also the Package containing two pr. socks & 1 handkerchief sent by Ma, which came all right. Tell her that I was very glad to get them and will prize them highly not only on account of their real worth, but because they were made at home and came from home.

If you will take a look at the map you can easily tell where we are now. We went from the mouth of the Red River to Simmsport to meet Banks retreating army. Remained there two or three days till the army crossed the Atchafalaya River and then marched to this place on the Miss River. Arrived here day before yesterday evening. It is very dry hot & dusty & marching was severe. Banks army is much demoralized. Saw cousin John Remley, Wm. Morton &Allen Eddy. We are having a pretty rough time of it. My health is good.

Have not time to write more.

Your Brother, G A Remley

39[5] — Sunday, June 12, 1864 — H'd Qrs 22nd Iowa Infty — Baton Rouge, Louisiana

Dear Pa,

After waiting a long, long time for a letter from home, yesterday evening I at last had the satisfaction of receiving yours of the 29th of May. You certainly allowed a long time to elapse between the letter I received yesterday and the one preceeding it dated May 2nd. It lacked just one day of being four weeks!! You need not wait to hear from me when we are on the move to learn where to direct your letters, for the mail always follows us up no matter where we go, therefore, don't refrain from writing on the grounds that you fear the letters will not reach me. Since I was at home last Fall I have written on an average four letters a month, writing you once a week as regularly as circumstances would permit, on the other hand I have received from home hardly any letters enough to average one in the two weeks. I know you have frequently said that I can imagine all about how you are and how you are getting along at home. That is all very true I can imagine almost anything, but that is not the thing. I may not have any fears in regard to your personal safety as you have for me, or in other words the cause of my desire to hear from you may be somewhat different from that of yours to hear from me, but that does not necessarily imply that there is a difference in the intensity of the desire; and besides I derive as much pleasure in reading a letter from home as you do in reading one from me and if I am willing to give you that pleasure (if indeed it is a pleasure) <u>frequently,</u> I think it nothing but right that I should be gratified by having it reciprocal. I would rather receive a letter, cheerful and affectionate, from home than anywhere else, it cheers me and does me good, and I have curtailed all other correspondence that I might not have any reason for neglecting home communication; but if they fail or dwindle down to an occasional letter the supply not being equal to the demand, the deficiency must be supplied from other sources. You have the advantage of me in numbers and also in facilities for writing. If you would number your letters (and I am not so sure they are not so many but that they might be numbered), I could then always tell on receiving one whether there were any that had miscarried. I number mine, not because it does me any good, but for your satisfaction.

I am very sorry thus to occupy so much of my letter, but have done it only with the hope of disabusing your minds of an error that seemed to be gaining

March 24, 1864–June 12, 1864

ground, that is; that it is a matter of the highest importance for you to hear from me frequently and <u>equally</u> non-important for me to hear from you.

Hoping you will, at least, give the matter a fair and honest consideration I gladly dismiss the subject. You say in your last that you need rain very much in your part of the country. I wish we could share what we get here with you. There has not been a day since the first of this month that we have not had rain, more or less, generally more than the ground could absorb, so that the camp ground which is level is frequently flooded. This is the case just now; for the past two hours the rain has been falling in perfect torrents and having slacked for a short time nearly every one is out with spades ditching and draining the water out of the tents. My tent fortunately being on a little higher ground than most of them, is not inundated. Yesterday I made a bunk of cane and I am all right for a good nights sleep no matter how hard it rains, unless the water should flood my tent to the depth of eighteen inches or more.

I have a load of cane to make a shade in front of the tent, which I will have done tomorrow morning; provided it stops raining long enough. At present, however, there is no prospect of the rain stopping for a week, for it is pouring down again somewhat after the manner it did one time in the days of Noah. There is considerable lightning which I think is a very good thing for us, for the atmosphere will thereby be purified and, as a consequence, we will be more healthy. I think this is a very unhealthy place and will be much more so when the season is further advanced. I am told that last Summer there were some nine months men, from New England, stationed here and that between forty and fifty were buried every day. There are four or five funerals every day now. The country around the town in the rear was at one time nothing more than cypress swamps, but the trees have been cut off in a great degree and the ground partially dried off, but still it looks very <u>bilious.</u> Our sick list is gradually increasing though there are <u>now</u> no serious cases. A young man, John Buddy, son-in-law of M. L. Morris, member of company "F" but has always been absent from the Co. as clerk at different places was taken sick four or five days ago and died yesterday evening, was buried today. This is the first funeral we have had in our <u>camp</u> since last December.

Genl. Warren is now in command of District of Baton Rouge and he is coming down on the citizens living outside of the lines. Ladies are the principal persons who come inside the lines, for it is supposed that they can obtain what they want (provisions, etc.) easier than the men. The search at the picket lines going out is very strict and several ladies have been detected lately with contraband articles such as revolvers, gray cloth for uniforms, etc. concealed about their persons. One was relieved of 8 or 9 revolvers (Colts Navy) recently.

The left wing is yet at Morganzia Bend and it is hard to tell when they will be down for Genl. Lawler in command there wants to get the 22nd in his command and will not recognize Gen. Warren's order for them to be sent here immediately. It will be so when Warren gets an order from some higher authority. The 13th A. C. has no commander but is split up in Detachments. It is said that Genl. Herron will take command of the whole Corps shortly, until McClernand gets well.

I am very sorry to hear that you are not so well as usual. Hope you will soon get better. Am very glad to hear of the increasing prosperity of the Sunday School. If your crops need rain I would be glad to let you have some of what we have for it still comes with a steady patter. I wrote to Allie day before yesterday & to you on the 6th. Give my love to Ma & all

Your Affectionate Son, George A Remley

Chapter Seven

"We Will Have Some Fighting to Do"

— THE SHENANDOAH VALLEY CAMPAIGN —

46[1] — Sunday, July 24, 1864 — On board Steam Ship "Cahaba"
Dear Pa,
This is the seventh day we have been on the "bonny blue sea," and we are now within 4 miles of the mouth of the Chesapeake Bay and within 20 of Fortress Monroe, our destination. There is a Colonel on board who will start for Baltimore as soon as we land and by him I expect to send this just to let you know that I am all right and where to direct your letters. This is Sunday. Just a week ago to night we left New Orleans. We have for the most part a very smart voyage and as pleasant as could be expected where 1500 men are crowded into one ship. For the last two days it has been stormy and cool, raining a good part of the time. Have been kept back about a day by strong head winds.

The sea is rough now and it is as much as I can do to write here in the state room with a valise on my knee for a table, on account of the rolling of the ship.

All we know concerning our destination is that we are going to Fortress Monroe. Don't know where we will go from there. It is quite probable we will have some fighting to do before long. I am very anxious to hear the news. We will be right here when they make news.

I think you had better direct your letters to Fortress Monroe instead of Washington. The day we left New Orleans I received two letters — one from Milton written about the 27th of June and one from Howard written the 3rd & 4th of July. I have written frequently and as my letters are all numbered you can easily tell whether you got them all or not. I wish you would number yours.

Our boys have all been well excepting of course seasickness.

This room is so dark that I cannot see the lines — can hardly see what I am writing. I will write again the first opportunity after we land.

My love to all

Your Affectionate Son, Geo A Remley

Saturday, August 20, 1864 — Camp 22nd Iowa Infty
— Near Charlestown, Virginia
Dear Pa,
This morning I had the extreme satisfaction of receiving two letters from home dated August 11th and 12th and written respectively by yourself and Howard. I have not had an opportunity to write or send letters away from

camp since we left the vicinity of Washington on the 14th and indeed I do not know when this one will start for we have no regular communication with Harper's Ferry except by means of special dispatch carriers who do not have anything to do with the mail. You are right in supposing that we are in the Shenandoah Valley and as to getting "to the mountains of Va. before the summer is past" we think we are pretty near there now for the Blue Ridge is in plain view only a few miles off, east of us and the Alleghanies a little further off on the West. Our present camp is about four miles from Charlestown and eight from Berrysville on a direct road between the two and about twelve from Harper's Ferry.

We are for the present acting on the defensive waiting in the hourly expectation of being attacked. Our forces had advanced some distance beyond Winchester when [Jubal A.] Early was reinforced by [James] Longstreet's Corps and they were compelled to fall back to Berrysville and finally eight miles further to our present position. We joined them at Berrysville. There has been some fighting within the last few days, mostly by artillery and [Philip] Sheridan's cavalry.

On the 17th the rebels captured and burned a train loaded with supplies from Harper's Ferry just this side of Berrysville. I saw the smoking ruins when we passed. The train was guarded by "hundred day men" and the "rebs" rushed out of the woods near by with lighted torches taking them completely by surprise.

Notwithstanding the vigilance of our cavalry scouts several of the infantry pickets were killed yesterday and more wounded. We were camped in the edge of the woods bordering a large corn field and had the corn broken down for some distance around and everything ready for a fight. This is the case, in fact, all the time. I have not yet told you how we got into this part of the country. I will give you a short account of the march. Before daylight on the morning of the 14th we started and marching about four miles crossed the Potomac at "Chain Bridge" then taking the Leesburg road we kept on until two o'clock in the afternoon. Camped in a meadow on a small stream called Difficult Crick — very appropriately named for the bridge had been burned & it was hard work crossing. The next morning — Monday the 15th — promptly at 2 o'clock reveille beat and by 3 1/2 we were stumbling along the stony road in the dark. Marching very slowly through a rough, hilly country, we passed through a small town called Drainsville and stopped for the night near Broad Creek in a large timothy meadow.

At the usual hour the next morning the 16th we broke camp and crossing a good sized stream called Good Creek, we passed thro Leesburg about noon and camped just outside of the town. Leesburg is about the size of Lewisburg and like it is situated in a hollow. The inhabitants are mostly secesh but they don't say so themselves when union troops are around. On the 17th started again at half past three AM. This day we passed a beautiful little town called Hamilton. Inside of an upper story window where she could be seen by her neighbors, I saw a girl waving a small union flag and occa-

July 24, 1864–September 15, 1864

sionally throwing an apple to the passing soldiers. Marched about fifteen miles and went into camp as we supposed for the night but about five o'clock were ordered forward again. Some had to leave suppers half cooked, some half eaten & others went with none. It does not take the regiment more than about ten minutes to "pack up" and be ready to start. We took the Snickerville Road. Passed that place at the foot of the Blue Ridge and just at sunset reached the top of the mountain at a place known as Snicker's Gap. There is a spring of good, cold water on the very top of the mountain. When we began going down hill, then the "boys" broke loose and "yell" after "yell" ran from one end of the column to the other reminding me very much of the Vicksburg campaign. The Shenandoah river is about waist deep and we had to wade it. It must be a beautiful stream. I was sorry I could not see it by daylight. The moon shone brightly and the water is so clear that I could see the white pebbles on the bottom very distinctly. It was a novel sight to see the troops crossing. Most of the men took their pants off.

Reached Berryville, about six miles from the river by 12 o'clock PM having been on the road nearly ever since 3 1/2 that morning. The men were very tired many entirely worn out and for the last three miles the road was completely lined with them. I stood it very well. We had now joined the army under Sheridan and in place of going towards Winchester as we expected, took the Harpers Ferry road and retreating with the rest this far have taken a stand in advantageous position and are waiting for the enemy to attack us if he chooses to do so; if not we will be after him again soon. This is splendid country, the best I ever saw. We live mostly by foraging. Fresh meat, green corn and fruit are the principal articles of [forage]. The country has been pretty well "laid waste" by both armies. Out towards Winchester fences & everything are said to be destroyed and as we retreated the cavalry destroyed everything that would be of service to the enemy. This is the only part of the "Confederacy" that I have seen yet worth fighting for if that were the object.

There is a pretty large army on both sides here now and there may be some hard fighting before long. I have not time to write any more now but will the first chance.

Your affectionate son, George A Remley

56 — Tuesday, August 30, 1864 — In the field, Virginia
Dear Brother Milton,
My last intelligence from home was your letter of the 19th for which I desire to thank you and at the same time express the hope that you "continue in well doing."

Day before yesterday I wrote a few lines to Howard[2] and now I start this not knowing whether I will have time to finish it or when there will be a chance to send it away. When I wrote we were on the point of having our strong position on the hills in the vicinity of Harper's Ferry and starting up the valley in pursuit of the retreating rebels. Well about 7 o'clock that morning, with four (4) days rations in haversacks, we began the pursuit. Took the Charlestown "turnpike" and marching in close column for about two (2) miles, we stopped on account of hostile demonstrations made by the "rebs" in front. There was some cannonading and every thing looked favorable for a fight, but it didn't take place then. (It is liable to "come off" now at any time.) We stopped here on the rebel camp ground, for several hours, the men cooking their dinners in the mean time. When we came to hunt up our "contraband" to see about dinner behold, the coffee pot was missing, lost! We were in a fix; nothing but coffee and crackers to live on for the next four days and coffee pot lost! Nevertheless we got along the best we could without, that is by borrowing. I walked about a half a mile to get some roasting ears and hardly reached the corn-field when the bugle blew to "fall in." I pulled two ears of corn and hurried back to find the regiment in line ready to start forward again.

Not liking to be cheated out of my corn, I stripped off the outside husks, threw it into the fire and in a few minutes I had two "roasting ears" nicely cooked — steamed I suppose — and as sweet and well tasted as any you ever saw. That is the way we usually cook corn.

We continued our march with out interruption and passing thro' Charlestown — just one week since we passed it the other way — took the road leading to Winchester. The Court House in which John Brown was tried and condemned is completely riddled by cannon shots.[3] Several other buildings in the immediate vicinity have suffered in the same way and two or three have been burned, but beyond this the town is very little injured. It is a beautiful place but noted for its sympathy with treason. There are some rebel wounded there carefully nursed by the ladies. They don't like us much and the "attachment is reciprocal." We passed through the streets with martial music and Brass Bands playing. It being Sunday the "colored population" were all out in their finery and they at least had smiling faces and seemed perfectly delighted with the music.

About two miles from Charlestown we were again brought to a "stand still"; the rebels having taken up their old position of the 21st we could not do better than to occupy the works thrown up by the sixth corps on that day. Both armies hold exactly the same positions they did a little over a week ago, only the lines extend further to the right and not as far in the direction of the Blue Ridge. I say "both armies" but I can only speak certainly of ours; the greater part of the rebel force may be on its way to Richmond for all I know. Yesterday there was heavy skirmishing in front, but with what result I don't know, except that our skirmishers fell back about three miles, but that may have been done to draw the enemy on. A skirmish force for an army like this consists usually of two or three Batteries, a Division or more of cavalry, some times supported by infantry. There has been no firing in front to day. We are making our position here stronger every day, but I do not think there is much danger of our being attacked.

July 24, 1864–September 15, 1864

Our camp is in a beautiful, shady grove behind two lines of works and we are as free from thought of danger as if there were no enemy within a thousand miles. The works, in our part of the lines are formed of rails in such a way as to afford good protection against bullets. I believe I told you that our transportation was cut down to only one team & wagon to the regiment; well even that was left behind at Bolivar Heights and here we are without tents and with only part of our blankets & as a matter of course have the full benefit of the night air cool as it is, but that does not give us much trouble as long as the weather continues good as it has been for the last few days.

Apples are abundant and are brought into camp by the bushel. They are beginning to ripen and are eatable without being cooked. It is astonishing to see the quantity of green corn consumed by the army. A large field doesn't go far towards supplying it even for a few days. Corn will soon be too hard for use. The prices of provisions in the Commissary Department have risen and that makes the officers grumble occasionally. Fresh beef, for instance, killed here in the country is (18) eighteen cents per pound. As it is confiscated I can't see why it should be so dear. Sugar & salt pork instead of being about 12 or 13 cts. a pound is now .25 & other things in proportion.

The regular army ration has been reduced in some things, but there is no very material difference. A soldier's fare is unaffected by a change of prices as indeed it should be.

It not infrequently happens that barns and stacks of hay and grain are burned by our troops as we pass through country. This must seem pretty hard to the citizens but it is one of the invariable consequences of invasion no matter how civilized the people. If a citizen expresses his sympathy with the rebels openly to our men as is often the case, he is sure to suffer by it in some way.

One man trying to prove his loyalty by telling us how many relations he had in the Union army said he "had a nephew in the Invalistic Corps." "Ah!" said Col. Graham with a sober face "it must be the <u>Gum Elastic</u> Corps you mean." "Yes that was it," said the man and we all laughed but he never knew any better.

This happened on the other side of the Blue Ridge.

You must not think that soldiers are sober and solemn all the time as many suppose. They are generally cheerful, sociable and as full of fun as any body.

We have been notified since I began writing that the mail leaves at six o'clock, hence this will not be as long as it might have been other wise. Paper & writing materials will be scarcer with me until the field desk comes up. I hope this will not blur so that you cannot read it. If you have not sent stamps when this reaches home you need not do it. I succeeded in getting a dollars worth at Harper's Ferry the other day.

I sent two photographs in my last. Tell Clara one is for her. Allie promised me hers but I have not seen it yet. I would like to have Ma's & Pa's. Do not fail to write often.

Your Aff Brother, George A Remley

57 — Friday, September 9, 1864 — Camp near Berryville, Virginia
Dear Ma,
Last evening I had the pleasure of receiving your letter of Aug 28th. I had been looking for a letter from some of you for several days and had delayed writing partly on that account and partly because there was no chance to send letters away. Yesterday evening at the same time the mail came we received notice that one would leave immediately, but as I had none written of course I could not profit by it. My last was written to Milton while we were in camp two miles this side of Charlestown. On the 3rd we left that camp and marched to within a mile and a half of Berryville, our present position. On our arrival here that afternoon the 8th Corps, which was in the advance came upon the enemy suddenly and a sharp skirmish ensued, lasting until about 9 o'clock PM, in which our loss was 300 killed, wounded and missing. We took about seventy prisoners and one stand of colors. Night — a dark, cold, rainy night, put an end to the fighting; but if it had been morning instead of evening there would have been a general engagement for the enemy were in considerable force. About dusk the firing was very heavy and the 19th Corps was ordered up to support the 8th. I did not like the idea of going into a fight without having something to fight with, so I borrowed a gun from a sick man and got some cartridges, but as it happened did not have occasion to use them. We were soon formed in a line, on a low ground, immediately in the rear of the 8th Corps. In a short time it became quite dark and then a cold rain began to fall and you can easily imagine that the "situation" was by no means pleasant or comfortable. To make the matter worse the rebels soon began to throw shells over our way. The scene was grand, <u>fearfully</u> grand, but we were not in a position to <u>enjoy</u> it. It may look very well to see a shell describing a parabola through the air, leaving a streak of light in its path and then suddenly disappear in an indescribable flash of intense, glaring light, when it goes in any other direction, but when it comes almost directly towards one with its hissing, unearthly noise and perhaps bursts immediately overhead sending the fragments of iron in every direction, singing like nails shot from a common shot-gun <u>only more</u> so, the beauty and grandeur of the scene cannot be properly appreciated on account of its effect on the nervous system. Some of those thrown at us that night were percussion shells and struck in the ground in front of us without exploding, but most of them bursted in the air behind us and, as the pieces never fly backwards, we were perfectly safe. There was one man killed and another wounded in the regiment next to us on the left. About 9 o'clock the firing ceased and we all made ourselves as comfortable the rest of the night as we could under the circumstances. Making a pillow of my haversack, I lay down on one side of my rubber blanket and spent the night in vainly endeavoring to stretch the other side so that it would reach over me and keep out the cold and rain. Morning came at last, to the relief of all, and after spending two or three hours in getting into proper position, we had time to get some breakfast. Then we began to throw up fortifications immediately.

July 24, 1864–September 15, 1864

Whenever we stop, even for a few hours, in the vicinity of the enemy fortifications of some kind are thrown up: logs, rails, stones and everything available are brought into requisition and these covered with earth in such away as to form good protection and eventually make strong work, if we stay in one place long enough. Both sides do the same thing and then each is afraid to make the attack and the "flank movement" must be tried. Thus we are constantly changing ground, always near and skirmishing with the enemy and yet never coming to a general engagement. I believe that if Sheridan keeps Early out of Maryland & Pennsylvania until after the election, he will be doing all that Grant requires of him.

The main force of the rebels disappeared from our front on the 4th and since then the 6th & 8th Corps have moved off to the right in the vicinity of Summit Point four or five miles from here. Day before yesterday I sent with a reconnoitering force to within five miles of Winchester on the W & B turnpike. We found [Joseph E.] Johns[t]on's Brigade of rebels strongly posted across the road and after exchanging a few shots and driving in their pickets we turned around and came back to camp. The country has been pretty well devastated, fences destroyed (rails burned and stone fences thrown down) stock all driven off, orchards stripped of fruit and altogether it was the most desolate looking picture I ever saw. Dead horses along the roadside and new made graves gave evidence that it had lately been the scene of strife. On a board at the head of one grave I noticed the inscription "W.P. Davis. Staunton Artillery. Killed Sept 4th 1864." There are a few men yet in the country, but it is very doubtful whether they are union men as they pretend. They usually have a guilty look and most of them are, without doubt, the very persons who shoot stragglers, capture unguarded trains and on whom [John S.] Mosby mainly depends for support. I wish every one of them could meet the fate he deserves. I was very much surprised to learn what you told me of "David Creigh" and very sorry that such was his fate but I think that he, like thousands of others who have committed the same crime, fully merited it.

The weather for the last week has been cloudy & rainy and cool enough for November. I begin to dread the cold, wet & mud of the winter here, but there is one comfort, that is that we will not have to engage in active operations all the time, for that is impossible. We will probably go into winter quarters somewhere about the last of November, but I would greatly prefer going back to the Department of the Gulf. Since our successes at Mobile and Atlanta I do not think there is much probability of that, however. If it were not for the approaching Presidential election & the strife & party spirit engendered thereby, the prospect for peace would be much more favorable than at this time last year.

Just two years ago today we were mustered into the United States Services as a regiment. Two thirds of the time are gone and only one year of the present term remains and I do most sincerely hope that before it expires there will be no more necessity of soldiering.

The last year has seemed very short and upon the whole has passed away very pleasantly.

We have been in no battles, have had no <u>very</u> long fatiguing marches; in short, as a regiment we have been favored more than we should reasonably have expected.

During that time I have enjoyed good health indeed have not been sick a single day.

I am sure we have great cause to be thankful and I trust that will be as well at the end of another year.

Our Quartermaster and <u>one</u> regimental wagon were left back at Bolivar Heights consequently all baggage except what each one chose to carry was left behind. Adjutant Pryce and I have a little shelter tent, two blankets and a rubber bed with these we manage to get along very comfortably.

Our fare is not as extensive and varied as it might be but still it answers every purpose.

Corn has become too hard to roast or boil but now it is grated on graters made of canteens or pieces of tin or iron found around camp and made into mush or a kind of corn cake.

It would make you smile to see some of the dishes a soldier learns to prepare. It may be a very good thing for a man to know how to cook but I never expect to do much at the business.

I am glad to hear of Howard's prospect of obtaining a good situation this winter and hope he will succeed in obtaining it.

Tell Milton that if Howard leaves he will have a chance to put some of his surplus patriotism to some good use by staying at home to attend to things there, by doing it cheerfully too, that is very essential.

Tell him also that I don't know "what Pa intends doing with the Granary" and hope he will inform me.

I suppose you have a lovely time sometimes with the girls when they all get together. Louisa & Leila enjoy themselves finely I suppose.

The soiled appearance of this letter may be accounted for by the fact that paper envelopes & all has been carried in my pocket for more than a week that being the only mode of conveyance. Our team has just arrived this moment and I will soon have the field desk out then I will [have] plenty of writing material.

Give my love to Pa, Howard, Milton, Allie, Clara, Sidney & Freddie and believe me
As ever

Your Affectionate Son, George A Remley

Thursday, September 15, 1864 — Camp near Berryville, Virginia
Dear Brother Howard,
Your letter of the 4th and 5th inst. came to hand a few days ago. It was a good, long one, containing much domestic and other news, and I assure you was read with interest and pleasure. I am glad that you overcame your

drowsy propensities and resisted the temptation to read the "interesting Sunday School Book" for if you had not that letter would never have reached me, so instead of "doubting your judgment" I approve your decision (the letter being a good one) and think you will do well if you never show greater <u>want</u> of judgment.

Well, we still remain here in our "entrenched position near Berryville" and the prospect for our stay being protracted to an "indefinite length of time" seems as good now as when we first came. Our army is lying here watching and waiting, waiting for the enemy to attack us if he sees fit and watching to prevent him from getting into Pennsylvania or from leaving the valley to join [Gen. Robert E.] Lee at Petersburg. Reconnoitering parties, sometimes of infantry but more frequently of cavalry, are sent out every few days to feel for the rebels and ascertain as near as possible their strength and exact position. Day before yesterday a Brigade of Wilson's cavalry went about ten miles beyond Berryville and surprised & captured a rebel picket post, consisting of the 8th South Carolina Infty, in front of Kershaw's Div. It is <u>very</u> seldom that cavalry charges upon infantry but this time the surprise was so complete that the "rebs" had only time to fire one volley and start to run, before they were entirely surrounded, and without further resistance threw down their arms and surrendered. Our men say they never saw the rebels show so little fight. The prisoners numbered about 200 including a Colonel and about 20 line officers. They are veterans of 1861 and are a finer looking set of men than usually found among rebel prisoners. Their battle flag, tattered and torn by four years service was among the spoils. It must be very humiliating to the old soldiers, who have fought its folds ever since the commencement of the war to see it borne off in triumph by "the insolent foe." It is not certainly known, but it is confidently believed by those in authority that Early's entire force is here, none having been sent to reinforce Lee, and preparations to give the enemy a warm reception, in case he should attack us, are made accordingly. Every morning an hour or two before daylight the entire command is up, under arms, in line of battle; and at day-break the regiments are dismissed, thus we get an early breakfast and a good start in our day's work which consists for most of us, in <u>doing nothing.</u> At intervals all day yesterday the deep booming of cannon could be heard some two or three miles on our right and last night there was some firing on the picket line in our immediate front; in consequence of this, all available artillery was put in position along the works and we were roused up earlier than usual an attack being anticipated but no "Johnnies" made their appearance and at last "Aurora" came bringing the cheering assurance that "all was quiet along the lines." Except when relieved by something of this kind the monotony of the camp here is becoming as tiresome as it has been anywhere. 'Tis true we get the news from the Baltimore and Philadelphia daily papers the same day they are printed but that has become an old story with us.

The Presidential question is exciting considerable interest among the soldier and animated discussions upon the merits and demerits of the several candidates are becoming more frequent every day. The soldiers as a class are "true as steel" and will show at the coming election that they can fight for their country with <u>ballots</u> as valliantly as they do with <u>bullets.</u> If a vote were taken today there would probably be between thirty and forty votes cast for McClellan. I have not been able to find one who would endorse the resolutions adopted by the "Peace Convention" at Iowa City. Capt. Morsman is one of the strongest McClellan men in the Regiment.⁴ Capts. Morsman, Humphrey and Remick are the only men that "persuasion" among the officers. I gave the Republican to Capt Remick the other day and asked him to read those "resolutions" and whether he could endorse them. He read the preamble and thought it was "too bad" "outrageous." He went on down to the middle of the first resolution and threw the paper down in disgust, said he "couldn't go <u>that.</u>" Thus it is with the soldiers, however much of a Democrat or McClellan man he may be, he seems not to identify himself in any way with "copperheads." It is absolutely impossible for a <u>true</u> soldier to be a copperhead. We <u>all</u> hate them, despise them, yes even loathe them <u>ten thousand times</u> more than the armed traitors who oppose us in the field.

It is really amusing to hear them whine like "whipt curs" at the prospect of the draft and talk sending "committees" to Lincoln to persuade him to put a stop to "this terrible effusion of blood." Just as if any of their precious blood had been or ever would be shed as long as there was any plan their cowardly, craven hearts could devise to avoid it.

Let the draft — stern, uncompromising draft — be enforced and sweep as many of them into the rank as possible. I would like to be at home at the time of the organization of the militia companies for I shouldn't wonder if there would be stirring times. I hope you will elect good <u>sound</u> officers for your company. The oath Gov. Stone requires them to take before being commissioned is a bitter pill to copperheads and one I think they can hardly swallow.

A short time ago Edward Morgan, Co. "Y" received a "copperhead" letter (of the deepest dye) from one <u>Chrisman</u> from the River bottom settlement. It roused the indignation of the numbers of that company to such an extent that about a dozen of them wrote answers to it. I suppose he will think his list of soldier correspondents has increased wonderfully. I will send you a copy of it if I can get it. From beginning to end it was either an exhibition of his utter ignorance or a string of glaring <u>willful</u> falsehoods — having a <u>slight</u> acquaintance with the man I am unable to tell which. Such men are "treasuring up wrath against the day of wrath" for themselves for when the soldiers get back home they will not allow such treasonable sentiments as those expressed in the "Resolutions" of the Peace Party to be uttered with impunity. I hope that time will come soon.

It is getting late and I must close for I am an <u>early riser.</u>

Give my love to Pa, Ma, and all the family.

Your brother, George A Remley

Epilogue

October 4, 1864 — Camp 22nd Iowa Infantry — Harrisonburg, Virginia
Rev. James A. Remley
Dear Sir,
I have a leisure moment this evening and I think it my duty to write you in regard to the death of your Son, George, Sergeant Major of our regiment who was killed at the hard fought battle of Winchester on the 19th Ult.

For over a Year, Poor George, was my constant companion and bunkmate. Being Sergeant Major of the regiment his duties were in my office and we tented and messed together. His many noble qualities had so endeared him to me that I loved him as a brother. The boys in the regiment thought there was no such a man as George and they all loved him dearly. Always social and in good humor he had made himself beloved by all who knew him.

We lost many brave & good men on that fearful day but none are missed as much as George. Everyone seemed to have an interest in his welfare. His death cast a gloom over all. When the battle was over and those of us remaining were collected together, on almost every lip lingered the words "Poor George was killed, he was a noble good fellow."

I will endeavor to relate to you as near as possible the circumstances connected with his death, on the morning of that day we marched from Berryville and reached the vicinity of the battlefield about 10 AM. At 11 we formed a line of battle preparatory to advancing and charging the enemy's position. We were in the act of drinking a little coffee which we made while lying there when the order rang along the lines "forward." We all sprang to our places and in a moment men were double quicking towards the enemy. A few moments before I had a talk with George and I advised him to assist in carrying off the wounded, for the following reasons: He had previous to this time a sword which he purchased while in Texas at the time of his appointment from Lieut. Schell who had resigned and gone home. This he gave to Capt. Davis a few days before the fight on account of the latter having lost his a week or so previous. In view of this fact I told him it was useless for him to go into the fight without any weapon. I will never forget his reply to me. "I came into the Army to fight and I am going to get me a gun." He went at once to a man whose courage had failed him and got his gun and took his place in the ranks. As I told you before the order came to move "forward." Between our lines and the enemy was an open field about 600 yards wide. We started across this field with a wild yell and in a few moments the enemy opened on us with musketry, grape and canister. Our men were a very conspicuous mark to the enemy as we were crossing and they took advantage of it by pouring in a terrible fire which mowed the men down like grass. In the middle of the field was a slight depression in the ground and having gained this shelter from the enemy's fire we went some slower. Thus far, George escaped and was in good spirits. Forward again was sounded along the line and we advanced over the crest of the hill. We were then ordered to commence firing. The enemy were not more than 50 to 100 yards distant posted in a heavy timber & protect by rifle pits. George fell just as we had reached the crest and was pierced by three balls, one passing through the right temple, one under the arm and the other through the abdomen. He expired almost instantly. Capt. Davis was also killed about the same time, and not more than 10 feet from where George fell. I was not able to get George from the field at the time. In fact our dead and wounded both lie on the battlefield until a very late hour the same evening. During the fighting this ground was occupied by the enemy late in the afternoon, but they merely passed over the ground without disturbing our dead or wounded, with the exception of rifling their pockets. I am sorry to say that the disgraceful act is too often done by both parties. I was very anxious to secure a few things on George's person to send to you, but I could not find anything but his pocketbook which they overlooked. It was in his jacket pocket. This was all I could find upon his body. His sword belt was upon him when he entered the fight but the enemy had taken this from him. His sword was also taken from the body of Capt. Davis. I would have like to had secured the sword and belt to send to you but it was impossible. He generally carried his Bible in his inside coat pocket but I could not find it that day. But I am of the opinion that he did not have it along this time, that he left it in the desk. It had worn his pocket so that he could not carry it. I can inform you when we receive our desk again. I am indeed happy to inform you that George was very fond of his Bible. You are doubtless aware of this fact. It was the <u>vade mecum</u> of his army life. It was his rule, invariably to read a few chapters before retiring at night. For this purpose while in camp he used to keep his Bible in the pigeon hole of the desk before him. Frequently during the day when he had a leisure moment he would read his Bible. Indeed, morally, George had not his equal in the army. He was as pure a christian as ever lived. There was nothing vile in him. In all my association in life I have never been acquainted with a young man possessed with such a pure and spotless character. He was a christian soldier in every sense of the word.

George's clothing and little trinkets were all left back with my <u>valise</u> and a great many little things were in the desk. I will collect them all together and send them to you when the campaign is over if I am fortunate enough myself to escape. I can not do it sooner as all our things were sent back to Harper's Ferry, we have not even a change of clothing with us. Should I fall in this campaign some one will surely do it. We buried George in his uniform on the battlefield. It was done rather hurriedly as were pushing the enemy at every point.

Epilogue

I do not seek to give you any consolation in your bereavement by this letter, but, being George's companion, I thought you perhaps would by glad to hear the circumstances attending his death from one who saw him fall on the battlefield. Indeed I thought so much of him, he was the noblest young fellow that ever I knew. I have written more than I intended when I commenced and will close.

From your friend, S. D. Price
Adjutant 22nd Iowa Volunteers

October 30, 1864 — Camp 22nd Regiment Iowa Volunteers — Cedar Creek, Virginia
Rev. James Remley
Dear Sir,
I am in receipt of your letter of date Oct. 19 and hasten to write a few lines in reply. You have no doubt ere this received my letter written at Harrisonburg about the beginning of the present month.

In that letter I aimed to give you all the particulars concerning the death of your Son Geo. and I believe answered all the queries you propose in your letter. I am very anxious to do any thing that I possibly can for you in this matter. George was a <u>bosom</u> friend of mine and as Serg. Maj. of the regiment, it is admitted by every one that his place can never be filled by one so faithful in the discharge of his duties. Since his death I have been performing all the duties of the office myself, not able to find any one competent to fill the vacancy left by George Remley.

I will state in answer to one of your questions that Geo. did not fall in the retreat, but while advancing under the enemy's fire. He was shot while in the act of raising his gun to fire and this was about 10 feet from where we halted about one half an hour before the retreat was ordered.

His grave can be identified. He was buried with 3 of his comrades in Co. F on the battlefield on the spot where he was killed and by our own men, a detail sent back by me for the purpose of burying the dead and I gave them particular instructions to bury Geo. so that his grave could be identified by his friends. The men are here and could point out the grave. But there are many difficulties in your way. These men might not be here, and our army may not be here at that time. I think you might find it, however, by going over the field about a mile or perhaps more from the Opequan, to the right of the pike leading from Berryville to Winchester. If our army or our corps ever goes into Winter Quarters in the valley, you could get one of our men to show you the grave, but I do not think we will.

I informed you in my letter that I would express his effects to you as soon as we would get them. They have arrived today. I find his <u>Bible</u> in the desk before me also his "sewing case." He has several articles of clothing, pair of pantaloons, shirts, etc. & also several little nic nax.

I have his woolen blanket on this whole campaign. The morning we started from Berryville (about two o'clock) in the dark I got his blanket and he got mine and so I have had his ever since. I intend to send it to you, however, as it is the very identical blanket he drew at Camp Pope and may be highly prized by you, and has been through every campaign in which we have been engaged. I will have some difficulty in sending these things as there is no express office any nearer than Martinsburg and I could not get to go their for this purpose. I will hang [on]to them until I do get a chance. Our books & papers have arrived and I am very busy, you will have to excuse my lead pencil & haste. I miss my assistant George Remley very much. I don't think I can ever finish my reports as he could have done it. I am glad you are acquainted with my Uncle M. M. Jones. I write to him often. If you meet him, give him my respects. Again tendering my sympathy in your bereavement for your brave & noble George.

              I am your friend, S. D. Price

★ ★ ★

After the deaths of George and Lycurgus, family needs often interrupted the educational pursuits of Howard M. Remley. Howard graduated from the University of Iowa with a bachelor of arts degree in 1869, a law degree in 1872, and a master of arts degree in 1873. Howard entered into law practice with his brother Milton in 1872 in Anamosa, Iowa. After Milton moved to Iowa City in 1874, Howard practiced alone until joining with Thomas R. Ercanbrack. Howard was appointed to the 18th Judicial District Court of Iowa in 1896. After declining reappointment in 1902, Howard joined his son James in practice; their partnership lasted until Howard's death in 1932.

Howard married Mary E. Underwood, also a graduate of the University of Iowa. The Howard Remleys had ten children, all of whom graduated from the University of Iowa. Five of the children of Howard and Mary Remley married and had children who attended the University.

Milton Remley received a bachelor of arts degree in 1867 and a master of arts degree in 1872 from the University of Iowa and in 1868 was admitted to the bar. Milton practiced law in Anamosa, Iowa, with J. S. Stacy (1868–1872) and with his brother Howard (1872–1874). From 1874 to 1881, Milton practiced with A. E. Swisher in Iowa City. With the exception of a few short partnerships, including one with his brother Frederick A. Remley, Milton continued in solo practice. In 1888 he made an unsuccessful bid for the Republican nomination for Iowa attorney general; six years later Milton made a successful run for the same office, serving as Iowa attorney general from 1895 to 1901. In 1869 Milton married Josephine Dennis of Tiffin, Iowa. They had four children, all of whom graduated from the University of Iowa. None of Milton's grandchildren attended the university, however, because all four moved out of state after graduation. Milton delivered an address to George A. Remley Post, Grand Army of the Republic, of Oxford, Iowa, on September 19, 1886, twenty-two years after the death of his older brother at the third battle of Winchester. At the end of his address, Milton along with his mother, brother

Epilogue

Howard, and sister Alice presented the post with a flag "as a small token of our high appreciation of your love and tender regard for him we loved."[1]

Alice Remley graduated from the University of Iowa in 1868 with a bachelor of science degree. In the early 1860s, while George and Lycurgus were serving in the 22nd Iowa, Howard, Milton, and Alice were all in attendance at the university. The three siblings shared a house and chores, Alice doing the cooking while the "boys" did the rest of the housework. After graduation Alice married John D. Glass, an attorney and later a state senator. The Glasses made their home in Mason City, Iowa, and had two children who survived to maturity.

Clara Remley received her bachelor of arts degree from the university in 1876. She taught school in Iowa and Kansas before retiring in 1889 when she moved to Mason City, where she opened a book and stationery shop. Jane Remley lived with Clara during this period until Mrs. Remley's death in 1893. Clara remained in Mason City until her death in 1934. She never married.

Sidney Remley attended the University of Iowa until forced to withdraw because of illness. Sidney died in 1877, two years after the Reverend James Remley's death in 1875.

Frederick A. Remley graduated from the university in 1880 with a bachelor of arts degree. After graduation he entered the law firm of (Milton) Remley & Swisher in Iowa City and read law under them. He was admitted to the bar in 1884, the same year he started a partnership with Milton. Frederick gave up law in 1887 and entered the Baptist seminary in Morgan Park, Illinois. He remained there until 1890 when he moved to Leipzig, Germany, to pursue advanced theological studies. Frederick joined his mother and sisters in Mason City after receiving his doctorate in philosophy. Frederick died in 1908.

Biographical Directory

Atherton, John B.—Twenty-eight years old and a resident of Knoxville, Iowa, Atherton enlisted on August 22, 1862, as an adjutant. On September 9 he was commissioned into Field and Staff, 22nd Iowa Infantry, and was promoted to major on September 17. Atherton was wounded slightly at Vicksburg, Mississippi, on May 22, 1863, and resigned his commission on June 8, 1863.

Borland, Charles—Borland was a student and later an instructor at the University of Iowa in Iowa City. Borland enlisted in 44th Iowa Infantry in May 1864. The 44th was a three-month regiment, and Borland mustered out with his regiment on September 15, 1864.

DeCamp, William M.—DeCamp, a forty-year-old physician, enlisted in the 1st Iowa Infantry in April 1861. DeCamp was injured in the battle of Wilson's Creek. He mustered out with his regiment in August 1861. One year later, DeCamp enlisted in the 22nd Iowa Infantry and mustered into Company G. He was wounded in the battle of Port Gibson on May 1, 1863. DeCamp was promoted to second lieutenant on January 8, 1863, and to first lieutenant on May 27, 1863. He was discharged for disability on April 26, 1865.

Gohen, Lewis—A twenty-year-old resident of Oxford, Iowa, Gohen enlisted in August 1862 as a private.

Haddock, William G.—A thirty-year-old resident of Iowa City, Haddock enlisted as a second lieutenant in August 1862. Haddock resigned his commission January 10, 1863.

Handy, George W.—Handy was twenty years old when he enlisted as a first sergeant in the 22nd Iowa Infantry. He was promoted to second lieutenant on January 8, 1863, and to first lieutenant on March 28, 1864. Despite being wounded at the battle of Winchester on September 19, 1864, Handy continued to serve and mustered out with his regiment on July 25, 1865.

Johnson, Charles (Charlie or Charley)—Johnson enlisted in Company F, 22nd Iowa, on August 20, 1863.

Johnston, James—A twenty-eight-year-old resident of Johnson County, Iowa, Johnston mustered in as a private on August 26, 1862.

Kibler, George—An eighteen-year-old from Johnson County, Iowa, Kibler mustered in as a private.

Klenk, John—A resident of Oxford, Iowa, Klenk enlisted in August 1862 as a private.

Logan, Lewis—A twenty-five-year-old resident from Oxford, Logan mustered in as a corporal.

Mars, George F.—A resident of Iowa City and family friend, Mars is referred to as "Mr. Mars" in all Remley family correspondence. From October 1864 through October 1865, Mars boarded with the Remley family in Oxford. Mars paid for his board with cash and by working on "Nemora," the Remley family farm.

Montgomery, James—A twenty-eight-year-old resident of Johnson County, Iowa, Montgomery mustered in as a private on August 26, 1862.

Peabody, Oren—A thirty-seven-year-old resident of Newton, Iowa, Peabody enlisted as assistant surgeon in August 1862. In May 1863, Peabody was promoted to surgeon, 23rd Iowa.

Pool, Harvey Simeon—An eighteen-year-old resident of Johnson County, Iowa, Pool mustered in as a drummer on August 26, 1862.

Porter, John W.—A resident of Iowa City, twenty-three-year-old Porter enlisted on July 26, 1862, as a first lieutenant. On September 10, he was commissioned into Company F, Iowa 22nd Infantry. He was promoted to adjutant on December 20, and on January 29, 1863, he resigned his commission.

Remley, Elias Frank—The thirty-six-year-old Remley of Marion, Iowa, mustered into the 24th Iowa in September 1862.

Remley, John W.—The nineteen-year-old Remley enlisted in the 28th Iowa in August 1862. He mustered out with his regiment in July 1865.

Rutter, Henry—A resident of Johnson County, Iowa, twenty-seven-year-old Rutter enlisted as a corporal in August 1862. He was promoted to first corporal on July 1, 1864.

White, William H.—White, a resident of Iowa City, enlisted as surgeon in the 1st Iowa in 1861. A year after mustering out of the 1st Iowa, White enlisted in the 22nd Iowa, also as surgeon. White resigned his commission December 14, 1863.

Notes

1 — "Among the Barren Hills of Missouri"

1. Lewis Logan enlisted as a third corporal. Rutter is Henry Rutter of Johnson County, Iowa, who enlisted as a corporal. *Roster and Record of Iowa Soldiers in the War of the Rebellion: Together with Historical Sketches of Volunteer Organizations, 1861–1866,* 6 vols. (Des Moines: E. H. English, 1908–1911; http://www.civilwardata.com/) (hereafter cited as *RRIS*).

2. Throughout their letters, George and Lycurgus refer to their younger brothers, Howard (b. 1843) and Milton (b. 1844), as "the boys." Frederick (b. 1853) and Sidney (b. 1857) were generally excluded from this reference.

3. Dr. Silas Totten, president of the University of Iowa in Iowa City, resigned his position August 19, 1862. Richard Totten, Dr. Totten's son and a student at the university, took part in a pro-South rally and from the platform denounced the Northern cause. The younger Totten was "pursued by an angry crowd from which he escaped, never to return to Iowa City." Dr. Totten, who shared his son's Southern sympathies, resigned his position shortly thereafter; however, the Tottens did continue to reside in Iowa City for at least several more months (Theodore A. Wanerus, "Presidents of the University," *Iowa Alumnus* 9 [1911–1912]: 105). Richard Totten wrote his friend George Remley of his family's impending move: "We expect to leave Iowa City in about two weeks, of which I am very glad as I have learned to dislike the place very much" (Richard Totten, Iowa City, Iowa, to George A. Remley, Rolla, Missouri, October 12, 1862, Pearce Civil War Collection, Navarro College, Corsicana, Texas [hereafter cited as PCWC]). Charles Borland, another University of Iowa student, wrote George in April 1863 that the Tottens remained in Iowa City (Charles Borland, Iowa City, Iowa, to George Remley, Memphis, Tennessee, April 8, 1863, PCWC).

4. Reverend O. M. Spencer served as president of the university from 1862 through 1867.

5. Professor E. M. Guffin is listed in every General Catalog of the university from 1856 to 1861 as principal of the Preparatory Department. In the faculty meeting minutes Guffin's presence is noted on September 21 and 23, 1862. In the latter meeting, Guffin recommended Charles Borland for a position in the Preparatory Department. "Faculty: Minutes of Meetings, 1860–1890," box 21, folder 9, Manuscript File, Archives, Special Collections Department, University of Iowa Libraries, Iowa City, Iowa.

6. In 1862 Theodore S. Parvin served as president of the Johnson County Soldiers' Relief Association. Benjamin F. Shambaug, "The State University of Iowa and the Civil War," *Iowa and War* 8 (1918): 12–13.

7. Mitchel's name does not appear in the university catalog or elsewhere in university records.

8. Wanerus blames a lack of funding from the state and other financial problems for the reduction of salaries ("Presidents of the University," 106). The university had closed for lack of funds in 1858 and did not reopen until 1860. "This Family Tree Grows on Our Campus," *Iowa Alumni Review* 7 (1954): 6.

9. *RRIS* mistakenly lists Lewis Yenter as Lewis Yonter.

10. A mess is a group of men who join together to share cooking duties. For biographical information on members of the Remley mess, see individual listings in the biographical directory.

11. During the 1861–1862 school year, Lycurgus attended Chicago University. He may have transferred to Chicago when the University of Iowa closed between 1858 and 1860. By 1861, however, the University of Iowa had reopened, and George Remley had enrolled. For unknown reasons, Lycurgus did not join George at Iowa City for the 1861–1862 school year.

12. George is probably paraphrasing Matthew 26:45: "Then cometh he to his disciples, and saith unto them, Sleep on now, and take your rest: behold the hour is at hand, and the Son of man is betrayed into the hands of sinners."

13. A polyglot Bible contains several versions of the same text in different languages. James Remley spoke Latin and had taught his children to do the same; therefore, it is not unusual that George would acquire a polyglot Bible. According to family history, when the Reverend Remley would visit Dean Currier's Latin classes at the University of Iowa, Currier would turn his classes over to Remley. James E. Remley, Anamosa, Iowa, to Loren Hickerson, Iowa City, Iowa, July 20, 1949, Special Collections Department, University of Iowa Libraries, Iowa City, Iowa.

14. This letter is probably no longer extant as it is not part of the James Remley Family Papers in the Pearce Civil War Collection at Navarro College or of other known collections of Remley family papers.

15. "Blackjack oak," also known as "black oak," is another name for the emory oak, a medium-sized evergreen tree with a straight trunk, rough black bark, rounded crown, and shiny yellow-green leaves.

16. Missouri did not secede from the Union, though it remained a deeply divided state throughout the Civil War. According to James McPherson, in July 1861 the state convention, which had adjourned in March after rejecting secession, "constituted itself the provisional government of Missouri, declared the state offices vacant and the legislature nonexistent, and elected a new governor and state officials." Meanwhile former governor Claiborne Jackson, a proslavery Democrat, called the former (pro-South) legislature into session at Neosho in November 1861. The legislature adopted an ordinance of secession, and the Congress in Richmond admitted Missouri as a Confederate state three weeks later; however, the Confederate state government of Missouri was driven from the state soon after seceding and "existed as a government in exile for the rest of the war." James M. McPherson, *Battle Cry of Freedom: The Civil War Era* (New York: Oxford University Press, 1988), 292–93. See also Michael Fellman, *Inside War: The Guerrilla Conflict in Missouri during the American Civil War* (New York: Oxford University Press, 1989).

17. "Crackers (hard bread)" are hard tack or hard crackers, which are three-inch square crackers made of flour, salt, and water. Hard tack would last for months without spoiling.

18. Mit is shorthand for Milton Remley, younger brother of George and Lycurgus.

19. A common cure-all for afflictions of all types in the 1860s, blue mass pills were small, blue pills containing, among other things, mercury.

20. Jeff's identity is unknown despite the fact that he is mentioned by George, Lycurgus, and several other family members.

21. William Zoll married Jane Alderson Remley's sister, Sarah Martha, in December 1848. The Zolls were residents of Warrensburg, Missouri.

22. See George's letter of September 24–25, 1862.

23. The Sibley tent was invented by U.S. Army officer Henry Hopkins Sibley, who modified the basic design of an Indian tepee. Measuring eighteen feet in diameter by twelve feet high, Sibley's tent was supported by a single pole resting on an iron tripod thus allowing the tent to be tightened or relaxed. At the top of the tent a circular hole, which was covered with a cap in inclement weather, provided ventilation. The Sibley tent generally sheltered twelve men, though at times as many as twenty men would share one tent. Sibley, who patented his design in 1858, reached an agreement with the U.S. government whereby Sibley would receive five dollars for every tent they used; however, when the Civil War broke out and Sibley joined the Confederate Army, he lost all federal revenue. David J. Eicher, *The Longest Night: A Military History of the Civil War* (New York: Simon and Schuster, 2001), 119.

24. A Philadelphia lawyer is a shrewd attorney adept at the discovery and manipulation of legal technicalities.

25. Atherton was promoted to major on September 17, 1862. Porter received the appointment to adjutant on December 20, 1862. *RRIS*.

26. Second Lt. William G. Haddock did not receive a promotion. Haddock later resigned his commission (January 10, 1863) while at Rolla, Missouri. *RRIS*

27. Jayhawking was a widely used term for "free-form foraging." Michael Fellman notes: "'Jayhawkers' was the term applied to Kansas Raiders, and 'jayhawking' became a term widely applied to free-form foraging by Union troops in the state [Missouri] and eventually nationwide." Fellman, *Inside War*, 35.

28. See James Remley's letter dated October 22, 1862.

29. The two letters Lycurgus refers to are probably no longer extant.

30. Alice "Allie" Remley (b. 1848), Clara (b. 1854), Howard, Milton, Frederick, and Sidney are all siblings of George and Lycurgus (see also chap. 1, n. 2).

31. Lycurgus is probably referring to a shelter or "pup" tent. After 1862, the U.S. Army adopted the more portable shelter half or French "Tente d'Abai." Two shelter halves could be joined together into an inverted V structure housing two soldiers. "Thus," as Eicher notes, "two partners of the march would attach their tents at night, crawl inside, and with their heads exposed would often amuse themselves by barking like dogs, giving the whole affair the derisive name 'pup tent.'" Eicher, *Longest Night*, 119.

32. George is correct that only four members of the regiment had died since its arrival in Missouri; however, five men in all had died since the regiment's formation in August. Joel A. Priest, Company D, died October 10, 1862; Simeon Woodling, Company I, died October 27, 1862; and Charles Coons, Company G, died November 20, 1862. John W. Dunlap was discharged for disability on October 21, 1862, and died several weeks later in Iowa City. Noble A. Rogers, Company D, was the first death in the regiment; Rogers drowned September 18, 1862, before the regiment arrived in Missouri. *RRIS*.

33. James Remley's youngest brother, Samuel, ran a lumber and grist mill at Port Neches and Grigsby Bluff, Jefferson County, Texas. Samuel Remley is identified by W. T. Block as one of the few slaveholders in Jefferson County; in his correspondence with his brothers in Iowa, however, Samuel never mentions ownership of slaves. W. T. Block, "Smith's Bluff and Grigsby's Bluff, Texas"; available from http://www.wtblock.com/wtblockjr/smith.htm; accessed July 17, 2002. See also Howard M. Remley, "Remley Cousins Fighting Cousins: The Civil War, 1861–1865," unpublished manuscript in the possession of the editor.

34. Balloon framing is a system of wood-frame construction developed in the nineteenth century. Studs are continuous from the foundation sill to the top wall, and floor structures are hung from the studs. The entire house is held together by nails. Balloon-frame construction, which replaced traditional post-and-beam construction, was faster and required less skilled labor.

35. Foolscap is a size of paper that is typically sixteen by thirteen inches.

36. Sutlers were merchants authorized by the War Department to sell goods, frequently overpriced, to soldiers within military encampments. "Sutler tickets" were probably some form of credit extended by the sutler.

37. Seven members of the 1st Iowa Cavalry died in Missouri during November 1861, most at Benton Barracks, St. Louis. None of the seven is listed as having died in or near Rolla.

38. "Secesh" is a slang term for any person who supported secession.

39. George wrote this in response to his father's letter of October 22, 1862: "Jonathan Lengle and William Morton are both at home. Jonathan looks very well. He spent a considerable part of a day with us & I think is much improved by his connection with the army" (James Remley, Oxford, Iowa, to George and Lycurgus Remley, Rolla, Missouri, October 22, 1862, PCWC).

40. Howard wrote George and Lycurgus: "Pa made a trade today. You know Mr. Pine has owed Pa for a good while & as he could not get any money, Pa took his suckling colt for the debt $25, and as he did not raise any thing and must live, Pa bought a yearling colt for $35. Pa gives 100 bu[shels] of corn @ .25 the syrup they got and sundry other things, for it. Mr. Pine made another 'grand fizzle' this year. You know he was going to make syrup so fast, well he got a good 2 horse iron mill and let Creed [Vaughn] have the job for the third, and from all the cane they made nearly a barrel of thin stuff. Most of the cane soured just because Creed lacked energy & Mr. Pine sense. More over while they were so busy at the cane the cattle broke into the field destroyed everything corn, buckwheat, etc. Poor man, I am very sorry for him" (Howard Remley, Oxford, Iowa, to George and Lycurgus Remley, Rolla, Missouri, October 31, 1862, PCWC). Creed Vaughn was a cousin to Howard, George, and Lycurgus.

41. George's letter to Sidney and Frederick is probably not extant.

42. A quire of paper consists of twenty-four or twenty-five sheets of paper of the same size and quality.

43. Joseph H. Ledlie, 99th Illinois Infantry.

44. Captain Timothy M. Wilcox commanded Company G of the 3rd Missouri Cavalry.

45. George W. Handy was not removed from office. *RRIS*

46. Bushwhackers are guerrilla fighters.

47. George may be referring to cassimere, which is a plain or twilled woolen cloth used for suits.

48. A detachment of the 9th Cavalry, Missouri State Militia, along with men from the 1st, 2nd, and 11th Cavalries, Missouri State Militia; 3rd Iowa Volunteers; 3rd Indiana Battery; the Red Rovers, Missouri State Militia; and a detachment from the Merrill Horse, under the command of Col. John McNeil, engaged Confederate forces under the command of Joseph C. Porter at Kirksville, Missouri, on August 6, 1862. Five hundred Union men (the remaining 500 soldiers had been detailed to guard the train, ammunition, and horses while the other combatants dismounted for battle) fought house to house against an estimated 2,500–3,000 men of the Confederate Missouri Brigade. The Confederates were driven out of town and across the

Chariton River. McNeil's men, exhausted from their thirty-two day pursuit of Porter's forces, did not pursue the fleeing soldiers. Union losses were 5 killed and 32 wounded; Confederate losses were 150 killed, 300–400 wounded, and 47 captured. Of the 47 prisoners, 15 had been captured by Union forces before and "upon their own admissions had been discharged on their solemn oath and parole of honor not to again take arms against their country under penalty of death." McNeil ordered the men shot. *The War of the Rebellion: A Compilation of the Official Records of the Union and Confederate Armies,* 128 vols. (Washington, D.C.: Government Printing Office, 1880–1901), ser. 1, 13:211–19 (hereafter noted as *OR*).

49. William J. Schell enlisted in Company B, 1st Iowa Infantry, in May 1861. The 1st Iowa, organized as a three-month regiment, was immediately sent to Missouri. On August 10, 1861, the 1st Iowa Infantry was actively engaged in the battle of Wilson's Creek, Missouri, and was noted for its exemplary action on the battlefield. Schell mustered out with the regiment on August 21, 1861. One year later, Schell enlisted in the 22nd Iowa Infantry, Company F, as a 2nd sergeant *(RRIS)*. See also Lycurgus's letter dated August 21, 1862. For a full-length treatment of the battle of Wilson's Creek, see William Garrett Piston and Richard W. Hatcher III, *Wilson's Creek: The Second Battle of the Civil War and the Men Who Fought It* (Chapel Hill: University of North Carolina, 2000). For a history of the 1st Iowa Infantry written by one of its members, see E. F. Ware, *The Lyon Campaign in Missouri: Being a History of the First Iowa Infantry* (Iowa City, Iowa: Camp Pope Bookshop, 1991).

50. George's story was probably told in the missing letter to Sidney and Frederick. See George's letter dated December 25, 1862.

51. The battle of Murfreesboro, also known as the battle of Stones River, occurred December 31, 1862, to January 3, 1863, when the Union Army of the Cumberland under the command of William S. Rosecrans engaged Braxton Bragg's Army of Tennessee near Murfreesboro, Tennessee (McPherson, *Battle Cry of Freedom,* 580–83; Eicher, *Longest Night,* 419–28). Eicher notes: "both sides claimed a victory of sorts, and neither had actually achieved one."

52. Samuel N. Alderson, 9th Missouri State Militia Cavalry, Company G, was in the battle of Kirksville in July–August 1862. The editor was unable to connect Alderson's family line to Lycurgus's Alderson family line.

53. Second Lt. Bennett F. Newgent, Wachman's Battery, Missouri Light Artillery.

54. Lycurgus mistakenly names the battle of Hartville as the battle of Hartsville. The battles of Springfield and Hartville, Missouri, were part of Confederate Col. John S. Marmaduke's raid into Missouri in January 1863. On January 8, Marmaduke's forces advanced on the Union garrison at Springfield, Missouri, an important Federal communications center and supply depot. Heavy fighting continued until after dark when Confederate forces withdrew from the area. Brig. Gen. Egbert B. Brown, commander of the Union forces, was injured in the assault. On January 9, a column of men led by Col. Joseph C. Porter led the second prong of the raid into Missouri, assaulting Union posts around Hartville before moving on to Marshfield where on January 10 he joined forces with Marmaduke's column. In the meantime Union Col. Samuel Merrill and his men arrived in Hartville. When Merrill found the garrison had already surrendered, he took his men in pursuit of the Confederates. The two forces were soon engaged in an intense four-hour battle. The Union soldiers were forced to retreat back to Hartville where they established a line of defense. The Confederates suffered heavy losses and were forced to abandon the raid and return to Arkansas. *OR,* ser. 1, 22(pt. 1):178–211.

55. Men were sent in "every direction" to commandeer teams to "haul away government property."

56. Lycurgus's journal is probably no longer extant.

57. George's letter is probably no longer extant.

58. This is actually the fifth letter written home. Lycurgus did not include the letter he wrote home on January 23 in his count. The letter written by George on January 23 to Howard is no longer extant (see chap. 1, n. 65).

59. John W. Porter resigned his commission on January 29, 1863, at Rolla, Missouri. *RRIS*.

60. Warren's arrest and subsequent replacement by Stone was indeed just a rumor.

61. The battle of Batesville, Arkansas, occurred February 4, 1863, when the 4th Missouri Cavalry drove General Marmaduke's forces out of Batesville. When some of the fleeing Confederates were unable to crowd onto the ferry boats, they swam the White River to escape capture by the Union forces.

62. The letter or letters referred to are probably no longer extant.

63. Lycurgus is referring to the Enrollment Act of 1863, passed by Congress on March 3, 1863. McPherson, *Battle Cry of Freedom,* 600–601.

64. Charles Able is listed as Charles Abel in the *RRIS;* Able (Abel) is not listed in the roster as a deserter. Smith Purcell (Pursell in the roster) deserted February 27, 1863.

65. Sibley tents proved too cumbersome for active use and were replaced by "shelter" or "pup" tents.

66. The Remley barn had been under construction since the fall of 1862. In October Howard described their efforts to George and Lycurgus: "The barn don't get along very fast & is needed very much, most of the hewing is done and as soon as we get done with the corn we will go at it in earnest. The lumber will be on the middle of Nov. We would be at it now if we could hire hands, but hands are very scarce." Howard Remley, Oxford, Iowa, to George and Lycurgus Remley, Rolla, Missouri, October 31, 1862, PCWC. See also letter of November 11, 1863, in chap. 4.

67. Milton was "guilty" of wooing, or courting a young lady or ladies.

68. See George's letter dated March 14, 1863.

69. Eleven men are listed on the roster as deserters between August 1862 and March 1, 1863; two of these are from Company F (Benjamin Bailey and Smith Pursel or Purcell). Charles Able (Abel) is not listed as a deserter; however, Lycurgus wrote home that Able had deserted (see chap. 1, n. 64). From March 1–19, seven more men deserted, including three from Company F: Alonzo Chapman, George Chapman, and Jefferson Chapman. The Chapmans deserted March 19. *RRIS*.

70. The deserters may have been John R. McNamara and Sylvester Stackweather, both of Company K and both of whom deserted Saturday, March 14. *RRIS*.

71. The letter referred to by Lycurgus is probably no longer extant.

72. Col. Samuel Merrill was responsible for the defense of Hartville, Missouri, during Confederate Col. John S. Marmaduke's raid into Missouri in January 1863.

2 — "He Died in Hope of a Blissful Immortality"

1. For a history of the Vicksburg campaign, see Edwin C. Bearss, *The Campaign for Vicksburg,* 3 vols. (Dayton, Ohio: Morningside, 1986).

2. The battle of Belmont, Missouri, occurred November 7, 1861, when Grant routed the Confederate troops at Belmont. Surrounded by Confederate reinforcements from Columbus, Kentucky, Grant's forces were forced to withdraw and return to Cairo. McPherson, *Battle Cry of Freedom,* 396.

3. Island No. 10 was as much an obstacle to Northern shipping on the Mississippi as Columbus had been. A combined land and river operation isolated the Confederate garrison at Island No. 10, and on April 7, 1862, Union forces captured more than 4,000 men as well as guns and equipment (McPherson, *Battle Cry of Freedom,* 415; Eicher, *Longest Night,* 202–4). McPherson estimates 7,000 Confederates surrendered at Island No. 10 while Eicher places the number at 4,538.

4. Elias F. Remley. See Biographical Directory.

5. See Biographical Directory.

6. James Remley was teaching at Marengo, Iowa, about twenty miles northwest of Oxford. Before his enlistment, Lycurgus had taught school there as well.

7. Picket guard, or picket duty, refers to the practice of posting soldiers along the perimeter of the camp to keep out unauthorized individuals and warn of attack.

8. Jacob Sigafoose, Company K, died April 6, 1863, and Samuel Q. White, Company G, died April 8, 1863, both at Milliken's Bend, Louisiana.

9. James Remley disputed this statement in his next letter, dated April 28, 1863.

10. Grant ordered McClernand to clear a path from Milliken's Bend to a position along the Mississippi River south of Vicksburg. As part of this movement, Porter was ordered to run the Vicksburg batteries with the ironclads and move south to rendezvous with McClernand below Vicksburg where his boats could be used to transport troops across the river. Eleven of the ironclads survived the shelling and arrived at Hard Times, Louisiana, south of Vicksburg, where they joined Grant's forces. See Eicher, *Longest Night,* 443.

11. The USS *Henry Clay* was sunk.

12. The letter is probably no longer extant.

13. George's casualty accounts are correct. Eighteen men were killed and fifty-seven were wounded; one-third of those casualties occurred on the *Benton* (*Official Records of the Union and Confederate Navies in the War of the Rebellion,* 30 vols. [Washington, D.C.: Government Printing Office, 1894–1922], ser. 1, 24:608–28). The *Benton* was hit forty-seven times and had its plating pierced repeatedly. The *Tuscumbia* had been hit eighty-one times, which left its casements in ruins and one engine damaged nearly beyond repair. See also Eicher, *Longest Night,* 458–59; and Warren Grabau, *Ninety-eight Days: A Geographer's View of the Vicksburg Campaign* (Knoxville: University of Tennessee Press, 2000), 136–38.

14. The pickets were the forward pickets of Gen. John S. Bowen's force. Bowen's force had moved south from Grand Gulf toward Port Gibson to meet the advancing Union army. Eicher, *Longest Night,* 459.

15. The Confederate forces at Port Gibson were outnumbered four to one. Pemberton's failure to mass troops at Grand Gulf and Port Gibson gave Grant a much needed "foothold" to launch his successful campaign for Vicksburg. Eicher, *Longest Night,* 459–61; Grabau, *Ninety-eight Days,* 154–67.

16. At the battle of Port Gibson there were 23,000 Union and 6,500 Confederate soldiers engaged. Federal losses were 131 killed, 719 wounded, and 25 missing. Confederate losses were 68 killed, 380 wounded, and 384 missing.

17. George is referring to the first and second assaults on the Confederate fortifications at Vicksburg. The first assault occurred May 19 and the second May 22.

Earlier in the campaign the forces had been engaged in the battles of Raymond (May 12), Jackson (May 14), Champion's Hill (May 16), and Big Black River (May 17). Company F had been detailed as Carr's Provost Guard, so they were not actively engaged in these battles.

18. The 22nd Iowa, except for Company F, played a significant role in Grant's failed second assault on the fortifications at Vicksburg on May 22. Grant's forces lost 659 killed, 3,327 wounded, and 155 missing, almost as many casualties as in the previous five battles in the campaign for Vicksburg. Graham was captured and later paroled. McPherson, *Battle Cry of Freedom,* 633; Eicher, *Longest Night,* 469.

19. See George's letter of May 6, which he continued on May 7 and completed on May 8.

20. The battle of Raymond, Mississippi, occurred May 12, 1863. Eicher, *Longest Night,* 463; McPherson, *Battle Cry of Freedom,* 629–30.

21. The battle of Jackson, Mississippi, occurred May 14. Eicher, *Longest Night,* 463–65; McPherson, *Battle Cry of Freedom,* 630.

22. The battle of Champion's Hill occurred May 16. Eicher, *Longest Night,* 465–67; McPherson, *Battle Cry of Freedom,* 630. According to McPherson, the battle of Champion's Hill was the "key battle of the [Vicksburg] campaign."

23. Elias Frank Remley was not in the battle of Champion's Hill because he had been wounded in battle a day earlier. Frank Remley died of disease at a Memphis, Tennessee, hospital on June 2, 1863.

24. The battle of Big Black River occurred May 17. Eicher, *Longest Night,* 467; McPherson, *Battle Cry of Freedom,* 631.

25. George is referring to the actions of the 22nd Iowa during the second assault on Vicksburg (see chap. 2, n. 18).

26. Andrew J. DeVault, Company H; Eli F. Lynch, Company E; and William K. Rush, Company E, died of disease on June 3, 1863. Nicholas Russell, Company I, and John Swaggart, Company C, were killed that same day. *RRIS.*

27. Charles Tippenhauer, of Johnson County, Iowa, was killed June 13, 1863. *RRIS.*

28. Mr. Saxton delivered the news of Lycurgus's death to the family, George's letters not having yet arrived in Iowa (see chap. 2, n. 27).

29. Grant relieved McClernand of his command on June 18, 1863. Despite McClernand's personal claims of great accomplishments during the Vicksburg campaign, Grant remained unhappy with McClernand's performance. McClernand was replaced by Maj. Gen. E. O. C. Ord. Eicher, *Longest Night,* 471.

30. Word of Lycurgus's death two weeks earlier had not yet reached William and Sarah Zoll.

3 — "A Bright and Glorious 'Fourth'"

1. Confederate Gen. Joseph E. Johnston failed to arrive in Vicksburg to relieve Pemberton. After the surrender of Vicksburg, Johnston withdrew to Jackson. Johnston retreated from Jackson on July 16.

2. Between July 16 and August 29, 1863, George Remley was granted a furlough and returned home to Oxford, Iowa. George's letter of August 29 was written during his trip to rejoin his regiment in Louisiana.

3. The destruction of the *City of Madison* was believed to be the work of Confederate saboteurs, the first of thirteen similar acts by Confederate agents in August

and September 1863. *OR,* ser. 1, 48(pt. 2):194-96.

4. Gallinippers are very large American mosquitoes. A gar is a fish with an elongated body resembling that of a pike and long, narrow jaws.

5. See George's letters of April 1 and 11, 1863.

6. Port Hudson was the last Confederate stronghold on the Mississippi River. After the fall of Vicksburg, the Confederate forces at Port Hudson surrendered. For a full account of the siege of Port Hudson, see Lawrence Lee Hewitt, *Port Hudson: Confederate Bastion on the Mississippi* (Baton Rouge: Louisiana Sate University Press, 1987).

4 — "Our Grand Expedition . . . into Texas"

1. A hogshead is a cask or barrel capable of holding about sixty-three gallons.

2. George is referring to the 1863 campaigns. Several state elections occurred in the fall of 1863 including Iowa's gubernatorial election. Republican William M. Stone, former colonel of the 22nd Iowa Infantry, ran against War Democrat James M. Tuttle for the Iowa governorship. Stone won the election by a margin of thirty thousand votes.

3. Milton was enrolled at the University of Iowa.

4. See chap. 4, n. 2.

5. Samuel Remley (see chap. 1, n. 33).

6. The "memento" George mentions is a note from his father included in Howard and Jane Remley's letter.

5 — "Into Texas Proper"

1. This letter is unnumbered.

2. This letter is apparently a continuation of another letter dated ca. December 5, 1863, which is probably no longer extant.

3. No. 13 is incomplete. See George's letter dated December 8, 1863. No. 14 is probably no longer extant.

4. Alice and Milton were both students at the University of Iowa.

5. DeCrow's Point is also spelled DeCros Point.

6. George mistakenly calls a "Norther" a "Northerner."

7. Creed Vaughn is cousin to George and Howard (see chap. 1, n. 40).

8. See Howard Remley's letter dated October 14, 1863. "Copperhead" is the slang term for a Northerner who sympathized with the Southern cause during the Civil War.

9. Private Franklin W. Butler, Iowa City, died December 22, 1863. *RRIS.*

10. George sent his family an ambrotype. An ambrotype is a positive picture made of a photographic negative on glass backed by a dark surface and encased. Ambrotypes are inherently fragile because the image is printed on glass, hence George's concern that it might be broken before reaching Iowa.

11. Refers to Major Dana's General Orders Nos. 14 and 15.

12. Refers to Ecclesiastes 3. See verse 1: "To every thing there is a season, and a time to every purpose under heaven." See also verse 8: "A time to love, and a time to hate; a time of war, and a time of peace."

13. See Biographical Directory.

14. See chap. 4, n. 2.

15. Lincoln reinstated McClernand to his command in January 1864.

16. Samuel Remley.

17. See chap. 5, n. 9.

6 — "To Bid His <u>Dulcina</u> Farewell"

1. Dr. Alfred B. Lee died April 4, 1864, in Iowa City while home on leave.

2. The James Remley Family Papers collection includes two letters written to E. Rust of Matagorda Island, Texas, from Lavaca, Texas. These are most likely the letters to which George refers.

3. In June 1863 the French army captured Mexico City and overthrew the republican government of Benito Juarez in an attempt by Louis Napoleon to reestablish French presence in the region. Napoleon named Hapsburg Archduke Ferdinand Maximilian as emperor of Mexico. The United States refused to recognize Maximilian as the leader of Mexico; however, the Confederate government formed alliances with anti-Juarez groups in the provinces bordering Mexico and offered to recognize Maximilian if he would help the South obtain French recognition. See McPherson, *Battle Cry of Freedom,* 683–84.

4. George is referring to a deep, usually suppurative inflammation of the finger, especially near the end or around the nail.

5. Letters 37–38, one of which was presumably written to Allie, are probably no longer extant.

7 — "We Will Have Some Fighting to Do"

1. Letters 40–45, assuming George's numbering system is consistent, are probably no longer extant.

2. The letter is probably no longer extant.

3. Abolitionist John Brown, who, along with his sons and other supporters, captured the arsenal at Harpers Ferry, Virginia, on October 16, 1859, as part of Brown's plan for an armed black insurrection in northern Virginia. Col. Robert E. Lee and his militia quickly overran Brown's position, and Brown was captured, tried, and sentenced to hang. Brown was hanged December 2, 1859.

4. Gen. George McClellan ran against Lincoln in the 1864 presidential election.

Epilogue

1. Milton Remley, "An Address on the Life of George Alderson Remley," delivered before the George A. Remley Post 183, G.A.R. of Oxford Iowa, September 19, 1886, 14.

Index

Able, Charles, 42, 174n64
African Americans, 93, 94, 97, 99, 103, 104, 135, 154; regiments of, 108, 126, 142. *See also* slavery; slaves
Alderson, Samuel, 173n52
Algiers, La., 87, 89
Allender, R. G., 59
Arcadia, Mo., 44
Atherton, Joseph B., xx, 10, 12, 17, 167, 171n25
Atlanta, Ga., 157

Banks, Nathaniel, xxvi, 84, 98, 99, 103, 128, 142, 143, 146, 147–48
Batesville, Ark., 38, 39, 40, 41; battle of, 174n61
Baton Rouge, La., 148
Battles. *See* names of specific engagements
Bayou Beauf, La., 87–88, 90
Bayou Teche campaign, xxvi, 92–105
Belmont, Miss., battle of, 52, 175n2
Benton Barracks (St. Louis, Mo.), xvi, 4, 6
Benton, William P., 85, 118, 122
Berryville, Va., xxvii, 152, 153, 156, 158, 160, 163
Berwick City, La., 106
Black River Bridge, Miss., battle of, xxi–xxii, xxviii, 65, 67, 175n24
Bloomington, Ill., 88
Borland, Charles E., 80, 85, 108, 126, 130, 167, 169n3, 169n5
Bovie, E. H., 58
Bragg, Braxton, 173n51
Brashear City, La., 88, 90, 93, 95, 101, 102, 105
Brown, John, xi, 154, 178n3
Brownsville, Tex., 103, 105
Bruinsburg, Miss., xix
Buddy, John, 149
Bull Run, Va., first battle of, xiii
Cairo, Ill., 51, 86, 88
Camp Pope (Iowa City, Iowa), xv, 4, 5, 54, 164

Camp Sigel (Rolla, Mo.), 6–7, 8
Carr, Eugene A., xviii, xxi, 6, 53, 64, 65, 66, 68, 76, 77, 81, 85
Carrollton, La., 87, 89, 91, 94, 105
Carthage, La., 57, 59
Cedar Creek, Va., battle of, xxvii, xxviii
Champion's Hill, Miss., battle of, xxi, 67, 143
Charlestown, Va., 154, 156
Chattanooga, Tenn., 101
Chicago University, 170n10
Christian Times, xxx, 5, 6, 14, 17, 32, 96, 107, 121, 126
City of Madison, destruction of, 86, 176n3
Columbus, Ky., 52
Confederate Army: guerillas and, xvii
conscription, xiii, 47, 129
Copperheads, xxv, 97, 112, 129, 160, 177n8
Cree, Alfred B., 5, 24, 25, 29, 41, 54, 72, 75, 77, 85, 86, 87, 90, 101, 113, 114, 118, 126, 127, 141
Creigh, David, 157
Curtis, Samuel R., 30

Dana, Napoleon, 122, 128, 177n11
Davenport Gazette, 17
Davenport, Iowa, 88, 140
Davidson, John Wynn, xvii, 37, 38, 39
Davis, D. J., 62, 77, 106, 161, 162
Davis, Jefferson, xvii, 97
Davis, Lorenzo, 32
Davis, W. P., 157
DeCamp, William M., 16, 64, 167
DeCrow's Point, Tex., xxvii, 108, 118, 125, 128. *See also* Port Cavallo, Tex.
Dennis, Josephine: and marriage to Milton Remley, 164
desertions: from Confederate Army, 120, 128–29; from Union Army, 22, 42, 48
destruction, pillaging, 33–34, 44, 49
disease, xiv, xvi, xxiii
Dix, John, 84
Dunlap, J. W., 20

Index

Early, Jubal A., xvii, 152, 159
Eddy, Allen, 32, 148
Eddy, William, 32
Eighteenth Indiana Infantry, 117, 120
Eighteenth Iowa Infantry, 22
Eighth Army Corps, 156
Eighth Indiana Infantry, 117, 120
Eighth Iowa Infantry, 31
Eighth South Carolina Infantry, 159
Eleventh Wisconsin Infantry, 62, 116, 117, 123
Emancipation Proclamation, 21
Emory, Silas, 97
Ewing, Silas, 129

Farmington, Mo., 42
Farragut, David G., 61
Fifteenth Army Corps, xxi
First Iowa Battery, xx
First Iowa Cavalry, 22, 172n37
First Iowa Infantry, 62, 173n49
foraging, xx, xxvi, 7, 19, 40, 44, 49–50, 99, 100, 103
Fort Sumter, S.C., xiii
Fort Wyman, Mo., 17
Fortieth Iowa Infantry, 80
Fourteenth Iowa Infantry, 31
Franklin, La., 104
Franklin, Mo., 7
Franklin, William B., xxvi, 94
furloughs, 42, 45, 48

Galveston, Tex., 87, 91
Georgetown, Canada, 23, 26
Gettysburg, Pa., battle of, 83
Glass, John D.: and marriage to Alice Remley, 165
Glover, John, 25
Gohen, Lewis, 10, 20, 48, 58, 112–13, 125, 135, 138, 167
Graham, Harvey, xv, 10, 20, 30, 106, 135, 137, 140, 141, 147, 155; wounded and captured during second assault on Vicksburg, Miss., 65
Grand Army of the Republic, George A. Remley Post (Oxford, Iowa), 164, 178n1
Grand Gulf, Miss., 61, 143
Grant, Ulysses S., 46, 47, 53, 81, 99, 137, 175n10; and Vicksburg, xviii, xix, xxiii–xxiv, xxvi

guerillas, 8–9, 29, 47, 53, 87
Guffin, E. M., 3, 169n5

Haddock, William G., 12, 29, 167, 171n26
Hamilton, Va., 152
Handy, George W., 3, 25, 29, 167, 172n45
Harpers Ferry, Va., 152, 153, 155, 162; John Brown's raid at, xi, 154
Harper's Weekly, xxx, 17, 32, 35
Harris, Charles Lofer, 53
Harrison, W. H., 5
Harrisonburg, Va., 161
Hartsock, Virgil S., 138
Hartville, Mo., battle of, 31, 173n54
Helena, Ark., 47, 52, 89
Herron, Francis J., 9
Hobart, Franklin, 17
Hoffer, John, 146
Hopwood, William D., 45, 59, 135
Houston, Mo., 25, 29, 35, 37, 40, 49

Illinois, xii
Indiana, xii
Indianola, Tex., xxvii, 115–30, 132
Iowa: and Civil War, xii, xiii, xxv; and conscription, xiii; and gubernatorial elections of 1863, 96, 177n2; and statehood, xii
Iowa City, Iowa, xii, xxix, 3, 4, 6, 8, 13, 17, 20, 21, 26, 27, 34, 37, 45, 54, 55, 59, 80, 86, 88, 96, 109, 129, 137, 138, 140
Iowa City Republican, xxx, 5, 6, 30, 32, 48, 54, 83, 85, 96, 107, 108, 111, 119, 121, 126, 139, 160
Iron Mountain, Mo., xvii, xviii, 42, 46, 47
Ironton, Mo., 39, 44
Island No. 10, 52, 175n3

Jackson, Miss., 83; battle of, xxi, 65, 66, 175n21; siege of, xxiv–xxv, 84
Jayhawking, 12, 171n27. *See also* foraging
Johnson, Charles, 88, 96, 100, 105, 107, 110, 111, 118, 130, 135, 138, 167
Johnson County, Iowa: and James Remley, xii; and loss of men at Vicksburg, 69
Johnson, Ira, 26
Johnston, James, 5, 167
Johnston, Joseph E., xxiv–xxv, 77, 157, 175n1
Jones, Samuel, xiv, xv

Index

Kentucky, xii
Kibler, George, 5, 168
Kirksville, Mo., battle of, 29, 172n48
Kirkwood, Samuel J., xiv, xv, xxix, 4, 12, 73
Klenk, John, 10, 45, 98, 101, 168
Kurtz, Joe, 59

Lavaca, Tex., 126
Lawler, Michael K., xviii, xix, xx, xxii, 75, 77, 83, 149
Ledlie, Joseph, 24, 172n43
Lee, Alfred B., 137
Lee, Robert E., 83, 159
Leesburg, Va., 152
Lenderman, John, 45
Lengle, Jonathan, 22, 32, 172n39
Lewisburg, Va., 152
Lincoln, Abraham, xii, xiii, 49, 97, 177n15, 178n4; and conscription, xiii; and re-election, 160
Logan, Lewis, 3, 4, 5, 10, 11, 27, 32, 45, 55, 58, 69, 92, 105, 107, 113, 118, 130, 135, 138, 168, 169n1
Longstreet, James, 152
Loudon Technical Institute (Va.), xiii
Lovelace, C. F., 59
Luce, William C., 34, 45, 96

Magruder, John B., 116, 119, 120, 129
Manassass, Va., first battle of. *See* Bull Run, Va., first battle of
Marengo, Iowa, 54, 58, 59, 65, 73, 82
Marmaduke, John S., 173n54
Mars, George F., 121, 123, 127, 135, 138, 142, 146, 168
Maryland, xii
Matagorda Bay, Tex., 105, 106, 108, 116, 119
Matagorda Island, Tex., xxvii, 106, 125, 128, 131–42, 143
McClellan, George B., Jr., 160, 178n4
McClernand, John A., xviii, xix, xxi, 53, 54, 76, 78, 123, 129, 143, 150, 175n10, 177n15
McCordel, Mike, 59
McKee, William, 59
Meade, George, G., 84
Memphis, Tenn., 47, 52, 144
Merrill, Samuel, 49, 173n54, 174n72

Michigan, xii
Milliken's Bend, La., xviii, 51, 52, 53, 54, 56, 89
Mississippi River, 29, 35, 52, 59; control of, xvii
Missouri: Confederates in, 32; and divided allegiance, xvi; and government, Confederate, 170n16; and government, Union, 170n16; and guerilla warfare, 32, 33–34, 78–79; and homefront, 33; and secession, 170n16; and union residents, 31–32
Missouri Compromise, xi
Mobile, Ala., 100, 125, 157
Montgomery, James, 5, 168
Morgan, Edward, 160
Morganzia Bend, La., 147, 149
Morton, William, 22, 32, 148, 172n39
Mosby, John S., 157
Murfreesboro, Tenn., battle of, 30, 173n51
Mustang Island, Tex., 106

New Carthage, La., xviii, 55, 56, 59
New Iberia, La., 93, 94, 100, 101, 104
New Madrid, Mo., 45
New Orleans, La., 18, 84, 87, 88, 91, 93, 98, 99, 101, 108, 114, 117, 142, 143, 144–45, 146, 147, 151
Nineteenth Army Corps, 91, 94, 100, 146, 156; and rivalry with Thirteenth Army Corps, 95
Ninth Cavalry, Missouri State Militia, 30, 172n48
norther, 109, 114, 115, 125, 126, 132, 133, 177n6
Northwest Ordinance, xi

Oberlin College, xi
Ohio, xii
Opelousa, La., 99, 100, 101
Ord, E. O. C., 78
Osterhaus, Peter J., 64
Oxford, Iowa, xii, 10–11, 13, 18, 79, 119

Parvin, Theodore, 3, 169n6
Peabody, Oren, 24, 70, 168
Peace Democrats. *See* Copperheads
Pemberton, John C., xxi, xxii, xxiii–xxiv, 81
Perkins Plantation (La.), xix, 71, 73
Petersburg, Va., 159

— 181 —

Index

Pilot Knob, Mo., 39, 44, 46
Pleasant Hill, La., battle of, 146
Pocahontas, Ark., 35
Pool, Harvey Simeon, 5, 168
Port Cavallo, Tex., 106–15. *See also* DeCrow's Point, Tex.
Port Gibson, Miss., 61, 70; battle of, xix–xx, 61–65, 143, 175n15, 175n16
Port Hudson, La., xvii, 57, 89; siege of, 177n6
Porter, David Dixon, xviii
Porter, John W., 10, 12, 13, 16, 19, 25, 28, 29, 35, 41, 59, 168, 171n25, 174n59
Porter, Joseph C., 29, 172n48, 173n54
Price (Pryce), Samuel D., 127, 129, 158, 161–64
Pryce, Samuel D. *See* Price, Samuel D.
Purcell, Smith, 42

Raymond, Miss., 67; battle of, xx, 66, 175n20
Red River campaign, 143, 144, 146
Remley, Alice (sister), 18, 28, 29, 33, 36, 43, 45, 49, 50, 55, 58, 60, 73, 78, 80, 83, 86, 96, 108, 129–30, 131, 144, 155, 158, 165, 171n30
Remley, Clara (sister), 22, 23, 28, 36, 46, 49, 86, 96, 97, 105, 107, 131, 135, 138, 155, 158, 165, 171n30
Remley, Elias Frank (cousin), 52, 67, 168, 175n4, 175n23
Remley, Frederick (brother), 18, 22, 23, 28, 36, 46, 49, 96, 105, 107, 113, 135, 136, 138, 158, 165, 169n2, 171n30
Remley, George: and ambrotype, 124–25; and church attendance, xxix, 5–6, 26, 102, 126, 145; death of, 161–64; and death of Lycurgus Remley, 80, 114; drawings of, 56; and education at University of Iowa, xiii; and health, 23–24, 28, 41, 58, 76, 83–84, 86, 94, 107, 121, 138, 141; and literary interests, xxx, 86, 114; military service of: —, and assignment to Provost Marshal's office, 117–18, 122; —, and Black River Bridge, battle of, xxi; —, and bravery at third battle of Winchester, 161–64; —, and camp life, 4, 6, 8, 19, 25, 81–82, 90, 92, 94, 98, 100, 107, 108, 110–12, 127, 132–33, 134, 144, 149, 155; —, and detail as nurse for Lycurgus, 72; —, in field hospital, xxx–xxxi; —, and furlough, 88–89; —, and guarding Confederate prisoners, 67–68; —, and guarding Southern property, 21, 98–99; —, and marching, 7, 66, 100, 104, 153, 154; —, and probable reasons for enlistment, xiv; —, and promotion to sergeant, 129; —, and second assault on Vicksburg, Miss., xxii; —, and Shenandoah Valley campaign, xxvii; —, and third battle of Winchester, xxvii–xxviii, 161–64; and views on: —, blasphemy, 102; —, card playing, 102; —, Confederate prisoners, 22; —, conscription, 137, 160; —, Copperheads, 47, 129; —, deserters, 128–29; —, disloyalty in North, 47, 129, 137, 160; —, draft, 129, 137, 160; —, gambling, 102; —, Louisiana, 88, 90, 93, 94, 104; —, marriage, 121, 132; —, McClellan, George B., 160; —, Missouri, 7–8, 26; —, northers, 109, 114, 115, 125, 126, 132, 133, 177n6; —, plantation life, 57, 92, 94; —, profanity, 102; —, religion, 46, 64, 74–75, 105, 126, 139, 162; —, Republicanism, xxix; —, slaves, 57; —, Southern whites, 26, 40, 49, 56, 86, 104, 120, 128–29, 131–32, 145, 152, 155; —, Texas, 115, 128, 135, 136; —, war, 20, 46, 47, 102, 113–14, 131–32; writings of, 14, 17
Remley, Howard M. (brother), 9, 11, 13, 14, 18, 19, 23, 26, 27, 29, 32, 36, 44, 46, 60, 65, 76, 80, 81, 86, 87, 90, 92, 96, 97, 98, 102, 103, 105, 107, 108, 110, 112, 119, 126, 127, 131, 135, 136, 139, 140, 144, 147, 151, 153, 158, 164, 165, 169n2, 171n30
Remley, James (father), xii, 3, 5, 6, 9, 10–11, 15, 18, 28, 31, 33, 34, 35, 36, 37, 38, 39, 51, 54, 56, 59–60, 61, 65, 70, 71, 73, 76, 79, 82–83, 102, 106–7, 108, 110, 115, 121, 125, 126, 127, 131, 134, 138, 142, 144, 146, 147, 148, 151, 155, 160, 165; and concern for health of George Remley, 83, 93, 96; and death of George Remley, 161–64; and death of Lycurgus Remley, 82–83; and move to Iowa, xii; and professions: —, as Baptist minister, xii, 55, 60; —, as farmer, 10, 13, 17, 18, 45, 54, 110, 138, 158; —, as

— 182 —

Index

teacher, xii, 59–60, 170n13; and views on: —, Civil War, 11, 14, 18, 59–60; —, death of Lycurgus Remley, 82–83; —, military service, 18; —, religion, 11, 14, 18, 59–60, 82–83; —, slavery, xii–xiii;

Remley, Jane Alderson (mother), xii, 6, 9, 11, 23–28, 33, 36, 42, 43, 46, 49, 58, 70, 73, 74, 75, 79–80, 102, 107, 108, 117, 131, 133, 138, 142, 144, 147, 155, 156, 160, 164, 165; and concern for health of George Remley, 83; and death of Lycurgus Remley, 79–80, 82, 85, 86, 91, 96, 97–98, 105

Remley, John (cousin), 52, 58, 59, 67, 91, 101, 147, 148, 168

Remley, Lycurgus, 80, 82, 175n28; and church attendance, xxix, 5–6; death of, 74–75, 79–80, 114; drawings of, 10, 17; education of: —, and expulsion from Loudon Technical Institute; —, and University of Iowa, xiii; and health, 9–10, 11–12, 13, 15, 23, 28, 31, 34, 35, 38, 38–39, 41, 58, 65, 67, 70, 71–72, 73–74; and literary interests, xxx; military service of: —, and Black River Bridge, battle of, xxi; —, and camp life, 4, 6, 10, 11, 16; —, and enlistment, 3; —, and hospitals, 15; —, and marching, 32, 44; —, and Port Gibson, battle of, 70; —, and probable reasons for enlistment, xiv; —, and promotion to sergeant, xv, 3; and views on: —, card playing, 11; —, deaths in regiment, 77; —, Louisiana, 54; —, Missouri, 9; —, plantations, 53; religion, xxix–xxx, 43; —, Southern whites, 29, 32, 44; swearing, 11; —, war, 13, 44–45; writings of, 11, 14, 17, 34, 45

Remley, Milton (brother), 9, 23, 28, 35, 35, 43, 44, 45, 60, 70, 73, 74, 78, 96, 97, 108, 129–30, 131, 138, 139, 147, 151, 153–54, 156, 158, 164, 169n2, 170n18, 171n30

Remley, Samuel (uncle), 137, 171n33

Remley, Sidney (brother), 19, 22, 23, 26, 28, 36, 46, 49, 96, 105, 113, 135, 136, 138, 158, 165, 169n2

removal of Confederate property to Texas, 94

Richmond, La., xviii, 56

Rolla, Mo., xvi, 6, 7–8, 10, 11, 15, 18, 19, 24, 25, 28, 29, 31, 34, 35, 36, 37, 38, 39, 40, 41, 45, 58, 59

Rolston, J., 58
Rosecrans, William S., 47, 173n173
Ruppert, Michael, 45
Rutter, Henry, 3, 55, 168, 169n1

Salem, Ark., 39
Salem, Mo., 25, 29, 31
sanitation commissions, 85
Saxton, Walter, 75, 76, 79, 80, 82
Schell, William, 3, 29, 137, 141, 161, 173n49
secessionists, 49, 56
Second Missouri Artillery, 32
Seventeenth Army Corps, 146
Shenandoah Valley campaign, xxvii–xxviii, 151–63
Sheridan, Philip, xxvii, 152, 153
Sherman, William T., xxi, xxv, 65
Simmsport, La., 146, 147
Sixth Iowa Cavalry, 54
Sixty-Ninth Indiana, 133
slavery, xi, 33, 79
slaves, 22, 53, 94, 171n33
Snicker's Gap, Va., 153
Spencer, Oliver M., xxix, 3, 169n4
Springfield, Mo., 6, 12, 19, 22, 31, 33; battle of, 31
St. Genevieve, Mo., xviii, 42, 44, 46, 48, 51, 52, 54
St. Louis, Mo., xvi, 4, 6, 7, 8, 20, 26, 35, 37, 46, 48
St. Martinsville, La., 104
Stone, William M., xv, xvii, xx, 19, 20, 37, 38, 39, 40, 42, 45, 49, 85, 123, 135, 160, 174n60; elected governor of Iowa, 95, 96, 177n2; wounded during second assault on Vicksburg, 65
Subbury, Peter, 58
sutlers, 114, 122, 134, 172n36

Texas, 20, 120; weather of, 109, 114, 115, 125, 126, 132, 133, 177n6
Third Iowa Cavalry, 38, 39
Third Missouri Cavalry, 25, 29
Thirteenth Army Corps, xviii, 53, 87, 89, 103, 103, 123, 129, 135, 143, 146, 150; incorporated into Nineteenth Army Corps, xxvii; and rivalry with Nineteenth Army Corps, 95; transferred to the Department of the Gulf, xxvi, 95, 98, 99

Index

Thirty-Third Illinois Infantry, 117, 120
Tidd, H. A., 73
Totten, Richard, xxix, 23, 26, 169n3
Totten, Silas, xxix, 3, 26, 169n3
Tuttle, James M., 95, 96, 177n2
Twentieth Iowa Infantry, 109
Twenty-Eighth Iowa Infantry, 52, 58, 67, 143, 146
Twenty-First Iowa Infantry, xix–xx, 38, 39, 49, 51
Twenty-Fourth Iowa Infantry, 52, 58, 67, 141, 143, 146
Twenty-Second Iowa Infantry, xix, 81, 84, 86, 87, 90, 91, 97, 99, 123, 137, 140, 142; assigned to the Army of the Shenandoah, xxvii; assigned to the Department of the Gulf, xxvi, 89; battles of: —, at Big Black River, xxi–xxii, xxviii; —, at Cedar Creek, xxvii, xxviii; —, and second assault on Vicksburg, Miss., xxii, xxviii; —, and Shenandoah Valley campaign, xxvii; —, and third battle of Winchester, xxvii–xxviii; and chaplains, xxix, 14, 16, 43, 102, 105, 117; and Company F, xvi, xxi, 7, 39, 41, 45, 48, 51, 55, 65, 66, 84–85, 90, 106, 118, 127, 135, 137, 147, 163; and deserters, 22, 174n69, 174n70; —, punishment of, 48; and discipline, xvi, 16; and furloughs, 134–35, 139; and health, 75, 105; incorporated into Nineteenth Army Corps, xxvii; ordered to Texas, xxvi; ordered to Virginia, xxvii; and organization, xiv, 4; regional origins of, xiv; and trip to Missouri, 6–9
Twenty-Seventh Wisconsin Infantry, 80
Twenty-Third Iowa Infantry, 38, 39, 45, 67, 109, 140, 142

Underground Railroad, xi
Underwood, Mary E.: and marriage to Howard M. Remley, 164
United States Christian Commission, 143
University of Iowa, xii, xxix, 3, 129, 131, 147, 164, 165, 170n11

U.S.S. *Benton,* 56–57, 61, 175n13
U.S.S. *Henry Clay,* 56, 175n11
U.S.S. *Tuscumbia,* 61, 175n13

Vaughn, E. C. "Creed," 112, 172n40
Vermillionville, La., 96, 98, 99, 100, 103, 104
Vicksburg, Miss., xvii, xviii, 20, 30, 41, 42, 46, 47, 51, 52, 53, 54, 55, 56, 57, 59, 61, 65, 84, 85, 87, 88, 89; first Union assault on, 65, 175n17; second Union assault on (May 22, 1863), xxii, xxviii, 65, 175n17, 175n18; siege of, xxii–xxiv, 68 to 81; Union campaign for, 174n1, 175n10; Union capture of, xxiii–xxiv, 57, 81, 98
Virginia, xii, xiii

Warren, Fitz Henry, 25, 29, 35, 37, 40, 107, 117, 122–23, 134–35, 141, 149, 174n60
Warrensburg, Mo., 30, 33, 78
Washburne, C. C., 107
Waynesville, Mo., 12, 19
Westcott, Albert, 35
West Plains, Mo., 40, 41, 45, 53
West Virginia, xii, xiii
White, William H., 11, 12, 14, 16, 20, 24, 45, 67, 70, 71, 72, 77, 85, 168
Wilcox, Timothy M., 24, 29, 172n44
Williamsburg, Va., 93
Wilson's Creek, Mo., battle of, 29, 173n49
Winchester, Va., 153, 154, 163; battle of (third), xxvii–xxviii, 161–64
Wisconsin, xii

Yazoo City, Miss., 51
Yenter, Lewis, 4, 5, 10, 11, 23, 27, 45, 48, 55, 58, 59, 65, 69, 75, 87, 91, 92, 96, 98, 101, 105, 107, 113, 118, 130, 135, 137–38, 141, 169n9

Zoll, Sarah M., 11, 34, 35, 170n21
Zoll, William, 10, 17, 30, 33–34, 35, 78–79, 85, 170n21; and Civil War, 11, 33, 36, 78–79